The Culinary Arts Institute

Book design: Edmar

Illustrations: Karen Rolnick

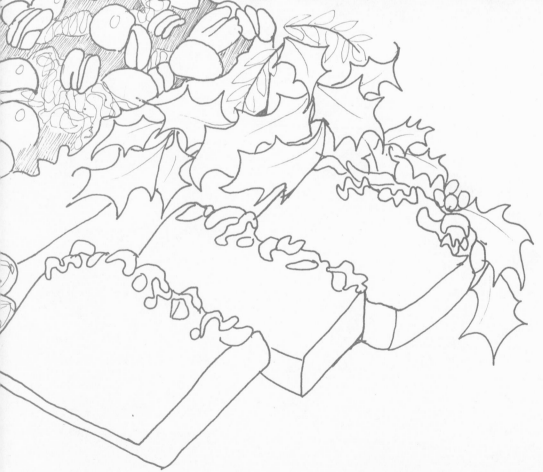

Christmas COOKBOOK

Culinary Arts Institute
A DIVISION OF DELAIR PUBLISHING COMPANY INC.

ISBN: 0-8326-0635-9

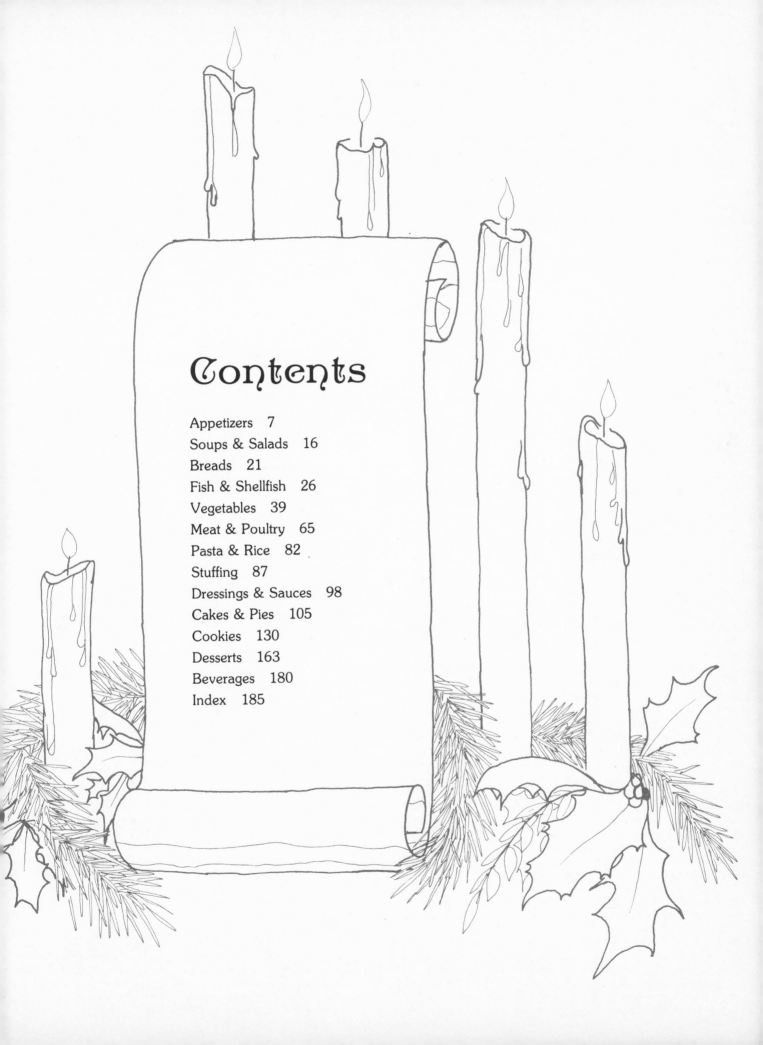

Contents

Appetizers

Cocktail Meatballs

1	large onion, minced
2	tablespoons olive oil
1½	pounds freshly ground round steak (half each of lamb and veal)
3	tablespoons cracker meal
2	cups firm-type bread, crusts removed
2	eggs
6	tablespoons chopped parsley
2	teaspoons oregano, crushed
1½	teaspoons mint
2	tablespoons vinegar
	Salt and pepper to taste
	Flour
	Olive or corn oil for deep frying heated to 365°F

1. Brown half of onion in 2 tablespoons oil in a small frying pan. Mix with the uncooked onion and add to meat in a large bowl. Add the remaining ingredients except flour and oil. Toss lightly with two forks to mix thoroughly.
2. Dust hands with flour. Roll a small amount of meat at a time between palms, shaping into a ball.
3. To heated fat in deep fryer, add the meatballs a layer at a time. Fry until browned on all sides (about 12 minutes). Serve hot.

30 to 40 meatballs

Baked Clams Oregano

12	clams
3	tablespoons minced onion
	Salt and pepper to taste
1	teaspoon oregano
1	teaspoon minced parsley
5	tablespoons olive oil
	Juice of 1 lemon

1. Open clams. Arrange side by side in a small baking dish.
2. Combine onion, salt, pepper, oregano, parsley, olive oil, and lemon juice. Spoon on clam meat.
3. Bake at 325°F about 7 minutes, or until clams curl slightly at the edges.

3 servings

Clam and Walnut Stuffed Mushrooms

20	large mushrooms
½	cup butter or margarine
1	clove garlic, minced
1	can (10 ounces) minced or whole baby clams, drained
1	cup soft bread crumbs
½	cup chopped walnuts
¼	cup chopped parsley
¼	teaspoon salt
¼	teaspoon black pepper
	Walnut halves (optional)
	Parsley sprigs (optional)

1. Rinse mushrooms and pat dry. Remove stems and chop (about 1 cup); set aside
2. Melt butter in a large skillet. Use about 3 tablespoons of melted butter to brush on mushroom caps. Place caps in a shallow pan.
3. To butter remaining in skillet, add garlic and reserved chopped mushroom stems; saute 2 minutes. Add clams, bread crumbs, nuts, parsley, salt, and pepper; mix well.
4. Spoon stuffing into mushroom caps, piling high.
5. Bake at 350°F about 12 minutes, or until hot.
6. If desired, garnish with walnut halves and parsley sprigs.

20 stuffed mushrooms

Shrimp Cocktail, Seviche Style

1½	lbs. cooked shrimp, shelled, deveined, and chilled
1	firm ripe tomato, peeled and diced
¼	cup thinly sliced green onions with tops
¼	cup thinly sliced celery
½	cup lime juice
1½	teaspoons salt
3	teaspoons soy sauce
¼	teaspoon Worcestershire sauce
½	clove garlic, minced

1. Dice the chilled shrimp into a bowl and combine with remaining ingredients; toss lightly to mix well. Chill in refrigerator, covered, about 8 hours.
2. Serve very cold on cocktail sea shells lined with leaf lettuce. Or, if desired, spoon cocktail mixture into ripe avocado halves brushed with lime juice.

6 servings

Shrimp Cocktail

1½	lbs. fresh shrimp with shells
3	cups water
3	tablespoons lemon juice
1	tablespoon salt
1	bay leaf

1. Wash shrimp in cold water.
2. Drop shrimp into a boiling mixture of water, lemon juice, salt, and bay leaf.
3. Cover tightly. Simmer 5 min. or until shrimp are pink and tender.
4. Drain shrimp and cover with cold water to chill. Drain shrimp again.
5. Remove tiny legs. Peel shells from the shrimp. Cut a slit along back (outer curved surface) of shrimp to expose the black vein. With knife point, remove vein in one piece. Rinse the shrimp quickly under running cold water. Drain them on absorbent paper. Store in refrigerator until ready to use.
6. Serve shrimp on **lettuce** or **curly endive** with **Peppy Cocktail Sauce (below).**

About 3 cups shrimp

Hot Shrimp Appetizer: Follow recipe for Shrimp Cocktail. Arrange shrimp on broiler rack. Brush with a mixture of ½ **cup butter or margarine,** melted, and **3 tablespoons lemon juice.** Place under broiler about 2 in. from heat for 3 to 5 min., or until shrimp are thoroughly heated. Insert wooden picks. Serve immediately with **Peppy Cocktail Sauce.**

Shrimp With Peppy Cocktail Sauce

1	cup ketchup
1	tablespoon lemon juice
1	tablespoon prepared horseradish
1	teaspoon onion juice
¼	teaspoon Worcestershire sauce
	Few drops Tabasco
1	tablespoon sugar
½	teaspoon salt
1½	lbs. fresh shrimp with shells, cooked, peeled, de-veined, and chilled

1. Mix thoroughly in a small bowl all ingredients except the shrimp; refrigerate until ready to serve.
2. To prepare cocktail, line 6 chilled sherbet glasses with chilled lettuce or curly endive. Arrange about 5 shrimp in each glass and top with cocktail sauce.

6 servings

Cheese Balls

4	ounces Cheddar cheese, shredded (about 1 cup)
1	teaspoon flour
¼	teaspoon salt
	Dash pepper
1	egg white
	Oil for deep frying

1. Mix cheese, flour, salt, and pepper.
2. Beat egg white to stiff, not dry, peaks. Fold beaten egg white into cheese mixture. Form into small balls, using a rounded tablespoon of the mixture for each.
3. Heat the oil to 365°F in a wok. Fry the cheese balls, a few at a time, until brown. Serve while warm.

12 cheese balls

Planning Appetizers

There is no limit to the kinds of meat, poultry, fish, cheese, vegetables, and fruits that can be used. Though imagination and ingenuity are the only limiting factors in selecting appetizers, there is one rule that should be followed—*avoid repeating any food in the main part of the meal that has been used in the appetizers.* Remember that they are a part of the whole menu; select them to harmonize with the rest of the meal. Choose them for complementary flavors, for contrast of texture and color and variety of shape. Picture the serving dishes, trays, and other appointments as you plan the menu.

Pimiento-Crab Meat Strata Supreme

1   can (7½ oz. Alaska King crab meat, drained and flaked
½   cup finely chopped celery
¼   cup finely chopped onion
¾   cup mayonnaise
     Few grains cayenne pepper
12   slices white bread, crusts removed
     Butter or margarine softened
3   jars or cans (4 oz. each) whole pimientos, each pimiento cut in 2 or 3 large pieces
1   lb. Swiss cheese, shredded
5   eggs
3   cups milk
1   teaspoon salt
1/8   teaspoon pepper
¼   teaspoon dry mustard

1. Mix crab meat, celery, and onion. Blend in a mixture of the mayonnaise and cayenne pepper. Set aside.
2. Spread both sides of the bread slices with butter. Place half of the bread in one layer in a greased 3-quart shallow baking dish; reserve remainder.
3. Arrange half of the pimiento pieces over the bread, half of the crab mixture, and a third of the shredded cheese. Repeat layering using remainder of crab mixture, pimiento, and second third of the cheese. Cover with reserved bread and sprinkle with the remaining cheese.
4. Beat remaining ingredients together until frothy and blended. Pour over all. Let stand 1 hour.
5. Bake at 425°F 1 hour, or until puffed and browned.
6. Garnish top with three well-drained whole pimientos arranged in a bell cluster with green pepper strips between the bells. Nestle a small parsley bouquet at center.

6 to 8 servings

Cheese Ball

2 pkgs. (8 oz. each) cream cheese
1/2 lb. sharp Cheddar cheese, shredded
2 teaspoons grated onion
2 teaspoons Worcestershire sauce
1 teaspoon lemon juice
1 teaspoon dry mustard
1/2 teaspoon paprika
1/2 teaspoon seasoned salt
1/4 teaspoon salt
1 can (2¼ oz.) deviled ham
2 tablespoons finely chopped parsley
2 tablespoons finely chopped pimiento, thoroughly drained
Finely chopped pecans (about ⅔ cup)

1. Soften the cream cheese in a small mixer bowl, beating with electric beater. Beat in the Cheddar cheese, onion, Worcestershire sauce, lemon juice, dry mustard, paprika, seasoned salt, salt, and deviled ham until mixture is creamy.
2. Stir in the parsley and pimiento. Cover and rerigerate several hours, or until cheese mixture is firm enough to handle.
3. Shape into a ball and coat evenly with the chopped pecans. Wrap in moisture-vaporproof material and refrigerate until ready to serve. Or blend nuts with snipped parsley or snipped slices of dried smoked beef before coating. Serve with assorted crackers and small thin cocktail rye-bread slices.

1 Cheese Ball (About 3 Cups)

Cream Cheese Dainties

Apricot, Strawberry, or Mincemeat Filling, below
1/2 cup butter
1 package (3 ounces) cream cheese
1 teaspoon sugar
1 cup all-purpose flour

1. Prepare desired filling or fillings and set aside.
2. Beat butter and cream cheese until well blended. Mix in sugar and then flour. Divide dough in half and chill thoroughly.
3. On a lightly floured surface, roll each half of dough to 1/16-inch thickness. Use floured 2-inch cookie cutters to cut about 3 dozen "bases."
4. Transfer bases to cookie sheets. Spoon about ¼ teaspoon filling in center of each cookie.
5. Cut remaining dough with the same size cutters. Use cut-out cookies or with 1-inch cutouts.
6. Bake at 375°F 6 to 8 minutes. Remove immediately to wire racks to cool.

About 5 dozen cookies

Apricot Filling: Mix 1/2 cup apricot preserves with 1/2 teaspoon lemon extract.

Strawberry Filling: Mix 1/2 cup strawberry preserves with 1/2 teaspoon almond extract.

Mincemeat Filling: Mix 1/2 cup prepared mincemeat with 1/2 teaspoon orange extract.

Note: If desired, make tart shells from dough. Roll dough to 1/16-inch thickness and cut out rounds with a 2¾-inch cookie cutter. Carefully line well-buttered 2¼x¾-inch tart pan wells with rounds of dough; prick with a fork. Bake at 375°F 8 to 10 minutes, or until lightly browned. Cool; remove from pans. Fill with fruit or cream filling.

About 3 dozen tart shells

Mushroom Cheese Mold

2 packages (8 ounces each) cream cheese, softened
½ pound Cheddar cheese, shredded (about 2 cups)
1 clove garlic, crushed
1½ teaspoons brown mustard
¼ teaspoon salt
1 can (3 to 4 ounces) mushroom stems and pieces, drained and chopped
¼ cup finely chopped onion
2 tablespoons finely diced pimiento
2 tablespoons finely chopped parsley
Sliced mushrooms (optional)
Parsley (optional)

1. Combine cheeses, garlic, mustard, and salt in a bowl. Add chopped mushrooms, onion, pimento, and parsley; mix well.
2. Turn mixture into a lightly buttered 3-cup mold. Refrigerate until firm.
3. Unmold onto serving platter. Garnish with sliced mushrooms and parsley, if desired. Serve with **crackers.**

3½ cups spread

Marinated Pimiento Piccante

3 tablespoons red wine vinegar
2 cloves garlic, minced
1 bay leaf
½ teaspoon salt
½ teaspoon pepper
2 tablespoons olive or other cooking oil
2 tablespoons chili sauce
2 jars or cans (7 oz. each) whole pimientos, drained and torn in half or in large pieces
1 can anchovy fillets
¼ cup slivered ripe olives
1 tablespoon lemon juice

1. Put the vinegar, garlic, bay leaf, salt, and pepper into a saucepan; simmer 5 minutes.
2. Blend in oil and chili sauce; pour over pimientos. Let stand about 3 hours.
3. To serve, drain pimientos and garnish with anchovy filets and ripe olives. Drizzle lemon juice over all.

6 servings

Zucchini Vinaigrette

6 medium-sized zucchini
1 pkg. Italian salad dressing mix
¼ cup white wine vinegar
½ cup salad oil
2 tablespoons finely chopped green pepper
2 tablespoons finely chopped parsley
¼ cup finely chopped green onion
3 tablespoons sweet pickle relish

1. Cut ends from each zucchini and slice lengthwise into 6 pieces. Cook in a small amount of boiling salted water about 3 minutes, or until crisp-tender. Drain if necessary and cool; put into a shallow dish.
2. While zucchini is cooling, combine the remaining ingredients in a jar with a tight-fitting lid. Cover and shake vigorously to mix well.
3. Pour vinaigrette sauce over zucchini. Chill 4 hours or overnight. Serve on antipasto tray.

Avocados Stuffed with Cauliflower Salad

2 cups very small, crisp raw cauliflowerets
1 cup cooked green peas
½ cup sliced ripe olives
¼ cup chopped pimiento
¼ cup chopped onion
 Oil and Vinegar Dressing (see page 17)
 Salt to taste
6 small lettuce leaves
3 large ripe avocados
 Lemon wedges

1. Combine all ingredients, except lettuce, avocados, and lemon wedges; stir gently until evenly mixed and coated with dressing.
2. Refrigerate at least 1 hour before serving.
3. When ready to serve, peel, halve, and remove pits from avocados. Place a lettuce leaf on each serving plate; top with avocado half filled with a mound of cauliflower salad. Serve with lemon wedges.

6 servings

Mushrooms a la Grecque

1 pound fresh mushrooms or 2 cans (6 to 8 ounces each) whole mushrooms
⅓ cup olive oil
⅓ cup dry white wine or apple juice
¼ cup water
1 tablespoon lemon juice
¾ cup chopped onion
1 large clove garlic, minced
1½ teaspoons salt
1 teaspoon sugar
½ teaspoon coriander seed (optional)
¼ teaspoon black pepper
2 cups carrot chunks
½ cup pimento-stuffed olives

1. Rinse, pat dry, and halve fresh mushrooms or drain canned mushrooms; set aside.
2. In a large saucepan combine oil, wine, water, lemon juice, onion, garlic, salt, sugar, coriander, and black pepper. Bring to boiling; add carrots.
3. Cover and simmer for 15 minutes. Add mushrooms and olives. Return to boiling; reduce heat. Cover and simmer for 5 minutes.
4. Chill thoroughly, at least overnight.
5. To serve, thread mushrooms, carrot chunks, and olives on skewers or spoon into a bowl. Serve as hors d'oeuvres.

8 to 10 hors d'oeuvre portions

Suggested Foods for an Antipasto Tray

1. Meats—**Salami,** sliced thin; **prosciutto,** sliced thin; **capocollo,** sliced thin.
2. Vegetables—**mushrooms,** pickled; **peppers,** pickled or raw; **tomatoes,** sliced or with **olive oil; radishes, celery; finocchio (fennel); pimiento, pickled vegetables** (carrots, eggplant, zucchini); **olives,** green or ripe; **artichokes,** pickled or with **lemon.**
3. Eggs—Hard-cooked, sliced.
4. Fish—**Sardines; tuna** pieces or chunks; **anchovies** around **capers** or around **stuffed olives.**
5. Greens—**Lettuce,** head or leaf; **romaine; chicory; endive.**
6. Cheese—**Mozzarella,** sliced; **Provolone,** sliced; **Gorgonzola,** sliced.

Northern Italy Antipasto

Salami, sliced thin; **prosciutto,** sliced thin; **artichokes,** pickled or with lemon; **pickled mushrooms; anchovies** around **capers** or around **olives; tuna,** pieces or chunks; **lettuce; Hard-Cooked Eggs.**

Southern Italy Antipasto

Salami, sliced thin; **sardines; anchovies; peppers,** raw; **celery** and **fennel; olives; pimiento; pickled vegetables; radishes; lettuce; cheese** (Mozzarella, Provolone or Gorgonzola).

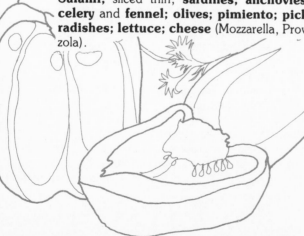

Tomato Toast

¼ cup finely chopped onion
2 tablespoons butter or margarine
Italian-style tomatoes (canned), drained
1 teaspoon sugar
1/8 teaspoon salt
1 egg yolk, fork beaten
½ teaspoon Worcestershire sauce
¼ cup shredded Parmesan cheese
4 slices white bread, toasted, crusts removed, and toast cut in quarters
Snipped fresh parsley or crushed dried basil or oregano

1. Add onion to heated butter in a heavy saucepan and cook until tender, stirring occasionally.
2. Force enough of the drained tomatoes through a sieve to yield 1½ cups. Add to onion with sugar and salt; cook, stirring occasionally, until liquid evaporates and mixture is thick (about 25 minutes).
3. Stir a small amount of tomato mixture into egg yolk; blend thoroughly and return to saucepan. Cook and stir 5 minutes.
4. Mix in Worcestershire sauce and half of cheese; spread generously on toast quarters. Sprinkle half of appetizers with the remaining cheese and half with the parsley.
5. Broil appetizers 3 to 4 inches from heat until bubbly. Serve hot.

16 appetizers

Eggnog Fondue

2 eggs, beaten
2 tablespoons sugar or honey
1/8 teaspoon salt
1½ cups milk
½ teaspoon vanilla extract
3 tablespoons arrowroot
3 tablespoons dark rum
Nutmeg
Fruitcake, cut into ¾-inch pieces

1. Beat together eggs, sugar, and salt. Stir in milk and vanilla extract.
2. Pour eggnog into a nonmetal fondue pot. Mix arrowroot with 1 tablespoon rum and stir into the eggnog.
3. Cook over medium heat until mixture thickens, stirring occasionally. Stir in remaining rum.
4. Keep fondue warm while dipping fruitcake pieces.

6 to 8 servings

Soups & Salads

Chestnut Soup

2	cups blanched chestnuts
3	cups water
2	cups milk, scalded
2	tablespoons minced onion
4	tablespoons butter
2	tablespoons flour
1	teaspoon salt
1/4	teaspoon pepper
1/8	teaspoon celery salt
	Dash nutmeg
1	cup cream or evaporated milk
	Chopped parsley

1. To shell and blanch chestnuts: wash and discard those that float. Dry and with a sharp knife make a cross on both sides of the nuts. Place in a baking dish with 1 teaspoon shortening, bake in a hot (450°F.) about 10 minutes.
2. Cool and remove shell and brown skin with knife.
3. Cook chestnuts in water until tender, press through a sieve and add milk. Cook onion in butter until tender, but not brown.
4. Blend in flour, salt, pepper, celery salt and nutmeg. Add milk stirring constantly. Cook 5 minutes, add cream, heat to boiling, garnish with parsley and serve, for 6.

Almond Soup

5	cups milk
1/2	pound blanched almonds, ground twice
5	bitter almonds (optional)
1	teaspoon almond extract
2	cups cooked rice
1/3	cup sugar
1/4	cup raisins or currants

1. Heat milk just to simmering in a large saucepan.
2. Add all the ingredients; stir until well mixed. Cook over low heat 3 to 5 minutes.
3. Serve hot as is traditional for Christmas, or chill before serving.

About 2 quarts

Red Vegetable Salad

1 pint cherry tomatoes, stems removed, cut in half
20 radishes, sliced
1 small red onion, sliced
3 tablespoons wine vinegar
2 teaspoon salad oil
1 teaspoon salt
2 teaspoons snipped fresh mint
1/8 teaspoon freshly ground white pepper
Lettuce leaves

1. Combine all ingredients except lettuce leaves in a medium bowl; refrigerate covered 2 hours, stirring occasionally.
2. Serve vegetables on lettuce.

4 to 6 servings

Salade Nicoise

Salad Dressing, below
3 medium-sized cooked potatoes, sliced
1 pkg. (9 oz.) frozen green beans, cooked
1 clove garlic, cut in half
1 small head Boston lettuce
2 cans (6½ or 7 oz. each) tuna, drained
1 mild onion, quartered and thinly sliced
2 ripe tomatoes, cut in wedges
2 hard-cooked eggs, quartered
1 can (2 oz.) rolled anchovy fillets, drained
3/4 cup pitted ripe olives
1 tablespoon capers

1. Pour enough salad dressing over warm potato slices and cooked beans (in separate bowls) to coat vegetables.
2. Before serving, rub the inside of a large shallow salad bowl with the cut surface of the garlic. Line the bowl or a large serving platter with the lettuce.
3. Unmold the tuna in center of bowl and separate into chunks.
4. Arrange separate mounds of the potatoes, green beans, onions, tomatoes, and hard-cooked eggs in colorful groupings around the tuna. Garnish with anchovies, olives and capers.
5. Pour dressing over all before serving.

6 to 8 Servings

Salad Dressing: Combine in a jar or bottle ½ cup olive oil or salad oil, 2 tablespoons red wine vinegar, a mixture of 1 teaspoon salt, ½ teaspoon pepper, and 1 teaspoon dry mustard, 1 tablespoon finely chopped chives, and 1 tablespoon finely chopped parsley. Shake vigorously to blend well before pouring over salad.

About ⅔ Cup

Christmas Eve Salad

1 cup diced cooked beets
1 cup diced tart apple, not peeled
1 cup orange sections
1 cup sliced bananas
1 cup diced pineapple (fresh or canned)
Juice of 1 lime
Oil and Vinegar Dressing (see below)
Shredded lettuce
1/2 cup chopped peanuts
Seeds from 1 pomegranate

1. Drain beets well. Combine beets, apple, oranges, bananas, and pineapple. Refrigerate until ready to serve.
2. Add lime juice to beet-fruit mixture. Add desired amount of dressing and toss until evenly mixed and coated with dressing.
3. To serve, make a bed of shredded lettuce in salad bowl. Mound salad on top. Sprinkle with peanuts and pomegranate seeds.

8 to 10 servings

Oil and Vinegar Dressing: Mix 2 **tablespoons white wine vinegar, 1½ teaspoons sugar,** and **¼ teaspoon salt.** Add **⅓ cup salad oil;** mix well.

Poinsettia Salad

1 No. 2½ can pears
½ cup red cinnamon drops
3 tablespoons vinegar
1 bunch watercress
4 teaspoons grated sharp
Cheddar cheese
Lime French Dressing
(page 98)

1. Combine syrup from pears with cinnamon drops and vinegar and heat to boiling. Cut each pear half into 4 lengthwise slices to represent petals and simmer in syrup for 20 minutes, or until well colored. Chill.
2. Arrange watercress on 4 salad plates. On each arrange 8 petals, clockwise, each curving toward the center to represent a flower.
3. Sprinkle 1 teaspoon grated cheese in center of each flower, and serve with dressing.

Serves 4

Christmas Wreath Salad

6 slices pineapple
1 head romaine
Angelica
½ cup red cinnamon drops
Whipped Cream Dressing
(page 98)

1. Arrange 1 slice pineapple on romaine on each plate. Cut angelica to represent holly leaves and arrange on pineapple.
2. Sprinkle cinnamon drops at intervals between the leaves to represent holly. Fill center of pineapple ring with whipped cream dressing.

Serves 6

Salad Pointers

A salad is only as good as its makings so select the ingredients with care. Greens should be fresh, crisp, and dry, vegetables garden fresh, and fruits firm, fully ripe, and free from blemish. When using canned products, choose those of good quality and appearance.

Chill all salad ingredients, bowls, and plates thoroughly. With the exception of a few hot salads, coldness is essential to the appeal of all salads.

Trim and rinse greens under running cold water, handling them carefully to avoid bruising. Shake off the excess moisture and then gently pat dry before putting them into a plastic bag or the vegetable drawer and into your refrigerator. Wet greens not only make watery salads, they present a surface to which an oil dressing cannot cling.

Greens should always be broken or torn, never cut (except in the case of head lettuce which is to be served in wedges or quarters).

Tomatoes may be peeled or not, as your family prefers, for use in salads. Unpeeled tomato shells or tomato cups are sturdier and keep their shape better; peeled ones are easier to cut with a fork.

Tomato wedges or chunks should be added to tossed salads just before serving, as their juice tends to make the dressing watery.

Shrimp Salad Duo Elegante

2   lbs. cooked shrimp, peeled and deveined
½   cup chopped pickled watermelon rind (reserve ½ cup syrup)
⅔   cup lime juice
4   teaspoons French dressing mix
2   pkgs. (3 oz. each) strawberry-flavored gelatin
1½ cups boiling water
1   can (29 oz.) pear halves, drained (reserve 1½ cups syrup)
1½ cups sliced celery
¼   cup coarsely chopped pistachio nuts
French Mayonnaise

1. Put shrimp into a large shallow dish and pour a mixture of the reserved syrup, lime juice, and French dressing mix over the shrimp; cover and marinate 2 hours, turning occasionally. Drain, reserving marinade; set shrimp aside.
2. Dissolve gelatin in boiling water; stir in 1 cup of the marinade and the reserved pear syrup; chill until gelatin is slightly thickened.
3. Pour gelatin into a 2-quart ring mold to ¼-inch depth; set remaining gelatin aside. Cut three pear halves in half lengthwise, and arrange, rounded side down, in bottom of mold; chill until gelatin is just set, but not firm.
4. Meanwhile, cut remaining pears and 2 cups of the shrimp into small pieces; add to remaining gelatin with the watermelon rind and blend well.
5. Spoon mixture over layer in mold and chill until firm, about 3 hours.
6. Combine remaining shrimp (about 2 cups) with celery, nuts, and the French Mayonnaise; toss lightly to mix. Refrigerate.
7. Unmold salad onto a chilled large serving plate and garnish mold with salad greens. Spoon shrimp mixture into the center.

8 to 10 servings

French Mayonnaise: Mix together ½ cup mayonnaise, ¼ cup clear French dressing, and ¼ teaspoon horseradish.

Molded Lobster Elegance

2½ env. unflavored gelatin
1   cup cold water
3   egg yolks
1   cup strong chicken broth, cooled (dissolve 2 chicken bouillon cubes in 1 cup boiling water)
1¼ teaspoons salt
¼   teaspoon pepper
2   teaspoons grated onion
1   teaspoon prepared mustard
1   teaspoon prepared horseradish
3   cups cooked lobster meat
3   tablespoons lemon juice
1½ cups chilled heavy cream, whipped
¼   cup finely chopped toasted almonds
¼   cup finely chopped celery
¼   cup finely chopped pimiento-stuffed olives

1. Soften the gelatin in the cold water in a small bowl. Set aside.
2. Meanwhile, beat the egg yolks in the top of a double boiler. Add the broth gradually, stirring constantly. Mix in the salt and pepper. Stirring constantly, cook over simmering water until smooth and slightly thickened 5 to 8 minutes.
3. Remove from simmering water, immediately add the softened gelatin, and stir until gelatin is dissolved. Stir in the grated onion, mustard, and horseradish. Cool; chill until mixture is slightly thickened.
4. Cut the lobster meat into small pieces and put into a large bowl. Drizzle lemon juice evenly over lobster.
5. Fold whipped cream into the slightly thickened gelatin mixture. Mix almonds, celery, and olives with the lobster. Pour the whipped cream mixture over lobster and fold together. Turn mixture into a 1½-quart mold. Chill until firm, 4 to 5 hours overnight.
6. Unmold onto a chilled serving plate. Garnish with watercress.

10 to 12 servings

Crab Meat Salad

Cooked Pineapple Salad Dressing, page 100
2 cups boiling water
2 pkgs. (3 oz. each) lemon-flavored gelatin
½ teaspoon salt
1 cup cold water
3 tablespoons cider vinegar
¼ cup large-curd creamed cottage cheese, sieved
½ cup coarsely chopped salted almonds
½ cup finely chopped celery
¼ cup finely chopped green pepper
1 tablespoon grated onion
2 teaspoons chopped pimiento
¾ lb. fresh crab meat, separated in pieces (bony tissue removed)
½ cup chilled heavy cream, whipped
Fresh pineapple, thinly sliced pieces

1. Prepare salad dressing; chill thoroughly.
2. Pour boiling water over gelatin and salt in a bowl; stir until gelatin is dissolved. Blend in the cold water and vinegar. Chill until mixture is slightly thickened.
3. Thoroughly mix cottage cheese, almonds, celery, green pepper, onion, and pimiento with ½ cup of the salad dressing. Gently blend in crab meat.
4. Stir the crab meat mixture into slightly thickened gelatin. Turn into a 2-quart fancy mold and chill until firm.
5. Fold the whipped cream into the remaining salad dressing. Chill until ready to serve.
6. Unmold salad onto chilled serving plate and surround mold with the chilled sliced pineapple. Serve with the salad dressing.

About 8 servings

Breads

Christmas Bread

2	envelopes active dry yeast
2	cups scalded milk, cooled to 105° to 115°F
1	cup sugar
1	teaspoon salt
4	eggs (or 8 yolks), well beaten
½	cup unsalted butter, melted
7½	to 8 cups all-purpose flour
1½	teaspoons cardamom, pounded, or 1 teaspoon mastic
½	cup dried golden currants
¾	cup chopped walnuts
2	egg whites, beaten
4	tablespoons sugar

1. Sprinkle yeast over 1 cup warm milk in a small bowl; stir until dissolved. Set aside.
2. Reserve 2 teaspoons sugar for pounding with mastic, if using. Put sugar into a bowl and add salt, eggs, remaining 1 cup milk, and butter; mix well.
3. Put 7 cups flour into a large bowl. Stir in cadamon, or pound mastic with 2 tablespoons sugar (so it will not become gummy) and add. Make a well and add dissolved yeast, egg mixture, currants, and nuts; mix well.
4. Knead dough on a floured board, adding the remaining 1 cup flour as required. Knead dough until smooth (5 to 6 minutes).
5. Place dough in a greased bowl. Turn until surface is completely greased. Cover. Set in a warm place until double in bulk.
6. Punch dough down. Form into two round loaves and place in buttered 10-inch pans.
7. Cover and let rise again in a warm place until double in bulk.
8. Bake at 375°F 15 minutes. Remove from oven and brush with beaten egg whites, then sprinkle with sugar. Remove from oven and brush with beaten egg whites, then sprinkle with sugar. Return to oven. Turn oven control to 325°F and bake about 35 to 40 minutes, or until bread is done.

Kings' Bread Ring

2	packages active dry yeast or 2 cakes compressed yeast
½	cup water (hot for dry yeast, lukewarm for compressed)
½	cup milk, scalded
⅓	cup sugar
⅓	cup shortening
2	teaspoons salt
4	cups all-purpose flour (about)
3	eggs, well beaten
2	cups chopped candied fruits (citron, cherries, and orange peel)
	Melted butter or margarine
	Confectioners' Sugar Icing

1. Soften yeast in water.
2. Pour hot milk over sugar, shortening, and salt in large bowl, stirring until sugar is dissolved and shortening melted. Cool to lukewarm. Beat in 1 cup of the flour, then eggs and softened yeast. Add enough more flour to make a stiff dough. Stir in 1½ cups candied fruits, reserving remainder to decorate baked ring.
3. Turn dough onto a floured surface and knead until smooth and satiny. Roll dough under hands into a long rope; shape into a ring, sealing ends together. Transfer to a greased cookie sheet. Push a tiny china doll into dough so it is completely covered. Brush with melted butter.
4. Cover with a towel and let rise in a warm place until double in bulk (about 1½ hours).
5. Bake at 375°F 25 to 30 minutes, or until golden brown.
6. Cool on wire rack. Frost with Confectioners' Sugar Icing and decorate with reserved candied fruit.

1 large bread ring

Confectioners' Sugar Icing: Blend **1⅓ cups confectioners' sugar, 4 teaspoons water,** and **½ teaspoon vanilla extract.**

Helpful Hints About Breads

• To glaze tops of fancy breads and rolls brush before baking with slightly beaten egg white mixed with 1 tablespoon milk or water; or egg yolk slightly beaten with a little milk or water.
• To slice newly baked bread, cut with a hot knife.
• To butter bread for thin sandwiches, spread end of loaf with softened butter, then cut off a slice as thin a possible. Repeat buttering and slicing.
• To freshen rolls, place them in a heavy paper bag. Twist top of bag and place in a 400°F oven 10 to 15 minutes. (Or wrap securely in aluminum foil.)
• To prepare crumbs from dry bread, force through the fine blade of food chopper or place dry bread in a small plastic bag and crush with a rolling pin. Crush in an electric blender, if available. If using the food chopper, tie a paper bag onto end of food chopper to keep crumbs from scattering.

Norwegian Christmas Bread

1	cup milk, scalded
½	cup butter, softened
½	cup sugar
1	teaspoon salt
1	teaspoon ground cardamom
2	pkgs. active dry yeast
½	cup warm water
½	cup currants
½	cup coarsely chopped almonds
½	cup mixed candied fruit
1	tablespoon flour
5	cups all-purpose flour
1	egg, beaten
1	tablespoon sugar
⅛	teaspoon ground cinnamon

1. Pour scalded milk over butter, ½ cup sugar, salt, and cardamom in a bowl. Stir until butter is melted. Cool to lukewarm.
2. Soften yeast in the warm water.
3. Toss currants, almonds, and mixed fruit with the 1 tablespoon flour; set aside.
4. Add about 2 cups of the flour to milk mixture and beat until smooth. Stir in yeast, egg and then the fruit-nut mixture. Beat in enough of the remaining flour to make a soft dough.
5. Turn onto a lightly floured surface. Knead dough until smooth and elastic, 5 to 8 minutes. Form into a ball and place in a greased deep bowl. Turn dough to bring greased surface to top. Cover; let rise in a warm place until doubled, about 1½ hours.
6. Punch down dough and turn onto a lightly floured surface. Divide dough into halves and shape each into a round loaf. Place on a greased baking sheet. Cover; let rise again until doubled, about 1 hour.
7. Bake at 350°F 25 minutes. Brush tops with softened butter and sprinkle with a mixture of the sugar and cinnamon. Remove to wire racks to cool.

2 Loaves Bread

Fruit Bread

1	pound prunes
1	pound figs
1	pound dates
¼	cup raisins
¼	cup dried currants
1	tablespoon chopped candied citron
1	tablespoon chopped candied lemon peel
1	tablespoon chopped candied orange peel
¼	cup chopped blanched almonds
2	cakes yeast
4½	cups sifted flour
¼	teaspoon cloves
¼	teaspoon cinnamon
¼	teaspoon salt

1. Soak prunes and figs 1 hour in just enough water to cover.
2. Add dates and cook gently in the same water 20 minutes. Remove fruit, chop and mix with other fruit and nuts.
3. Reduce liquid to ¾ cup. Cool to lukewarm, add yeast and stir until well blended.
4. Add 2 cups flour, beating well. Let rise until light and spongy.
5. Add spices, salt, fruit mixture and remaining flour to make a stiff dough. Knead until smooth. Let rise until doubled in bulk.
6. Shape into oval loaves, brush with slightly sweetened milk and sprinkle with split almonds. Let rise again and bake in hot oven (425°F.) 45 minutes.
7. Makes 3 loaves. If desired, when cool, spread with icing and garnish with candied fruits and nut meats.

Cranberry Fruit-Nut Bread

2	cups all-purpose flour
1	cup sugar
1½	teaspoons baking powder
1	teaspoon salt
½	teaspoon baking soda
1¼	cups cranberries, cut in halves
½	cup walnuts, coarsely chopped
1	egg, well beaten
1	teaspoon grated orange peel
¾	cup orange juice
2	tablespoons melted butter or margarine

1. Mix flour with sugar, baking powder, salt, and baking soda in a bowl. Mix in cranberries and walnuts.
2. Blend egg, orange peel and juice, and butter in a bowl. Make a well in center of dry ingredients; add liquid mixture and stir only enough to moisten dry ingredients.
3. Turn into a well-greased and floured cooker bake pan or 2-pound coffee can. Cover bake pan with lid; or, if using coffee can, cover with 6 layers of paper toweling. Set in an electric cooker.
4. Cover and cook on High 3 to 4 hours.
5. Remove bake pan and let cool 10 minutes before removing bread.

1 loaf bread

Butter Pecan Shortbread

Shortbread:

1	cup butter
½	cup firmly packed light brown sugar
2¼	cups all-purpose flour
½	cup finely chopped pecans

Decorator Icing:

2	tablespoons butter
¼	teaspoon vanilla extract
1	cup confectioners' sugar
	Milk (about 1 tablespoon)
	Red and green food coloring

1. To prepare shortbread, beat butter until softened; add brown sugar gradually, beating until fluffy. Add flour gradually, beating until well blended. Mix in pecans.
2. Chill dough until easy to handle.
3. On a lightly floured surface, pat and roll dough into a 14x10-inch rectangle about ¼ inch thick. Cut dough into 24 squares. Divide each square into 4 triangles.
4. Transfer triangles to ungreased cookie sheets.
5. Bake at 300°F 18 to 20 minutes, or until lightly browned. Remove to wire racks to cool.
6. To prepare icing, cream butter with vanilla extract in a small bowl. Add confectioners' sugar gradually, beating until blended. Blend in enough milk for desired consistency for icing. Color one third of icing red and two thirds green. Force icing through a decorator tube to make a holly decoration on each cookie.

8 dozen cookies

Coffee Bread

½ cup finely chopped blanched almonds
1 cup milk or cream
1 pkg. active dry yeast
¼ cup warm water
½ cup butter
⅓ cup sugar
1 teaspoon salt
3½ cup sifted all-purpose flour
1 egg

1. Two baking sheets will be needed.
2. Set out finely chopped blanched almonds.
3. Scald milk or cream.
4. Meanwhile, soften dry yeast in ¼ cup warm water, 105°F to 115°F (Or if using compressed yeast, soften 1 cake in ¼ cup lukewarm water, 80°F to 85°F.)
5. Set aside.
6. Put into a large bowl butter, sugar, and salt.
7. Immediately pour scalded milk over ingredients in bowl. When lukewarm, blend in 1 cup all-purpose flour beating until smooth. Stir softened yeast and add, mixing well.
8. Add about one-half the flour to the yeast mixture and beat until very smooth.
9. Beat in 1 egg, well beaten.
10. Then beat in enough remaining flour to make a soft dough. Turn dough onto a lightly floured surface and allow dough to rest 5 to 10 minutes.
11. Knead dough.
12. Form dough into a large ball and put it into a greased, deep bowl. Turn dough to bring greased surface to top. Cover with waxed paper and towel and let stand in warm place (about 80°F) until dough is doubled.
13. Punch down with fist; pull edges of dough in to center and turn dough completely over in bowl. Cover and let rise again until nearly doubled. Punch down and turn dough out onto lightly floured surface. Divide dough into two portions and shape into oblong loaves.
14. Lightly grease the baking sheets.
15. Place loaves on baking sheets and brush with egg white, slightly beaten.
16. Sprinkle each loaf with one-half of a mixture of chopped almonds and sugar.
17. Cover and let rise about 45 min., or until dough is doubled.
18. Bake at 375°F 20 to 25 min.
19. Cool completely on cooling racks.

2 loaves bread

Christmas Rolls: Follow recipe for Coffee Bread. Instead of dividing dough for loaves, break off pieces of dough and roll with hands into strips 4 in. long and ½ in. thick. Coil each end in to center of strip. Place two coiled strips together so that coils are back to back. Or place two coiled strips at right angles, one on top of the other. Or shape strip into a half circle and coil ends in opposite directions. Press **1 raisin** into the center of each coil. Place rolls on greased baking sheets. Omit egg white and almond-sugar mixture. Cover and let rise until doubled. Bake at 375°F about 15 to 20 min.

About 4 doz. rolls

Fruit Bread, Milan Style

2 packages active dry yeast
¼ cup warm water
1 cup butter, melted
1 cup sugar
1 teaspoon salt
2 cups sifted all-purpose flour
½ cup milk, scalded and cooled to lukewarm
2 eggs
4 egg yolks
3½ cups all-purpose flour
1 cup dark seedless raisins
¾ cup chopped citron
½ cup all-purpose flour
1 egg, slightly beaten
1 tablespoon water

1. Dissolve yeast in the warm water.
2. Pour melted butter into large bowl of electric mixer. Add the sugar and salt gradually, beating constantly.
3. Beating thoroughly after each addition, alternately add the 2 cups flour in thirds and lukewarm milk in halves to the butter mixture. Add yeast and beat well.
4. Combine eggs and egg yolks and beat until thick and piled softly. Add the beaten eggs all at one time to yeast mixture and beat well. Beating thoroughly after each addition, gradually add the 3½ cups flour. Stir in raisins and citron.
5. Sift half of the remaining ½ cup flour over a pastry canvas or board. Turn dough onto floured surface; cover and let rest 10 minutes.
6. Sift remaining flour over dough. Pull dough from edges toward center until flour is worked in. (It will be sticky.) Put dough into a greased deep bowl and grease top of dough. Cover; let rise in a warm place (about 80°F) about 2½ hours.
7. Punch down dough and pull edges of dough in to center. Let rise again about 1 hour.
8. Divide dough into halves and shape each into a round loaf. Put each loaf into a well-greased 8-inch layer cake pan. Brush surfaces generously with a mixture of slightly beaten egg and water. Cover; let rise again about 1 hour.
9. Bake at 350°F 40 to 45 minutes, or until golden brown. Remove to wire racks to cool.

Croustade Basket

1 loaf unsliced bread
⅓ cup melted butter or margarine

1. Neatly trim the crusts from top and sides of loaf. Using a sharp pointed knife, hollow out center, leaving 1-inch sides and bottom.
2. Brush inside and out with melted butter. Place on a baking sheet.
3. Toast in a 400°F oven 10 to 15 minutes, or until golden brown and crisp. Fill with Scrambled Eggs.

Fish & Shellfish

Trout in Grapevine Leaves

1   jar (32 ounces) grapevine leaves, drained
4   medium trout, cleaned, with heads and tails left on
2   tablespoons olive oil
2   tablespoons butter, melted
2   teaspoons oregano
1   teaspoon dill
     Additional oil to brush outside of trout
     Salt and pepper to taste
2   lemons, cut in wedges

1. Rinse grapevine leaves thoroughly under cold running water to remove brine.
2. Rinse trout; pat dry.
3. Drizzle 2 tablespoons olive oil and butter in trout cavities. Sprinkle with oregano and dill. Brush oil on outside of fish. Season inside and out with salt and pepper.
4. Wrap each trout in 5 or 6 grapevine leaves. Refrigerate 1 to 2 hours.
5. To charcoal-broil, adjust grill 4 inches from heated coals. Grease a rectangular, long-handled grill on all sides. Place fish in the grill, side by side. Grill one side about 8 minutes, turn, grill until fish flakes easily with a fork (about 8 minutes more).
6. Discard browned outer leaves. Serve trout in remaining leaves. Garnish with lemon wedges.
4 servings

Note: Trout may also be broiled under the broiler. For easy turning, use a long-handled grill.

Fillet of Sole in White Wine

2   pounds sole fillets
½   cup dry white wine
½   cup chopped onion
3   tablespoons butter, melted
2   bay leaves, crushed
1   teaspoon chopped parsley
½   teaspoon salt
¼   teaspoon pepper

1. Put fillets into a greased shallow 2-quart casserole.
2. Mix wine, onion, butter, and dry seasonings. Pour over fish. Cover casserole.
3. Bake at 375°F 25 minutes, or until fish flakes easily when tested with a fork.

6 servings

Cod Sailor Style

2	pounds cod steaks, about 1 inch thick
2	cups canned tomatoes, sieved
¼	cup chopped green olives
2	tablespoons capers
1	tablespoon parsley
1	teaspoon salt
½	teaspoon pepper
½	teaspoon oregano

1. Put cod steaks into a greased 1½-quart casserole.
2. Combine tomatoes, olives, capers, parsley, salt, pepper, and oregano in a saucepan. Bring to boiling and pour over cod.
3. Bake at 350°F 25 to 30 minutes, or until fish flakes easily when tested with a fork.

4 servings

Codfish for Christmas

1	pound salted codfish (1 piece)
2	small onions, peeled
	Salt and pepper
3	medium (1 pound) tomatoes, peeled, seeded, and cut in pieces
2	cloves garlic, peeled
3	tablespoons oil
5	pickled chilies, seeded and cut in strips
3	canned pimentos, cut in strips
½	cup pimento-stuffed olives
1	tablespoon chopped parsley

1. Soak codfish several hours in cold water; change water several times.
2. Drain codfish and put into a saucepan; add 1 onion and water to cover. Bring to simmering, cover, and cook gently about 15 minutes, or until fish flakes easily when tested with a fork. Drain. Season with salt and pepper.
3. Meanwhile, puree tomatoes, remaining onion (cut in quarters), and garlic in an electric blender.
4. Heat oil in a skillet and add the red sauce. Cook until thicker, stirring occasionally. Mix in chili and pimento strips.
5. To serve, put the codfish on a platter, pour the sauce over it, and garnish with whole olives and parsley. Accompany with cooked rice.

About 4 servings

Baked Eel

Have eel skinned, split and backbone removed. Cut into 2 or 3 inch pieces, wash in salted water and dry thoroughly. Dredge with flour, season with salt and pepper, place in buttered baking pan and add ½ cup water. Cover. Bake in hot oven (400°F.) for 20 minutes or until eel is browned.

Pickled Octopus

1	small octopus (about 2 pounds)
½	cup olive oil
¼	cup white wine vinegar
	Juice of ½ lemon
1	tablespoon minced parsley
½	teaspoon marjoram
	Salt and pepper to taste

1. Beat octopus with the flat side of a metal meat hammer 15 to 20 minutes; it will feel soft and excrete grayish liquid.
2. Wash octopus thoroughly, drain, and cook in skillet without water until it becomes bright pink. Cut into bite-size pieces.
3. Make a salad dressing of the olive oil, vinegar, lemon juice, parsley, marjoram, salt, and pepper. Mix well.
4. Pour over octopus and store in the refrigerator in a covered container for 5 days before serving.
5. Serve cold as an appetizer.

4 to 6 servings

Stuffed Squid

32	squid, cleaned and tentacles removed
¾	cup olive oil
1	large onion chopped
1½	cups water
1	cup long-grain rice
½	cup chopped parsley
1	teaspoon mint
1	teaspoon basil
2	cloves garlic, crushed in a garlic press
½	cup pine nuts
¼	cup dried black currants
1	cup dry white wine
	Salt and pepper to taste
	Water
	Juice of 2 lemons

1. Reserve squid. Rinse tentacles in cold water. Drain and mince finely.
2. In a large saucepan, heat 2 tablespoons of the oil, add onion and minced tentacles and cook over low heat until tentacles turn pink. Add water. Heat to boiling. Reduce heat, add rice, parsley, mint, basil, garlic, pine nuts, currants, and ½ cup of the wine.
3. Simmer until liquid is absorbed. Season with salt and pepper. Cool.
4. Using a teaspoon, stuff each squid cavity loosely with the rice mixture. Arrange squid in rows in a large baking dish. Combine the remaining wine and olive oil with enough water to reach half the depth of the squid. Season with additional salt and pepper. Cover.
5. Bake at 325°F about 40 minutes, or until squid is tender. Drizzle with lemon juice just before serving.

8 servings

Note: Stuffing may also be used as a side dish. Stuff 16 squid. Put remaining stuffing in a baking dish. Add a little water, salt and pepper and cover. Bake at 325°F 30 minutes.

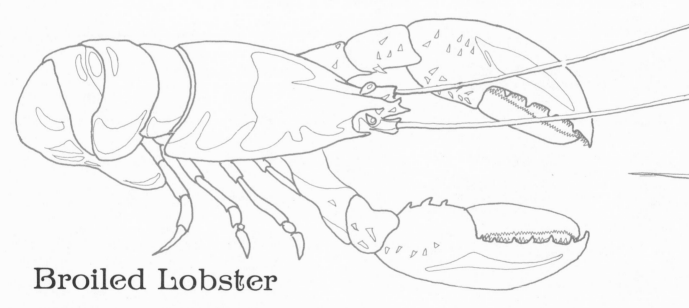

Broiled Lobster

Kill lobster by inserting sharp knife into joint where tail and body-shell come together, thus cutting the spinal cord. Place lobster on back, make deep incision at mouth and with a quick cut, split lobster legthwise to end of tail. Open and remove stomach, intestinal vein running length of body, liver and coral. Save liver and coral for sauce. Crack large claws. Spread lobster as flat as possible, place split side up on greased broiler; brush with melted butter, sprinkle lightly with salt and pepper. Broil slowly for 15 to 20 minutes or until delicately browned. Turn and broil 10 minutes longer on shell side. Serve at once with melted butter. Allow ¾ to 1 pound lobster per portion.

Baked Lobster — Prepare lobster as above, but bake in hot oven (425°F.) 15 to 20 minutes, instead of broiling.

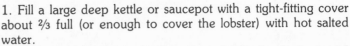
"Boiled" Lobster

Hot salted water (1 tablespoon salt per qt. water)
1   live lobster, about 1½ lbs
    Fresh dill or parsley
    Sauce for Lobster

1. Fill a large deep kettle or saucepot with a tight-fitting cover about ⅔ full (or enough to cover the lobster) with hot salted water.
2. Bring water rapidly to boiling. Grasp lobster by the back and plunge head first into the water.
3. Cover, bring water again to rolling boil. Reduce heat and simmer 15 to 20 min. Drain and cover with cold water to chill. Drain again. Place shell-side down on a cutting board.
4. Twist off the two large claws, the smaller ones and the tail. With a pair of scissors cut or with a sharp knife slit the bony membrane on the underside of tail. Remove and discard the intestinal vein. Using a sharp knife, cut completely through tail crosswise into 1½ in. pieces. With a sharp knife, cut lobster into halves; cut completely through entire length of body and through shell. Remove and discard the intestinal vein running lengthwise through center of body. Remove and discard stomach (a small sac which lies in the head) and spongy lungs (which lie in upper body cavity between meat and shell).
5. If present, remove and reserve the tomalley (green liver) and the coral (bright red roe) to be used along with the lobster meat or as a garnish. Using a sharp knife, cut the body crosswise into 1½-in. pieces.
6. Chill pieces of lobster and the claws in refrigerator. When ready to serve on the smorgasbord, arrange pieces of lobster and claws on a platter, shell-side up, to resemble a whole lobster. Garnish lobster with fresh dill or parsley.
7. Serve with Sauce for Lobster.

About 8 to 10 servings

Note: To use cooked lobster meat in food preparation, do not cut lobster into pieces. Spread tail shell apart and remove meat in one piece; remove meat from body shell. Disjoint the large claws and crack with a nutcracker. A nut pick may be helpful in removing meat from small joints and claws. Chill in refrigerator, cut and use as directed.

1¼ cups lobster meat

Lobster Fra Diavolo

    Marinara Sauce (page 103)
2   live lobsters (about 1½ pounds each)
½   cup red wine
    Few grains cayenne pepper

1. Prepare Marinara Sauce.
2. While sauce is cooking, fill a large, deep kettle about two thirds full with water. Bring to boiling and plunge lobsters, one at a time, head first into boiling water. Cover and boil about 8 minutes (Lobsters will turn pink.) Remove lobsters with tongs. With a sharp knife, slit underside lengthwise and remove stomach, lungs, and vein. Keep warm.
3. When sauce is cooked, stir in wine and cayenne, bring to boiling, and pour over lobsters. Serve immediately.

2 servings

Lobster Thermidor I

3   **live lobster, about 1½ lbs. each**
9   **tablespoons butter**
1½   **cups Medium White Sauce (one and one half times recipe, page 99; stir into sauce 3 tablespoons heavy cream after removing from heat)**
⅔   **cup chopped mushrooms**
2   **tablespoons chopped shallots or onion**
3   **tablespoons heavy cream**
2   **tablespoons white wine**
1   **teaspoon finely chopped chervil or parsley**
½   **teaspoon Worcestershire sauce**
½   **teaspoon dry mustard**
¼   **teaspoon salt**
1/8   **teaspoon cayenne pepper White wine (about ¼ teaspoon per shell)**
1   **egg yolk, slightly beaten**
2   **tablespoons whipped cream**
2   **tablespoons grated Parmesan cheese**

1. Purchase 3 live lobsters
2. Live lobsters may be killed at the market. (Or see Broiled Lobster, page 28). To kill and clean lobster.) Cut completely through shell to divide lobsters into halves; disjoint large and small claws.
3. Heat 6 tablespoons butter in a large heavy skillet with a tight-fitting cover.
4. Add halves of lobster, meat-side down, to skillet. Place large and small claws on top. Cover; cook slowly 12 to 15 min., or until tender. (Lobster meat cooked at a high temperature becomes tough and is difficult to remove from shell.)
5. Meanwhile, prepare medium white sauce.
6. Set aside.
7. Clean and chop mushrooms.
8. Heat 3 tablespoons butter in a saucepan.
9. Add the mushrooms and chopped shallots or onion.
10. Cook over medium heat until mushrooms are tender and lightly browned and onion is soft. Occasionally move and turn mixture with a spoon. Remove from heat.
11. Blend heavy cream, white wine, chevil or parsley, Worcestershire sauce and a mixture of dry mustard, salt and cayenne pepper into one half of the white sauce.
12. Add to the mushroom-onion mixture. Cook over low heat, until thoroughly heated, moving and turning mixture gently with a spoon.
13. When lobster is done, starting at tail, with first and second fingers, gently pry lobster meat from shells, reserving shells. Remove meat from large claws. Place the shells, cavity side up, on a baking sheet and heat at 325°F about 7 min., or until shells are heated.
14. Meanwhile, cut the lobster meat into 1-in. pieces and blend into the sauce.
15. Remove shells from oven and sprinkle white wine over interior of each.
16. Fill the lobster shells with the lobster mixture.
17. Pour remaining white sauce into the top of a double boiler. Stir over low heat until heated. Vigorously stir about 3 tablespoons sauce into egg yolk.
18. Immediately return mixture to top of double boiler. Stirring constantly, cook over simmering water 3 to 5 minutes. Remove from heat and blend in whipped cream.
19. Spoon over lobster mixture in the shells.
20. Set out grated Parmesan cheese.
21. Sprinkle 1 teaspoon of the cheese over each of the filled shells.
22. Place baking sheet on broiler pan with tops of food 2 to 3 in. from heat. Broil 2 to 3 min., or until lightly browned.

6 servings

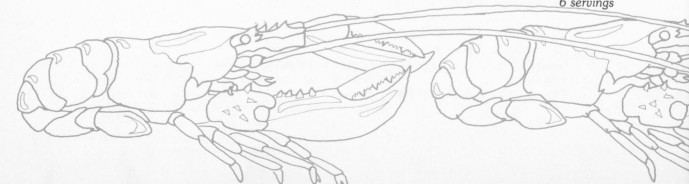

Lobster Thermidor II

1	**Boiled Lobster**
3	**mushrooms, sliced**
¼	**cup butter**
	Dash paprika
⅛	**teaspoon mustard**
1	**tablespoon minced parsley**
½	**cup sherry**
1½	**cups Cream Sauce (page 99)**
2	**tablespoons grated Parmesan cheese**

1. Cut lobster lengthwise into halves, remove meat and break it into small pieces.
2. Cook mushrooms 5 minutes in butter; add paprika, mustard, parsley, sherry and 1 cup cream sauce.
3. Mix well, fill lobster shell with mixture, cover with remaining sauce and sprinkle with cheese. Bake in hot oven (450°F.) about 10 minutes.

Serves 2

The cream sauce, may be seasoned more highly if desired. Increase mustard to 1 teaspoon, add 1 teaspoon grated onion and dash celery salt instead of parsley. Increase mushrooms to ¾ cup. Proceed as above.

Lobster Tails, Thermidor

2	**(1½ lbs. each) frozen rock lobster tails**
2	**tablespoons butter**
2	**tablespoons flour**
½	**teaspoon salt**
1	**teaspoon paprika**
⅛	**teaspoon Tabasco**
1	**teaspoon prepared mustard**
1½	**cups cream**
2	**cups (½ lb.) shredded Cheddar cheese**
1	**teaspoon Worcestershire sauce**
¼	**cup chopped green pepper**
½	**lb. fresh mushrooms, sliced lengthwise**

1. Drop frozen lobster tails into boiling salted water. Bring to boiling; simmer 25 to 30 minutes.
2. Meanwhile, heat the 2 tablespoons butter in a large saucepan. Stir in the flour, salt, and paprika and cook until mixture bubbles; blend in Tabasco and mustard. Add cream gradually, stirring until well blended. Bring rapidly to boiling and boil 1 to 2 minutes, stirring constantly. Remove from heat. Add cheese and Worcestershire sauce; stir until cheese is melted. Cover; set aside and keep warm.
3. Remove cooked lobster tails and place under running cold water for 1 minute, or until cool enough to handle. With scissors, cut along each edge of bony membrane on the underside of each shell; remove and discard the membrane.
4. Gently remove meat from shells, cut into ½-inch pieces, and add to sauce. Reserve shells.
5. Heat the ¼ cup butter in a skillet; add green pepper and mushrooms and cook about 5 minutes, or until mushrooms are lightly browned, stirring occasionally. Blend green pepper-mushroom mixture into the cheese sauce.
6. Fill lobster shells with mixture and top with a mixture of **2 tablespoons cracker crumbs, ¼ cup shredded Parmesan cheese,** and **2 tablespoons melted butter.**
7. Set under broiler 4 inches from source of heat 2 to 3 minutes, or until sauce is bubbly and top is lightly browned. Garnish base of each tail with watercress and serve immediately.

6 servings

Cooked Shrimp

1 lb. fresh shrimp with
    shells
2 cups water
3 tablespoons lemon juice
1 tablespoon salt

1. Wash the shrimp in cold water. Drop shrimp into a boiling mixture of remaining ingredients. Cover tightly. Simmer 5 minutes, or only until shrimp are pink in color. (Avoid overcooking as it toughens shrimp.) Drain and cover with cold water to chill. Drain shrimp again.

2. Remove tiny legs from shrimp; peel off shells. Cut a slit along back (curved surface) of each shrimp just deep enough to expose the black vein. With knife point remove vein in one piece. Rinse quickly in running cold water. Drain on absorbent paper. Store in refrigerator until ready to use.

1/2 to 3/4 Pound Cooked Shrimp

French Fried Shrimp

1½ pounds Boiled Shrimp
1 pint milk
1 egg
    Flour
    Corn meal or bread
    crumbs
1/8 teaspoon salt
    Dash pepper

1. Clean shrimp.
2. Mix milk with egg, and shrimp and let stand for 3 minutes.
3. Mix equal parts of flour and corn meal with seasonings.
4. Coat shrimp well with mixture. Cook in hot deep fat (375°F.) until brown. Shrimp will rise to the top of fat when cooked.
5. Drain on absorbent paper.

Serves 6

Shrimp De Jonghe

1 pound uncooked shrimp
2 tablespoons white wine
    Dash white pepper
2 teaspoons butter
2 slices dried bread or 1
    slice bread and 1 slice
    toast, crumbed
1 clove garlic, diced
2 tablespoons diced leek
1/8 teaspoon salt

1. Clean and rinse uncooked shrimp and arrange in shallow baking dish.
2. Add wine and pepper and dot with butter.
3. Add garlic, leek and salt to crumbs and rub to a smooth paste.
4. Spread on shrimp and bake at 350°F 20 minutes.
5. Serve at once in the baking dish, for 2.

Deep-Fried Shrimp

Vegetable shortening, all-purpose shortening, lard or cooking oil for deep-frying
2 lbs. fresh shrimp with shells
1 cup (3 slices) fine dry bread crumbs
2 eggs, slightly beaten
2 tablespoons milk
2 tablespoons paprika
1 teaspoon salt
1/4 teaspoon pepper
1/8 teaspoon cayenne pepper

1. About 20 min. before ready to deep-fry, fill a deep saucepan or automatic deep fryer one-half to two-thirds full with vegetable shortening, all-purpose shortening, lard or cooking oil for deep-frying.
2. Heat fat slowly to 350°F.
3. Peel shrimp, remove vein and set aside.
4. Put bread crumbs into a shallow pan or dish and set aside.
5. Mix in a bowl eggs, milk, paprika, salt, pepper and cayenne pepper.
6. Dip shrimp into egg mixture and then coat shrimp by rolling in bread crumbs.
7. Deep-fry in the heated fat only as many shrimp at one time as will lie uncrowded one layer deep in the fat. Fry shrimp 2 to 3 min., or until brown. Turn shrimp as they rise to surface and several times during cooking. Remove shrimp with a slotted spoon; drain over fat for a few seconds before removing them to absorbent paper.
8. Serve hot with lemon wedges and melted butter or chili sauce.

6 to 8 servings

Fried Shrimp De Luxe

2 lbs. Cooked Shrimp
2 eggs, fork beaten
1 1/2 cups of corn flake crumbs
1 env. (about 1 3/8 oz.) dry onion soup mix
1/4 cup chopped parsley
3 tablespoons shredded Parmesan cheese
Butter or margarine

1. Dip shrimp into egg, then into a mixture of the corn flake crumbs, soup mix, parsley, and cheese. (Store leftover crumb mixture, tightly covered, in refrigerator to use for coating meat, poultry, and shellfish, or as topping for casseroles.)
2. Fry the shrimp until lightly browned in hot butter in a heavy skillet.
3. Serve immediately.

About 8 servings

Fried Scallops

1 cup dry bread crumbs
1 teaspoon salt
½ teaspoon celery salt
1 pound scallops
1 egg
2 tablespoons water

1. Combine crumbs and seasonings.
2. Dip scallops into crumbs, then into egg diluted with water and dip into crumbs again.
3. Saute or fry in hot deep fat (365°F.) 4 to 5 minutes.
4. Serve with Tartare Sauce.

Serves 4

Broiled Scallops

1 pound scallops
French dressing (page 99)
(Seasoned crumbs)

1. Dip scallops into French dressing and roll in crumbs.
2. Place on greased baking sheet in a preheated broiler (550°F.) and cook for about 15 minutes, or until the scallops are browned.
3. Turn occasionally.

Serves 4

Use a fork when dipping scallops into crumbs to make crust smooth and even.

Boiled Hard-Shelled Crabs

Drop live crabs one at a time into boiling salted water to cover. Reheat water to boiling after adding each crab. Cook 20 to 25 minutes, drain and rinse.
Break off claws. Remove the hard top shell, working from tail end. Discard the spongy fiber and apron. Crack claws with a nut cracker. Remove meat, discarding all body spines. A 1-pound crab will yield about 1 cup of meat. Crab meat may be used instead of lobster in most recipes for lobster meat.

Deep-Fried Scallops

2 lbs. scallops
1 cup (about 3 slices) fine dry bread crumbs or corn meal
2 eggs, slightly beaten
2 tablespoons milk
2 tablespoons paprika
1 teaspoon salt
¼ teaspoon pepper
Tartar Sauce
Lemon wedges

1. Set out a deep saucepan or aoutomatic deep-fryer and heat fat to 365°F.
2. Set out scallops.
3. (If using frozen scallops, thaw following directions on package.) Rinse scallops in cold water. Set aside to drain on absorbent paper.
4. Put dry bread crumbs or corn meal into a shallow pan or dish and set aside.
5. Mix in bowl eggs, milk, paprika, salt and pepper.
6. Coat scallops, one at a time, by rolling in bread crumbs, dip in egg mixture and then coat again with bread crumbs.
7. Deep-fry in heated fat only as many scallops at one time as will lie uncrowded one layer deep in the fat. Fry 2 or 3 min., or until brown. Turn scallops as they rise to surface and several times during cooking. Remove scallops with a slotted spoon; drain over fat for a few seconds before removing them to absorbent paper.
8. Serve hot with Tartar Sauce and Lemon wedges.

6 to 8 servings

Deep-Fried Oysters: Follow recipe for Deep-Fried Scallops. Heat fat to 375°F. Substitute **1 qt. large oysters** for the scallops. Drain and pick over to remove any shell particles. (Reserve liquor for use in other food prepartion.)

Deep-Fried Clams: Follow recipe for Deep-Fried Scallops. Heat fat to 375°F. Substitute **1 qt. shucked clams** for the scallops.

Crab Ravigote

¼ cup butter
¼ cup flour
1 teaspoon salt
Few grains cayenne pepper
2 cups milk
⅔ cup chopped cooked green pepper
⅔ cup coarsely chopped pimento
2 tablespoons capers
2 teaspoons tarragon vinegar
2 cups lump crab meat
⅔ cup Hollandaise Sauce

1. Heat butter in cooking pan of a chafing dish; blend in flour, salt, and cayenne pepper; heat until bubbly. Gradually add milk, stirring constantly. Cook and stir until boiling; cook 1 minute.
2. Stir in remaining ingredients and heat thoroughly over simmering water.
3. Serve on **rusks.**

4 servings

Hollandaise Sauce: In the top of a double boiler, beat **2 egg yolks, 2 tablespoons cream, ¼ teaspoon salt** and a **few grains cayenne pepper** until thick with a whisk beater. Set over hot (not boiling) water. Add **2 tablespoons lemon juice or tarragon vinegar** gradually, while beating constantly. Cook, beating constantly with the whisk beater, until sauce is consistency of thick cream. Remove double boiler from heat, leaving top in place. Beating constantly, add ½ **cup butter,** ½ teaspoon at a time, until the butter is melted and thoroughly blended in.

About 1 cup

Elegant Party Crab Crepes

3   pkgs. (6 oz. each) thawed frozen or 2 cans (7½ oz. each) drained Alaska king crab, sliced
7   tablespoons butter or margarine
6   mushrooms, sliced through caps and stems
2   tablespoons minced onion
⅓   cup all-purpose flour
1   teaspoon rosemary leaves, crushed
½   teaspoon seasoned salt
     Few grains pepper
1½   cups chicken broth
1½   cups dairy sour cream
1   tablespoon snipped parsley
1   cup shredded Swiss cheese
     Paprika

1. Set out a heavy saucepan and a large shallow baking dish.
2. Prepare 16 to 18 crepes (use your favorite recipe); keep warm until ready to use. Have crab meat ready.
3. Heat in saucepan 1 tablespoon butter or margarine.
4. Add mushrooms and onion and cook until lightly browned.
5. Remove mushrooms with a slotted spoon and keep warm.
6. Add 6 tablespoons butter or margarine to the saucepan.
7. Blend in flour, rosemary leaves, salt and pepper.
8. Gradually add chicken broth, stirring constantly.
9. Cook and stir until boiling; cook about 2 min. and remove from heat.
10. Stir in dairy sour cream, a small amount at a time.
11. Mix in the mushrooms, the crab meat and parsley.
12. Spoon about ¼ cup filling along center of each crepe and roll up. Arrange, overlapping side down, in a single layer in the baking dish. Top with Swiss cheese.
13. Sprinkle with paprika.
14. Heat in 350°F oven 10 to 15 min., or until cheese is melted and crepes are thoroughly heated. Garnish with **sprigs of parsley.**

16 to 18 crab-filled crepes

Clams

There are two general types of clams, the soft clams and the hard or quahog clams. The latter group is divided into 3 classes: The littlenecks, small in size; the cherry stone, medium-sized; and the large chowder clams. The littleneck and cherry stone clams may be used uncooked.

When purchased the shells should be tightly closed or close at a touch as an indication of freshness. They may be opened with a knife or steamed open.

Steamed Clams

Wash clams in several waters, scrubbing shells well to remove any sand. Place in large kettle, using ½ cup of water to cover bottom of kettle. Cover kettle tightly, place over low heat and steam until shells open (about 15 minutes). Serve in the shells in soup plates, accompanying each serving with a small dish of melted butter to which a few drops of lemon juice have been added, and a cup of the hot clam liquor.

Steamed Mussels: Wash and cook mussels as above. Trim and discard horny beard. Serve as directed for Steamed Clams.

Clams for cocktails should be very chilly morsels; the sauce hot and spicy.

Fried Clams

1 quart fresh clams, shucked
2 eggs, beaten
2 tablespoons milk
2 teaspoons salt
   Few grains pepper
3 cups dry bread crumbs
   Oil for deep frying

1. Drain clams and set aside.
2. Combine egg, milk, salt, and pepper. Dip clams in egg mixture and roll in bread crumbs.
3. Heat oil to 350°F in a wok. Fry a few clams at a time in the hot oil 1 to 2 minutes, or until brown. Drain on absorbent paper.
4. Serve hot with tartar sauce.

About 6 servings

Oysters Rockefeller

4 dozen oysters in half shell
   Sauce
8 slices cooked bacon
2 cups cooked spinach
3 tablespoons minced parsley
6 celery hearts
2 green onion tops
1/2 teaspoon salt
1/4 teaspoon pepper
1/4 teaspoon paprika
1/2 cup butter, melted
6 tablespoons lemon juice
4 tablespoons cracker crumbs

1. Heat a 1-inch layer of rock salt in pans and arrange oysters in the half shell over the salt. Broil under moderate heat until edges begin to curl. Prepare sauce: Chop first 5 ingredients very fine.
2. Add remaining ingredients and heat to boiling. Pour hot sauce over each oyster, return pan to oven to brown the sauce slightly and serve at once, serving each guest a panful of oysters.
3. The salt is used to keep the oysters hot and to hold them upright.

Serve 8

Savory Oysters

6 slices crisp toast (2 cups crumbs)
1/2 cup butter or margarine
1 cup (8-oz. can, drained) mushrooms, finely sliced
1/3 cup chopped green pepper
1/2 clove garlic (insert wooden pick for easy removal)
1 qt. oysters
1/4 cup reserved oyster liquor
1/4 cup cream or milk
1 teaspoon Worcestershire sauce
1 teaspoon salt
1 teaspoon paprika
1/8 teaspoon mace
   Dash of cayenne pepper

1. Grease a 2-qt. casserole.
2. Prepare coarse crumbs from crisp toast.
3. Set aside.
4. Heat butter or margarine, mushrooms, green pepper, and garlic slowly about 5 min. in a large skillet, stirring occasionally.
5. Remove skillet from heat; discard garlic. Stir in toast crumbs, blending well. Set aside.
6. Drain oysters thoroughly, reserving liquor.
7. Remove any shell particles. Combine oyster liquor, cream or milk and Worcestershire sauce.
8. Set aside oysters and liquid.
9. Mix salt, paprika, mace and cayenne pepper.
10. Line bottom of casserole with one third of crumb mixture. Top with layers of one half of oysters, one half of seasonings and one third of crumb mixture. Repeat oyster and seasoning layers. Spoon liquid over oysters before topping with remaining mixture of crumbs.
11. Bake at 375°F 20 to 30 min., or until crumbs are golden brown.

6 to 8 servings

Oysters Piquante In The Half Shell

1   qt. (about 36) large oysters
1   cup mayonnaise
2   tablespoons chili sauce
1   tablespoon butter or margarine, melted
1 ½   teaspoons prepared mustard
1   teaspoon lemon juice
4   drops Tabasco
¼   teaspoon salt
  Few grains pepper
1/8   teaspoon paprika
1   cup buttered soft bread crumbs

1. Set out 12 small shell-shaped ramekins. (If oysters are purchased in shells, use deep half of each shell.)

2. Drain oysters; discard liquor; place 3 oysters in each ramekin or shell.

3. Blend the mayonnaise, chili sauce, butter, mustard, lemon juice, Tabasco, and a mixture of salt, pepper, and paprika. Spoon mayonnaise mixture over oysters. Top with the buttered crumbs.

4. Broil about 3 inches from source of heat 5 minutes, or until oysters begin to curl at edges and crumbs are golden brown.

12 servings

Vegetables

Cooked Artichokes

4   artichokes
1   tablespoon lemon juice
1   teaspoon salt
    Lemon slices
    Parsley sprigs
    Hot melted butter or
    margarine

1. Set out a large saucepot or kettle.
2. With a sharp knife cutting straight across, cut off 1 in. of the tops from artichokes.
3. Cut off stems about 1 in. from base and remove outside lower leaves. With scissors, clip off tips of uncut leaves and discard. Rinse artichokes under cold water and stand them upright in the saucepot. Add boiling water to a depth of 1 in. and lemon juice and salt.
4. Cook, covered, 35 to 45 min., or until a leaf can be easily pulled from artichoke. (Cooking time will depend upon size of artichokes.) If more water is needed during cooking, add boiling water.
5. Remove artichokes and drain upside down so all the water can run out. Cut off remainder of artichoke stem.
6. Serve immediately standing upright on serving platter. Garnish with lemon slices and parsley sprigs.
7. Accompany with individual serving of hot melted butter or margarine or individual servings of Hollandaise Sauce (page 35).

How to Eat Artichokes: Pull off each leaf and dip in melted butter or sauce. Eat only the tender part of leaf by drawing it between teeth. Discard less tender tip. Continue with each leaf until choke or fuzzy part in center is reached. Remove choke with knife and fork and discard. The heart or base may be eaten by cutting it with a fork and dipping each piece into the melted butter sauce.

4 servings

Chilled Artichokes: Follow recipe for Cooked Artichokes. Drain artichokes and chill in refrigerator until ready to serve. Chilled artichokes are usually served as a salad on individual serving plates. Accompany with individual servings of **mayonnaise, French Dressing** or any of its variations.

Artichokes in Mushroom Cream

2	packages (9 ounces each) frozen artichoke hearts
¼	cup butter
4	ounces mushrooms, coarsely chopped
2	tablespoons finely chopped onion
2½	tablespoons flour
¼	teaspoon salt
⅛	teaspoon white pepper
⅛	teaspoon ground nutmeg
¾	cup chicken broth (dissolve 1 chicken bouillon cube in ¾ cup boiling water)
¾	cup cream
2	egg yolks, slightly beaten
2	tablespoons snipped parsley
½	teaspoon capers
8	patty shells

1. Cook artichoke hearts according to package directions, substituting **seasoned salt** for salt. Drain and set aside.
2. Meanwhile, heat butter in cooking pan of a chafing dish; add mushrooms and onion. Cook, stirring occasionally, until mushrooms are lightly browned.
3. Blend in a mixture of the flour, salt, pepper, and nutmeg. Heat until bubbly. Remove from heat and add broth and cream gradually, stirring constantly; bring sauce to boiling and cook 1 to 2 minutes, stirring constantly.
4. Remove from heat and vigorously stir about 3 tablespoons of the mixture into egg yolks. Immediately return to double boiler. Cook over boiling water about 5 minutes, stirring slowly so mixture cooks evenly.
5. Mix in artichoke hearts, parsley, and capers. Heat thoroughly over simmering water.
6. Spoon mixture into warm patty shells. Replace patty shell tops or garnish with tiny fancy shapes cut from a crimson **cinnamon apple** or a **grenadine pear**.

8 servings

Stuffed Artichokes Sicilian

4	medium artichokes
1	teaspoon salt
⅔	cup (2 slices) fine dry bread crumbs
1	clove plus 3 slices garlic, sliced thin
1	teaspoon grated Parmesan cheese
1	tablespoon plus 1 teaspoon chopped parsley
1	teaspoon salt
¾	teaspoon pepper
2	tablespoon olive oil
2	cups boiling water

1. Set out a 10-in. dkillet with a tight-fitting cover.
2. Remove outside lower leaves and cut off stems from artichokes.
3. Cover with cold water. Add salt.
4. Let stand 5 to 10 min. Drain upside down.
5. Meanwhile, mix dry bread crumbs, garlic, Parmesan cheese, parsley, salt and pepper.
6. Set aside.
7. Spread leaves of artichokes open slightly and place 3 slices of garlic in each artichoke.
8. Sprinkle crumb mixture between leaves and over top of artichokes. Sprinkle with parsley.
9. Place artichokes close together in skillet so they will remain upright during cooking. Add boiling water.
10. Drizzle artichokes with olive oil.
11. Cover and cook about 30 min., or until artichoke leaves are tender.
12. To eat artichokes, pull out leaves, one by one.

4 servings

Artichokes with Anchovy Dressing: Follow recipe for Stuffed Artichokes Sicilian. When preparing artichokes, cut off the top of the leaves and cut out the choke from the center. Discard choke. Add to stuffing **4 anchovy fillets,** chopped. Fill center and between leaves with the stuffing.

Cooked Asparagus

2   **pounds asparagus**
     Boiling water
1   **teaspoon salt**

1. Wash the asparagus throughly and tie in 1 bundle or into 6 to 8 individual bundles. Place bundles upright with stems down in just enough boiling water to cover thick part of stalks.
2. Add salt and cook 10 minutes or until stalks are tender. Arrange bundles in water so tips are covered and cook 5 minutes longer. To serve season with pepper and butter.

Serves 6 to 8

With Hollandaise — Serve hot cooked Asparagus with Hollandaise Sauce (page 35) poured across the bunches and strip of pimiento over the sauce.

With Cheese Sauce — To vary, serve with Cheese Sauce (page 99).

Asparagus Supreme

2   **tablespoons minced onion**
2   **tablespoons butter or margarine**
1   **tablespoon flour**
½   **teaspoon salt**
½   **teaspoon paprika**
¼   **teaspoon dry mustard**
½   **teaspoon Worcestershire sauce**
1   **cup undiluted evaporated milk**
3   **pkgs. (10 oz. each) frozen asparagus pieces cooked and drained**
4   **oz. process sharp Cheddar cheese, shredded**
2   **tablespoons fine dry bread crumbs**

1. Cook onion in hot butter in a saucepan until onion is soft, but not browned. Blend in flour, salt, paprika, dry mustard, and Worcestershire sauce. Heat until bubbly.
2. Remove from heat. Add the evaporated milk gradually, stirring constantly. Bring to boiling; cook 1 to 2 minutes.
3. Turn asparagus into a 1-quart shallow baking dish. Pour sauce over asparagus and mix lightly with a fork. Sprinkle the cheese and bread crumbs over top.
4. Set under broiler with top of mixture 2 to 3 inches from source of heat and broil 3 to 5 minutes, or until crumbs are lightly browned and cheese is melted.

About 8 servings

Asparagus With Cheese Sauce

3   **lbs. asparagus**
2   **cups Cheese Sauce (page 99)**
6   **slices bread**
     Butter or margarine
     Few grains paprika

1. Break off and discard lower parts of stalks, as far down as they will snap, from asparagus.
2. Wash remaining portions of stalks thoroughly. If necessary, remove scales to dislodge any sand. Cook 10 to 20 min., or until asparagus is tender. (Or cook three 10-oz. pkgs. frozen asparagus.)
3. Meanwhile, prepare Cheese Sauce.
4. Keep sauce warm by setting it over hot water. Cover tightly.
5. Toast bread.
6. Spread one side of each slice with butter or margarine.
7. When asparagus is tender, drain if necessary. Arrange servings of asparagus on slices of toast. Spoon hot sauce over asparagus. Sprinkle each serving with paprika.
8. Serve immediately.

About 8 servings

Cooked Broccoli

2½   **pounds broccoli**
      Boiling water
1   **teaspoon salt**

1. Wash broccoli and split thick heads. Place broccoli in boiling salted water, with ends down and heads out of water. Cook uncovered 10 to 20 minutes. Then place all of broccoli under water and cook 5 minutes longer. Drain (makes about 4 cups).
2. To serve, season with pepper and butter.

Serves 6 to 8

With White Sauce — Combine with 1 cup White Sauce (page 99).

With Hollandaise Sauce — Serve cooked broccoli with 1 recipe Hollandaise Sauce (page 35).

Broccoli with Buttery Lemon Crunch

½   **cup coarse dry bread crumbs**
¼   **cup butter**
1   **tablespoon grated lemon peel**
3   **tablespoons butter**
1   **small clove garlic, minced**
½   **teaspoon salt**
      Few grains pepper
1½   **pounds broccoli, cooked and drained**

1. Lightly brown crumbs in ¼ cup butter in a large skillet. Remove from butter with slotted spoon and mix crumbs with lemon peel.
2. Put the 3 tablespoons butter, garlic, salt and pepper into cooking pan of a chafing dish. Heat until butter is lightly browned. Add broccoli and turn gently until well coated with butter. Top with "lemoned" crumbs.

About 6 servings

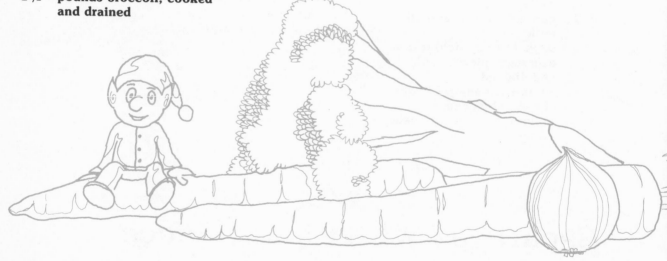

Brussels Sprouts and Grapes

1½   **pounds fresh Brussels sprouts, cut in half**
1½   **cups beer**
2   **teaspoons clarified butter**
¼   **teaspoon salt**
⅛   **teaspoon freshly ground white pepper**
1   **cup seedless white grapes**
      Snipped parsley

1. Simmer Brussels sprouts in beer in covered saucepan until tender (about 8 minutes); drain.
2. Drizzle butter over sprouts; sprinkle with salt and pepper. Add grapes; heat thoroughly. Sprinkle with parsley.

4 to 6 servings

Brussels Sprouts with Chestnuts

½   **lb. Brussels sprouts**
1   **beef bouillon cube**
½   **lb. chestnuts**
½   **teaspoon salt**
    Few grains pepper
    Few grains ground nutmeg
    Butter or margarine
¼   **cup buttered bread crumbs**

1. Cook Brussels sprouts; drain, reserving ½ cup liquid. Dissolve bouillon cube in liquid; set aside.
2. Rinse chestnuts, make a slit on two sides of each shell and put into a saucepan; cover with boiling water and boil about 20 minutes.
3. Remove shells and skins; return nuts to saucepan and cover with boiling salted water. Cover and simmer 8 to 20 mintues or until chestnut are tender; drain.
4. Mix chestnuts with Brussels sprouts. Turn one half of mixture into a buttered 1-quart casserole. Sprinkle with half of a mixture of salt, pepper, and nutmeg. Dot generously with butter. Repeat procedure. Pour beef broth over all. Sprinkle with buttered crumbs.
5. Heat in 350°F oven 15 to 20 minutes, or until crumbs are lightly browned.

4 servings

Carrot Ring

2   **cups diced Cooked Carrots**
½   **teaspoon minced onion**
1   **teaspoon salt**
⅛   **teaspoon pepper**
3   **eggs, well beaten**
1   **cup milk**

1. Combine ingredients. Pour into a buttered ring mold and bake in a moderate oven (350°F.) 40 minutes. Unmold and fill with seasoned Cooked Peas.

Serves 6

Cauliflower Supreme

½   **lb. fresh mushrooms sliced**
½   **cup butter**
½   **cup all-purpose flour**
1   **teaspoon salt**
2   **cups milk**
2   **pkgs. (10 oz. each) frozen cauliflower, cooked and drained**
6   **slices pasteurized process pimiento, cheese and Paprika**

1. Cook mushrooms in hot butter in a skillet until lightly browned. Remove mushrooms with slotted spoon and set aside.
2. Blend flour and salt into butter in skillet. Heat until bubbly. Add milk gradually, stirring constantly. Continue stirring and bring rapidly to boiling; cook 1 to 2 minutes. Stir in mushrooms.
3. Arrange half of cauliflower over bottom of lightly greased 1½-quart casserole. Cover with half of the sauce and 3 slices of cheese. Repeat layering. Sprinkle top with paprika.
4. Heat in 350°F oven about 15 minutes, or until cheese is melted and mixture is bubbly.

6 to 8 servings

Pineapple Glazed Carrots

1   **can (16 oz.) sliced carrots (about 2 cups, drained)**
1   **can (8½ oz.) pineapple tidbits (about ⅔ cup, drained)**
2   **teaspoons cornstarch**
½   **teaspoon salt**
⅔   **cup reserved carrot liquid**
⅓   **cup reserved pineapple syrup**
1   **tablespoon butter or margarine**

1. Set out a 1½-qt. saucepan.
2. Drain carrots and pineapple, reserving liquids.
3. Combine cornstarch and salt in the saucepan.
4. Mix carrot liquid and pineapple syrup and add gradually to cornstarch mixture stirring constantly.
5. Bring to boiling. Stirring constantly, cook about 3 min., or until the liquid is thick and clear. Stir in butter or margarine.
6. Add carrots and pineapple. Heat thoroughly.

4 or 5 servings

Roast Chestnuts

4   **pounds chestnuts**

1. Cut a cross on the flat side of each chestnut with a small sharp knife, being careful not to damage nutmeat. Spread in a large baking pan.
2. Roast in a 425°F oven about 30 minutes, or until done; shake frequently. Serve hot.

Candied Chestnuts

1   **lb. chestnuts**
1   **tablespoon cooking oil**
2   **cups sugar**
1   **cup water**
⅛   **teaspoon cream of tartar**

1. *To Remove Shells and Blanch Chestnuts*—Wash and make a slit in both sides of each chestnut shell. (*Follow either Method 1 or Method 2*)
2. *Method 1:* Turn chestnuts into a shallow pan and mix in oil. Bake at 450°F 20 min. Cool. Remove shells and all inner skins with a sharp knife.
3. *Method 2:* Put chestnuts into saucepan and add water to cover. Boil about 20 min. Drain immediately. Peel off shells and skins.
4. *To Glaze Chestnuts*—Turn blanched nuts into saucepan. Cover with boiling salted water. Cover. Simmer 8 to 20 min., or until tender when pierced with a fork. Set aside to drain.
5. Lightly butter a baking sheet.
6. Combine sugar, water and cream of tartar in the top of a double boiler with a tight-fitting cover. Stir over low heat until sugar is dissolved.
7. Increase heat to medium and bring mixture to boiling. Cover double boiler top and boil mixture gently 5 min. (This will dissolve any crystals that may have formed on sides of pan.) Uncover and continue cooking without stirring. Using a pastry brush dipped in water, wash down crystals from sides of pan from time to time during cooking. Cook to 300°F (remove from heat while testing). Immediately set double boiler top over gently boiling water.
8. If syrup becomes too thick, place over direct heat until proper consistency. With fork or candy dipper, dip nuts into syrup. Remove when they appear clear. Drain over saucepan for a moment. Dry on prepared baking sheet.

About 1 lb. Candied Chestnuts

Herbed Stuffed Mushrooms

* ¾   **pound mushrooms, chopped**
- ¼   **teaspoon salt**
- ⅛   **teaspoon freshly ground pepper**
- 1½   **teaspoons snipped fresh or ½ teaspoon dried basil leaves**
- 1   **tablespoon snipped parsley**
- ½   **cup chopped onion**
- 8   **large mushrooms, stems removed and sliced into rounds; reserve caps**
- 2   **tablespoons brandy**
- 1   **tablespoon clarified butter Parsley for garnish (optional)**

1. Process ¾ pound mushrooms, the salt, pepper, basil, parsley, and onion in a food processor or blender until thick and smooth. Layer ½ cup of the mushroom mixture in bottom of a baking dish.
2. Mix sliced mushroom stems, brandy, and butter. Fill reserved mushroom caps with mixture; place filled caps in baking dish. Spoon remaining mushroom mixture around mushrooms.
3. Bake at 400°F 20 minutes. Garnish with parsley.

4 servings

Note: This recipe is also excellent for a first course.

*If desired, chop mushrooms in food processor or blender, following manufacturer's directions.

Broiled Mushrooms

- 12   **large mushrooms**
- 2   **tablespoons butter**
- ¼   **teaspoon salt**
- ⅛   **teaspoon pepper**

1. Scrub mushrooms and remove stems. Place caps on greased broiler rack, cap side down, about 3 inches below source of heat.
2. Broil 3 minutes, then turn over and broil 3 minutes longer. Put a piece of butter in each cap, sprinkle with salt and pepper and broil until butter melts.
3. Serve on buttered toast.

Serves 6

Creamed Mushrooms

- 1   **pound mushrooms**
- 5   **tablespoons butter**
- ½   **teaspoon salt**
- ⅛   **teaspoon pepper**
- 2   **tablespoons flour**
- 1½   **cups milk**

1. Cut off all but ½ inch of mushroom stems.
2. Wash mushrooms thoroughly, dry and slice.
3. Cook mushrooms in butter until nearly tender; add salt, pepper and flour and mix well.
4. Add milk gradually and simmer 5 to 8 minutes, stirring constantly.

Serves 6 to 8

Sauteed Mushrooms

- 1   **pound mushrooms**
- 3   **tablespoons butter**
- ½   **teaspoon salt**
-    **Dash pepper**

1. Cut off all but ½ inch of mushroom stems.
2. Wash mushrooms thoroughly, leave whole or slice and cook, covered, in butter 10 to 15 minutes.
3. Season with salt and pepper.

Serves 6 to 8

Helpful Hints About Vegetables

• To freshen fresh asparagus, stand the stalks upright in icy cold water.

• To remove the skins from carrots easily, cover them with boiling water and let stand for a few minutes until the skin loosens.

• To keep cauliflower white while cooking, use half milk and half water; cook, uncovered, until just tender.

• To make celery curls, cut stalks (about 3 inches long) lengthwise into thin strips to within 1 inch of end. Place in cold water until strips begin to curl.

• To make celery very crisp, let stand in icy cold water to which 1 teaspoon sugar per quart of water has been added.

• To garnish lettuce leaves sprinkle some paprika on waxed paper and dip edges of leaves into it.

• To keep onions from affecting eyes, peel them under running water.

• To prevent odor while cooking onions and cabbage, add 1 tablespoon lemon juice or a wedge of lemon to the cooking water.

• To extract juice from onion, cut a slice from the root end and scrape juice from center outward, using edge of a teaspoon.

• To finely cut onion, peel, cut off a slice, then cut exposed surface into 1/8-inch squares as deep as is needed. Then slice across thinly.

• To keep fresh parsley, mint, and watercress fresh and crisp, wash thoroughly, shake off excess water, and place uncrowded in a glass jar; cover and refrigerate.

• To freshen withered parsnips, carrots, potatoes, cabbage, lettuce, etc., let stand in icy cold salted water.

• To keep leftover pimientos from spoiling, put into a small jar, pour enough cooking or salad oil over top to cover, and place, tightly covered, in refrigerator.

• To keep potato skins soft and tender enough to eat, grease them before baking.

• To prevent sweet potatoes and apples from discoloring after paring, place them in salted water at once.

• To remove skin from a tomato quickly, place fork through stem end and plunge tomato into boiling water for a few seconds, then into cold water. Or hold tomato over direct heat for a few seconds; remove from heat and break the skin at blossom end; peel skin back.

Mushrooms Magnifique

12	large fresh mushrooms, cleaned
2	tablespoons butter or margarine, softened
½	clove garlic, minced
¼	teaspoon salt
⅛	teaspoon thyme
½	cup finely chopped pecans
1½	tablespoons chopped parsley
½	cup heavy cream

1. Remove stem from mushrooms; finely chop enough stems to make ¼ cup; salt caps lightly.
2. Mix butter with garlic, salt, thyme, pecans, parsley, and chopped mushroom stems until well blended.
3. Heap mixture into mushroom caps and place in a shallow baking dish. Pour cream over all.
4. Heat in a 350°F oven 20 minutes, or until mushrooms are tender, basting several times.

12 Stuffed Mushrooms

Fried Mushrooms

½	lb. mushrooms
¼	cup butter or margarine
1	teaspoon minced parsley

1. Clean and slice mushrooms.
2. Heat in skillet butter or margarine.
3. Add mushrooms to skillet. Cook slowly, occasionally moving and turning gently with a spoon, until mushrooms are tender and lightly browned. Sprinkle with parsley.
4. Put mushrooms into a warm dish and serve immediately.

2 servings

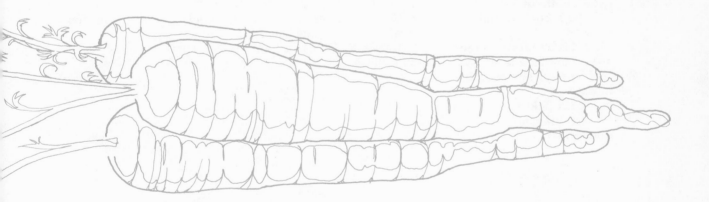

Mushroom Delight

1	lb. mushrooms
¼	cup butter or margarine
½	clove garlic, minced
2	tablespoons minced parsley
½	teaspoon salt
⅛	teaspoon pepper
1	cup dairy sour cream
1	tablespoon all-purpose flour

1. Clean and slice mushrooms.
2. Heat butter or margarine in a skillet over low heat.
3. Add the mushrooms and garlic, parsley, salt and pepper.
4. Cook over medium heat until mushrooms are tender and lightly browned, occasionally moving and turning them with a spoon.
5. Add to the mushrooms a mixture of sour cream and all-purpose flour.
6. Cook over medium heat, keeping mixture moving constantly, for about 5 min., until sauce is slightly thicker and thoroughly heated. Do not boil.
7. Serve on croutons or toast points.

6 servings

Creamed Onions and String Beans

8 small Cooked Onions
3⅓ cups Cooked Green Beans
1 recipe White Sauce (page 99)
Paprika

1. Combine vegetables and white sauce and heat thoroughly. Sprinkle with paprika.

Serves 6 to 8

Glazed Onions

4 tablespoons melted butter
3 tablespoons lemon juice
6 tablespoons honey
3½ cups Cooked Onions

1. Combine first 3 ingredients, add cooked onions and heat slowly 8 minutes or until onions are glazed.

Serves 6 to 8

Holiday Onions and Peas

¼ cup flour
1 teaspoon seasoned salt
¼ cup butter or margarine
2 cups milk
24 small white onions (about 1½ lbs.), cooked and drained
1 pkg. (10 oz.) frozen green peas, cooked and drained
2 tablespoons slivered pimiento
1 cup corn flakes
2 tablespoons butter or margarine

1. Blend a mixture of flour and seasoned salt into ¼ cup hot butter in a saucepan. Heat until bubbly. Stir in the milk and bring to boiling; cook and stir 1 to 2 minutes.
2. Mix onions, peas, and pimiento into sauce. Turn mixture into 1½-quart baking dish.
3. Coat corn flakes with 2 tablespoons hot butter in a skillet. Top creamed mixture with buttered corn flakes.
4. Heat in a 350°F oven until mixture is hot and bubbly, about 25 minutes.

About 8 servings

Glazed Onions

8 small (about 1 lb.) onions
¼ cup butter
2 tablespoons brown sugar

1. Clean onions.
2. Cook 15 to 25 min., or until onions are just tender.
3. Meanwhile, melt butter in a skillet.
4. Add and stir in brown sugar.
5. Stir over low heat until sugar is dissolved. Drain onions thoroughly. Dry onions by shaking pan over low heat. Add to butter-sugar mixture in skillet. Simmer a few minutes, or until onions are glazed. Turn several times to glaze.

4 servings

Creamed Onions: Follow recipe for Glazed Onions. Omit brown sugar mixture. Prepare **1 cup Thin White Sauce** (page 99); add onions and heat thoroughly.

Creamed Peas

4   cups cooked peas
2   cups White Sauce (page 99)

1. Combine cooked peas with white sauce.
2. Heat in oven or over direct heat.
3. Garnish with sieved hard-cooked egg yolks and sliced hard-cooked egg whites.

Serves 8

Creamy Peas

1   can (4 oz.) sliced mushrooms
3   slices bacon
1   tablespoon all-purpose flour
½   teaspoon seasoned salt
½   teaspoon crushed sweet basil
⅔   cup cream
1   teaspoon instant minced onion
1   can (16 oz.) green peas, drained
1   teaspoon diced pimiento

1. Drain mushrooms, reserving liquid.
2. Dice, panfry and drain bacon.
3. Put 2 tablespoons bacon dripping into skillet. Blend in a mixture of all-purpose flour, salt and sweet basil.
4. Heat until mixture bubbles. Add gradually stirring constantly, the mushroom liquid and cream.
5. Bring to boiling, stirring constantly. Mix in onion.
6. Stir and cook 1 to 2 min. Mix in mushrooms, green peas and pimiento.
7. Heat thoroughly. Toss with the bacon. Turn into a heated serving dish.

About 6 servings

Peas and Onions

3   cups Cooked Peas
1   cup tiny Cooked Onions
3   tablespoons heavy cream
½   teaspoon sugar

1. Combine vegetables, add cream and sugar and heat thoroughly.
2. Shake gently until vegetables are well coated with cream.

Serves 6 to 8

Peas And Onions With Lemon Butter

2   pkgs. (10 oz. each) frozen green peas
2   teaspoons sugar (added to cooking water)
1   jar (16 oz.) whole white onions
3   tablespoons butter or margarine
1   tablespoon brown sugar
½   teaspoon salt
¾   teaspoon pepper
1   tablespoon lemon juice
¼   cup water

1. Set out a heavy 1½-qt. saucepan.
2. Cook green peas and sugar until tender, following package directions, and drain thoroughly.
3. Meanwhile, drain onions.
4. Chop enough drained onions to yield ½ cup chopped. Set remaining onions aside.
5. Heat in saucepan butter or margarine.
6. Add chopped onion and cook over medium heat 5 min. Stir in brown sugar, salt, pepper, lemon juice and water.
7. Heat 2 to 3 min., then add cooked peas and remaining whole onions. Toss lightly and continue cooking until thoroughly heated.

About 8 servings

Peas and Mushrooms

2   **cups Cooked Peas**
1   **cup Sauteed Mushrooms**

Combine vegetables and serve hot.

Baked Potatoes

This is one of the most desirable methods of preparation. When potatoes are scraped and baked or baked in the skins, they retain most of their vitamins and minerals. If a soft skin is desired rub with fat before baking. Always break the skin immediately upon removal from the oven so steam may escape or potatoes will be soggy. Baked stuffed Irish potatoes when combined with poached eggs, chipped beef or sausage form attractive entrees for luncheons. Potatoes baked in the pan with meat absorb the delicious flavor of the meat besides serving as a garnish for the meat platter. Potatoes may be combined with meat or other vegetables and baked en casserole for one dish meals.

Mashed Potatoes

There are endless ways in which mashed potatoes may be combined and served. Preparing light and fluffy mashed potatoes, however, is an art. Add hot milk to boiled potatoes and beat hard with a potato masher or a fork, being sure no lumps remain in the potatoes. A very small amount of baking powder may be added to keep the potatoes white and light, but only hard beating will make them creamy. Be sure they are very hot when served. One pound or 3 medium-sized potatoes will make 2 cups mashed potatoes.

Idaho Potatoes On The Half Shell

6   **medium potatoes**
2   **teaspoons prepared**
     mustard
1   **tablespoon grated onion**
     Worcestershire sauce
½   **teaspoon salt**
     Buttered crumbs

1. Scrub potatoes and parboil for 20 to 30 minutes or until nearly cooked through.
2. Split partially cooked potatoes lengthwise into halves.
3. Spread each half with mustard, onion, sprinkle with Worcestershire sauce and salt. Top with buttered bread crumbs and bake in very hot oven (450°F.) 15 to 20 minutes or until potato is completely cooked and crumbs are brown.

Serves 6

4. *If desired, use 3 large potatoes allowing ½ potato for each serving. Instead of buttered crumbs, use chopped bacon.*

Slit baked potatoes as soon as they come from the oven, season and serve piping hot.

Fluffy Whipped Potatoes

6   **medium (about 2 lbs.) potatoes**
4   **tablespoons butter**
½   **cup hot milk or cream(adding gradually)**
¾   **teaspoon salt**
¼   **teaspoon paprika**
¼   **teaspoon pepper**

1. Wash, pare and cook potatoes.
2. Cook about 25 to 35 min., or until potatoes are tender when pierced with a fork. Drain. Heat potato masher, food mill or ricer and a mixing bowl by scalding them with boiling water. Mash or rice potatoes thoroughly. Whip in butter, milk or cream and a mixture of salt, paprika and pepper until potatoes are fluffy.
3. Whip potatoes until light and fluffy. If necessary, keep potatoes hot over simmering water and cover with folded towel until ready to serve.

About 6 servings

Mashed Turnips: Follow recipe for Fluffy Whipped Potatoes. Substitute washed, pared and quartered **turnips** for the potatoes. Omit milk or cream and paprika.

Hashed Brown Potatoes: Follow recipe for Fluffy Whipped Potatoes. Do not mash or rice. Dice potatoes and mix with **1 teaspoon salt** and **¼ teaspoon pepper.** Heat **⅓ cup fat** in a skillet. Add the potatoes, pressing into an even layer. Cook over low heat until a brown crust is formed on the bottom. Loosen edges and bottom of potatoes; shake skillet back and forth occasionally to prevent burning while browning. When potatoes are done. Lightly fold in half and serve on a warm platter.

Fried Parsnip Cakes: Follow recipe for Fluffy Whipped Potatoes. Substitute washed, pared and quartered **parsnips** for the potatoes. Cook about 30 min., or until tender. Omit paprika and add **2 tablespoons all-purpose flour.** Shape parsnip mixture into flat cakes. Heat about **¼ cup fat** in a skillet. Cook parsnip cakes over medium heat until golden brown and crisp on one side. Turn cakes and brown second side. Add extra fat when necessary.

Whipped Potato Ring: Follow recipe for Fluffy Whipped Potatoes. Spoon whipped potatoes onto warm serving platter to form a ring. Draw tines of fork around ring for patterned effect.

Scalloped Potatoes

6   **medium potatoes**
    Salt and pepper
2   **tablespoons flour**
4   **tablespoons butter**
    Milk

1. Pare potatoes and cut into thin slices. Place in a greased baking dish in 3 layers 1 inch deep, sprinkling each layer with salt, pepper and flour and dotting with butter.
2. Add milk until it can be seen between slices of potato, cover and bake in moderate oven (350°F.) until potatoes are tender when pierced with a fork, 1 to 1¼ hours. Remove cover for the last 15 minutes to brown.
3. Serve from baking dish.

Serves 6

Boiled New Potatoes

1½ **pounds small new potatoes**
¼ **cup butter, melted**
   Salt and pepper to season

1. Wash potatoes and cook with jackets on in boiling salted water to cover until tender, 15 to 20 minutes.
2. Peel. Pour butter over potatoes and season with salt and pepper. Juice of ½ lemon may be added to butter.

For 6

Parsley — Roll boiled potatoes in ½ cup chopped parsley.

Stuffed Potatoes

6 **medium-sized baking potatoes, baked**
½ **cup coarsely chopped onion**
½ **cup coarsely chopped green pepper**
3 **tablespoons butter or margarine**
1 **medium-sized tomato, chopped**
2 **tablespoons milk**
2 **tablespoons butter or margarine**
2 **teaspoons salt**
¼ **teaspoon white pepper**
1 **teaspoon paprika**
¼ **teaspoon crushed rosemary leaves**

1. While potatoes are baking, cook onion and green pepper in 3 tablespoons hot butter in a skillet. Add tomato and cook 1 minute.
2. Cut a thin lengthwise slice from each baked potato. With a spoon, scoop out each potato without breaking skin. Thoroughly mash or rice scooped-out potato. Whip in milk with remaining ingredients until potatoes are fluffy, Blend in vegetable mixture.
3. Pile mixture lightly into potato shells. Arrange on baking sheet. Sprinkle with paprika.
4. Bake at 400°F 20 minutes, or until thoroughly heated and lightly browned.

6 servings

Sauerkraut with Dried Peas (for Christmas Eve)

1 **cup dried split green or yellow peas, rinsed**
2⅔ **cups boiling water**
1 **quart sauerkraut, rinsed and drained**
½ **cup chopped mushrooms**
3 **cups water**
   Salt and pepper
1 **can (2 ounces) anchovies, drained**

1. Combine peas and 2⅔ cups boiling water in a saucepan. Bring to boiling and boil 2 minutes. Remove from heat. Cover and let soak 30 minutes. Bring to boiling; simmer 20 minutes.
2. Cover sauerkraut and mushrooms with 3 cups water in a saucepan; cover and cook 1 hour.
3. Add cooked peas to sauerkraut mixture. Season to taste with salt and pepper; mix well. Turn into a buttered baking dish. Top with anchovies. Cover.
4. Bake at 325°F 30 minutes.

4 to 6 servings

Sauerkraut with Dried Peas: Prepare Sauerkraut with Dried Peas; omit anchovies and baking. Fry **1 onion, chopped,** with ½ **pound salt pork or bacon,** chopped, until lightly browned. Blend in **2 tablespoons flour** and add **1 cup sauerkraut cooking liquid.** Cook and stir until smooth. Mix with sauerkraut and peas; heat thoroughly.

Baked Sweet Potatoes I

6   medium (about 2 lbs.) sweet potatoes or yams
1   tablespoon fat
1   tablespoon butter or margarine

1. Wash potatoes or yams and scrub with a vegetable brush.
2. Dry potatoes with absorbent paper. Rub potatoes well with fat.
3. Place potatoes on rack in oven and bake at 375°F 45 to 60 min., or until potatoes are soft when pressed with the fingers (protected from heat by paper napkin).
4. Remove potatoes from oven. To make each potato more mealy, gently roll potatoes back and forth on a flat working surface.
5. Cut a small cross in skin of each potato. Squeeze sides of potato until mealy portion is visible. Top each potato with butter or margarine.
6. Serve immediately.

6 servings

Lemon-Buttered Sweet Potatoes: Follow recipe for Baked Sweet Potatoes. While potatoes are baking, blend ½ **cup butter or margarine,** melted, **2 tablespoons lemon juice, ½ teaspoon salt,** and ⅛ **teaspoon pepper.** Keep mixture warm. Peel baked sweet potatoes and cut into halves or leave whole. Place in a baking dish and pour lemon-butter mixture over potatoes. Return to oven and bake 5 to 10 min. Spoon lemon-butter (in baking dish) over potatoes several times.

Baked Filled Sweets: Follow recipe for Baked Sweet Potatoes. While potatoes are baking, panbroil **12 (about ¾ lb.) pork sausage links.** Set aside to drain on absorbent paper and keep warm. Cut large baked potatoes into halves lengthwise. Or cut a thin slice from each small potato. With a spoon, scoop out inside without breaking skin. Mash or rice potatoes thoroughly. Whip in until potatoes are light and fluffy, **½ cup hot orange juice** (adding gradually), **3 tablespoons butter or margarine** and a mixture of **2 tablespoons brown sugar, 1 teaspoon grated orange peel, ¾ teaspoon salt, and ½ teaspoon cinnamon.** Whip potatoes until light and fluffy. Pile mixture lightly into potato shells, leaving surfaces uneven. Top each filled potato with two sausage links. Bake 8 to 10 min. longer, or until potatoes reheat and brown lightly.

Baked Sweet Potatoes II

Potatoes should be baked in their jackets to retain the most nourishment. Select uniform-sized, medium sweet potatoes. Wash, remove blemishes, and bake in a moderate oven (350°F.) until easily pierced with a fork, 30 to 40 minutes. Remove from oven, slit and insert a large piece of butter or margarine. Serve piping hot.
In place of butter use 1 tablespoon sour cream or butter that has been whipped with lemon juice.

Glazed Sweet Potatoes

6	sweet potatoes
1	cup brown sugar
¼	cup water
	Salt and pepper
	Butter

1. Boil potatoes until tender, drain and skin. Make a thick syrup of sugar and water.
2. Cut each potato in half, dip it in the syrup and place in a baking dish; season each piece with salt, pepper and butter.
3. Bake in a moderate oven (375°F.) until the potatoes are brown, about 15 minutes, basting occasionally with the syrup.

Serves 6 to 8

4. *Add ½ cup sliced Brazil nuts and 6 cloves to the syrup.*

Stuffed — Hollow centers from halves before glazing. Fill glazed potatoes with mincemeat or Cranberry Sauce. Heat throughly in oven.

Maple Candied Sweet Potatoes

6	medium sweet potatoes
½	cup maple syrup
1	tablespoon butter
1	teaspoon salt
1	cup apple cider
½	cup water

1. Boil potatoes in jackets until nearly tender.
2. Peel and slice into baking dish.
3. Heat remaining ingredients to boiling, pour over potatoes and bake in slow oven (300°F.) 1 hour.

Serves 6

Sweet Potatoes And Cranberries

6	large sweet potatoes
1½	cups Cranberry Sauce
3	tablespoons butter
⅓	cup brown sugar
1	teaspoon salt
½	cup finely chopped nuts

1. Boil potatoes in jackets until tender, peel, cut in halves lengthwise; scoop out halves slightly.
2. Place 6 halves in greased baking dish, fill centers with cranberry sauce, and top with remaining halves.
3. Hold potatoes together with toothpicks. Combine remaining ingredients and spread over potatoes. Bake in a moderate oven (350°F.) until lightly browned, about 20 to 25 minutes.

Serves 6.

Boiled Sweet Potatoes

	Sweetpotatoes
	Boiling water
	Salt

1. Sweet potatoes and yams are usually cooked with skins on.
2. Wash and rinse; cover with boiling salted water and cook until tender, 20 to 30 minutes.
3. Drain, peel and serve piping hot. Allow 1 medium potato to a serving.

Golden Glow Sweet Potatoes

6	medium (about 2 lbs.) sweet potatoes, cut into halves or quarters
12	marshmallows (3 oz.)
4	tablespoons butter or margarine
½	cup cream or milk
¼	cup firmly packed brown sugar
¾	teaspoon salt
1	teaspoon nutmeg
½	teaspoon cinnamon

1. Grease a 1½-qt. casserole.
2. Wash sweet potatoes and cook covered in boiling salted water to cover.
3. Cook about 20 min., or until tender when pierced with a fork. Drain. To dry potatoes, shake pan over low heat. Peel; mash or rice.
4. Meanwhile, cut marshmallows into crosswise halves and set aside.
5. Whip in butter or margarine and cream or milk until potatoes are fluffy and a mixture of brown sugar, salt, nutmeg and cinnamon.
6. Fold one half of the marshmallow slices into potatoes; pile lightly into casserole.
7. Bake at 350°F 15 min. Remove from oven and arrange remaining marshmallows around top of casserole. Bake 15 to 20 min. longer, or until marshmallows are lightly browned.

6 servings

Glazed Grapefruit Sweet Potatoes: Follow recipe for Golden Glow Sweet Potatoes. Omit marshmallows. Wash **1 grapefruit.** With a sharp knife, cut into ¼ in. crosswise slices; cut each into halves. Dip slices into mixture of **¼ cup honey** and **2 tablespoons melted butter or margarine.** Arrange a wheel of overlapping slices over potatoes in casserole. Drizzle remaining honey mixture over top. Bake 20 to 25 min., or until grapefruit is slightly browned.

Pecan Sweet Squash: Follow recipe for Golden Glow Sweet Potatoes. Use **3 pkgs. (10 oz. each) frozen squash;** cook following directions on package. If squash seems dry, moisten with necessary amount of **cream** or **orange juice.** Otherwise, omit cream and whip butter into squash. Turn squash into casserole; top with **½ cup (about 2 oz.) coarsely chopped pecans.** Bake 15 to 20 min., or until heated and nuts are toasted.

Sweet Potatoes With Orange

4	medium (about 1⅓ lbs.) sweet potatoes
¼	cup sugar
4	teaspoons grated orange peel
½	teaspoon salt
¼	teaspoon cinnamon
2	large oranges
¼	cup butter
½	cup orange juice

1. Grease a 1½-qt. casserole with a tight-fitting cover.
2. Scrub sweet potatoes.
3. Cook, covered, in boiling salted water for 10 min. Drain. Shake pan over low heat to dry potatoes. Peel. With a sharp knife, cut into crosswise slices ⅛ in. thick. Set aside.
4. Mix sugar, orange peel, salt and cinnamon. Wash oranges, cut away peel and cut into crosswise slices ¼ in. thick.
5. Set out butter.
6. Arrange one half of the potato slices in an even layer in the casserole. Cover with one half of the orange slices and sprinkle with one half of the sugar mixture. Dot with 2 tablespoons of the butter. Repeat layering. Pour orange juice over all.
7. Cover; cook in a 375°F oven about 40 min., or until potatoes are tender when pierced with a fork.

About 4 servings

Elegant Apricot Sweet Potatoes

½   lb. (1½ cups) dried
     apricots
2   cups water
6   medium (about 2 lbs.)
     sweet potatoes or yams
1   cup firmly packed dark
     brown sugar
3   tablespoons melted butter
1   teaspoon grated orange
     peel
2   teaspoons orange juice
¼   cup (about 1 oz.) pecan
     halves

1. A shallow 1-qt. baking dish will be needed.
2. Put dried apricots into a heavy saucepan.
3. Add water.
4. Bring water to boiling, reduce heat, and cook, covered, about 25 min., or until apricots are plump and tender when pierced with a fork. (Be careful not to overcook the fruit.) Remove saucepan from heat. Cool and drain well, reserving liquid.
5. Meanwhile, wash and scrub with a vegetable brush sweet potatoes or yams.
6. Cook 30 to 35 min., or until potatoes are tender when pierced with a fork. Drain potatoes and peel; cut into lengthwise slices about ½ in. thick.
7. Lightly grease the baking dish.
8. Set out brown sugar.
9. Arrange a layer of the sweet potatoes in the baking dish. Cover with a layer of apricots. Sprinkle with one half of the brown sugar. Repeat layers of sweet potatoes and apricots and sprinkle with remaining sugar.
10. Blend thoroughly ¼ cup of the reserved apricot liquid and melted butter, orange peel and orange juice.
11. Pour mixture over the layers.
12. Bake at 375°F 30 to 45 min., basting occasionally with liquid in bottom of baking dish. About 5 min. before sweet potatoes are done. Top with pecan halves.

6 to 8 servings.

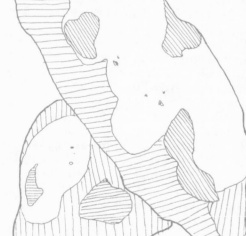

Maple Sweet Potatoes And Apples

6   medium (about 2 lbs.)
     sweet potatoes
1   cup maple syrup
     Few grains salt
4   large apples (about 1½
     lbs.)
⅓   cup buttered crumbs

1. Butter a 1½-qt. baking dish.
2. Wash, scrub and cook sweet potatoes.
3. Cook 30 to 35 min., or until tender when pierced with a fork.
4. Meanwhile, measure into a saucepan maple syrup.
5. Add salt.
6. Wash, quarter, core, peel and thinly slice apples.
7. Add apples to saucepan and cook over low heat until apples are just tender. Carefully turn apple slices to cook evenly. Remove from heat and set aside. Peel the cooked sweet potatoes. Cut into thin, crosswise slices. Arrange one half of the potato slices in the baking dish. Top with one half of the apple slices and syrup. Repeat layers, using remaining potatoes, apples and syrup. Sprinkle with buttered crumbs.
8. Bake at 350°F about 10 min., or until crumbs are lightly browned.

6 to 8 servings

Sweet Potato Pone I

4	medium (about 1½ lbs.) sweet potatoes or yams
⅔	cup butter or margarine
1	teaspoon grated lemon peel
1	teaspoon grated orange peel
½	teaspoon salt
½	teaspoon nutmeg
½	teaspoon cinnamon
½	teaspoon cloves
½	cup firmly packed brown sugar
4	eggs, well beaten
1	cup milk
⅓	cup molasses

1. Grease a 1½-qt. baking dish.
2. Wash sweet potatoes, pare, cover with cold salted water and set aside.
3. Cream until softened butter or margarine, lemon peel, orange peel, salt, nutmeg, cinnamon and cloves.
4. Add gradually brown sugar, creaming until fluffy after each addition.
5. Add eggs in thirds, beating thoroughly after each addition.
6. Stir in a mixture of milk and molasses.
7. Set aside while grating sweet potatoes.
8. Drain sweet potatoes and grate using medium-size grater (about 5 cups, grated). Blend grated potatoes into liquid mixture and pour into the baking dish. Set in a large baking pan and pour very hot water into pan to a 1-in. depth.
9. Bake at 350°F about 1 hr., or until top is crusty and lightly browned.

6 servings

Sweet Potato Pone II

1	cup sugar
½	cup butter
2	cups grated uncooked sweetpotatoes
½	cup milk
¼	teaspoon salt
1	teaspoon ginger
⅛	teaspoon cinnamon
⅛	teaspoon nutmeg
	Grated rind of 1 orange

1. Blend sugar and butter, add grated sweetpotatoes and milk.
2. Beat well. Add salt, spices and orange rind.
3. Place in shallow buttered baking pan and bake in slow oven (325°F) 1 hour.

Serves 8

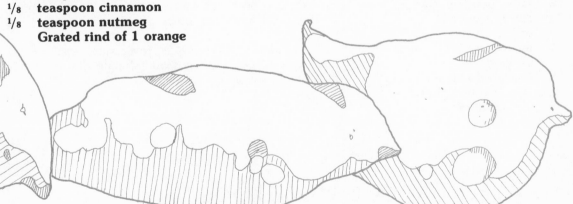

Orange Candied Sweet Potatoes

6	medium sweet potatoes
1	cup orange juice
½	teaspoon grated orange rind
1	cup water
1	sugar
¼	cup butter
½	teaspoon salt

1. Pare potatoes, slice in ¼-inch slices and arrange in a greased baking dish.
2. Combine remaining ingredients, heat to boiling, and boil until sugar is dissolved; pour over the potatoes. Cover and bake in moderate oven (350°F) until tender, about 45 to 60 minutes.
3. Baste occasionally. Uncover to brown during the last 10 minutes. If desired, a layer of marshmallows may be added and browned just before removing from the oven.

Serves 6

Sweet Potatoes With Applesauce

3   **large sweet potatoes**
¼   **cup butter**
¼   **cup brown sugar**
2   **cups thick Applesauce**

1. Pare sweet potatoes and cut into 1-inch cubes.
2. Cook for 15 minutes in rapidly boiling water.
3. Place sweetpotatoes in greased baking dish, dot with butter and brown sugar. Pour applesauce over potatoes.
4. Bake in moderate oven (350°F) until tender, about 30 minutes.

Serves 6

Sweet Potato Casserole

6   **sweet potatoes, cooked and sliced**
½   **cup brown sugar**
5   **tablespoons butter**
2   **oranges**
½   **cup orange juice**
¼   **cup strained honey**
¼   **cup fine bread crumbs**

1. In greased casserole, arrange a layer of sliced sweetpotatoes, sprinkle with 6 tablespoons brown sugar, dot with 4 tablespoons butter and cover with a layer of thinly sliced. unpeeled oranges.Repeat layers. Over all, pour orange juice with which honey has been mixed.
2. Combine bread crumbs with remaining 2 tablespoons brown sugar and 1 tablespoon butter and sprinkle over top. Cover casserole and bake in moderate oven (350°F.) 30 to 40 minutes, removing cover last 15 minutes.

Marshmallow Sweet Potatoes

8   **medium sweet potatoes**
2   **tablespoons butter**
½   **cup hot milk**
½   **teaspoon salt**
1   **teaspoon cinnamon or nutmeg**
¼   **teaspoon paprika**
1   **cup choppe walnuts**
½   **pound marshmallows**

1. Cook sweet potatoes until tender, remove skins and mash.
2. Add butter, milk, salt, cinnamon or nutmeg and paprika.
3. Beat until free from lumps and light and fluffy. Fold in walnuts.
4. Turn into a greased casserole, cover with marshmallows and bake in a moderate oven (350°F.) until mixture is heated through and marshmallows are brown.

Serves 8

Mashed Sweet Potatoes

6   **medium boiled sweet potatoes**
3   **tablespoons butter**
⅓   **cup hot milk**

1. Combine ingredients and beat until light and fluffy. It may be necessary to add more milk if potatoes are dry. Makes 4 cups mashed sweet potatoes.
2. Add dash of nutmeg.
3. Form mashed sweet potatoes into balls with a half with a half or a whole marshmallow in center of each.
4. Roll in shredded coconut and bake in a moderate oven (350°F.) until heated through and a delicate brown.
5. Form balls of mashed sweet potatoes and roll in crushed cereal flakes. Brown in the oven.
6. One or 2 eggs or egg whites, beaten, may be added to mashed sweet potatoes before shaping into balls and baking.

Serves 6

Sweet Potatoes in Orange Cups

2 cups mashed sweet potatoes
2 tablespoons butter
½ teaspoon salt
½ cup orange juice
3 large oranges
6 marshmallows, quartered

1. Combine sweet potatoes, butter, salt and orange juice. Mix well.
2. Cut oranges in halves, crosswise, and remove juice and pulp (use part of this juice, when mashing potatoes).
3. Scrub shells well.
4. Fill with the mashed potatoes and decorate with marshmallows.
5. Bake in hot oven (400°F.) about 15 minutes.

Serves 6

Sweet Potato Pie — Omit oranges and marshmallows. Increase butter to ⅓ cup, add 1 cup sugar, 4 eggs, beaten, 1 cup milk, 1 teaspoon cinnamon, ½ teaspoon nutmeg and 1 teaspoon grated orange rind. Mix well and bake in 2 pastry lined pans at 350°F. until firm.

Scalloped Sweet Potatoes and Apples

6 medium sweet potatoes, pared and cut in crosswise slices ¼ inch thick
1½ cups apple slices
½ cup firmly packed brown sugar
¼ cup butter or margarine, melted
½ cup apple juice
1 tablespoon lemon juice

1. Combine ingredients in an electric cooker.
2. Cover and cook on High 3 to 4 hours, or until sweet potatoes and apples are tender.

About 6 servings

Apple-Honey Sweet Potatoes

4 sweet potatoes
4 cooking apples
½ cup honey
¼ teaspoon nutmeg

1. Bake sweet potatoes at 350°F 45 minutes, or until tender.
2. Core apples and cut into thin slices. (To avoid darkening, brush with lemon juice.)
3. Peel baked potatoes and cut into ½-inch-thick slices.
4. Alternate layers of potatoes and apples in a greased 2½-quart casserole. Drizzle with honey and sprinkle with nutmeg.
5. Bake, covered, at 350°F 20 minutes, or until heated through.

6 servings

Pecan Sweet Potatoes

¼ cup butter or margarine
2 tablespoons cornstarch
¾ cup firmly packed brown sugar
½ teaspoon salt
2 cups orange juice
2 cans (23 ounces each) sweet potatoes, drained
¼ cup chopped pecans

1. Melt butter in a saucepan. Blend cornstarch, brown sugar, and salt; mix with butter. Gradually add orange juice, stirring until thickened and clear.
2. Put sweet potatoes into a 1½-quart casserole. Pour sauce over sweet potatoes. Sprinkle with pecans.
3. Bake, covered, at 350°F 45 minutes, or until heated through.

8 servings

Caramel Sweet Potatoes

⅓ cup butter
½ cup walnut pieces
1 cup firmly packed brown sugar
½ teaspoon salt
½ cup orange juice
6 medium (about 2 pounds) sweet potatoes, cooked
⅓ cup brandy

1. Melt butter in cooking pan of a chafing dish. Stir in walnut pieces. Cook over moderate heat until lightly toasted.
2. Remove walnuts from pan. Add brown sugar, salt and orange juice to butter remaining in cooking pan; stir to blend. Bring to boiling and boil 3 to 4 minutes, stirring occasionally.
3. Peel the sweet potatoes and cut in halves lengthwise. Add to the syrup with walnut pieces.
4. Place cooking pan over chafing dish burner. Heat the potatoes gently, basting with the syrup. Warm the brandy, pour over potatoes, and ignite. Serve when flames die out.

6 servings

Mallow Sweet Potato Balls

3 cups warm mashed sweet potatoes
Salt and pepper to taste
3 tablespoons melted butter
8 large marshmallows
1 egg
1 tablespoon cold water
1 cup almonds, blanched and chopped
Oil for deep frying

1. Season potatoes and add butter. Mold potato mixture around marshmallows, forming 8 balls with a marshmallow in center of each.
2. Beat egg and mix with cold water. Dip sweet potato balls in egg and then in almonds.
3. Slowly heat oil in a wok to 365°F. When oil is hot, fry sweet potato balls until brown, turning occasionally.

8 servings

Candied Sweet Potatoes I

6	**medium (about 2 lbs.) sweet potatoes**
⅓	**cup butter or margarine**
⅓	**cup firmly packed brown sugar**
¼	**teaspoon salt**

1. Set out a large heavy skillet and a large saucepan with a cover.
2. Scrub and cook sweet potatoes in boiling salted water.
3. Cook, covered 30 to 35 min., or until potatoes are just tender when pierced with a fork. Drain. Shake pan over low heat to dry potatoes. Peel them and set aside.
4. Heat butter or margarine in the skillet over low heat.
5. Blend in brown sugar and salt.
6. Heat until mixture bubbles. Add potatoes. Cook over medium heat, turning potatoes several times, about 20 min., or until they are well-glazed and thoroughly heated.

6 servings

Candied Sweet Potatoes II

6	**medium (about 2 lbs.) sweet potatoes**
1	**cup firmly packed brown sugar**
⅓	**cup water**
2	**tablespoons butter or margarine**
½	**teaspoon salt**
8	**marshmallows, quartered**

1. Grease a shallow baking pan.
2. Cook sweet potatoes.
3. While potatoes cook, combine brown sugar, water, butter or margarine and salt and boil together for 5 min.
4. Peel potatoes and cut into halves lengthwise. Dip potatoes in syrup and place, cut-side down, in baking pan. Add remaining syrup. Dot potatoes with marshmallow.
5. Bake at 400°F 20 min., basting occasionally with the syrup.

6 servings

Sweet Potatoes in a Basket

4 **medium (about 1¾ lbs.) sweet potatoes**
3 **large oranges**
2 **tablespoons brown sugar**
1 **teaspoon salt**
6 **marshmallow halves**

1. Scrub and rinse sweet potatoes.
2. Cook, covered, in boiling salted water 30 to 35 min., or until potatoes are tender when pierced with a fork.
3. While potatoes cook, cut oranges into halves crosswise.
4. With a spoon or grapefruit knife, remove pulp sections from inside dividing membranes. With scissors or knife trim and remove membranes from orange shells. Set aside orange shells, cut-sides down, to drain thoroughly.
5. Peel potatoes. Pour boiling water over potato masher, food mill or ricer and bowl to heat thoroughly. Mash or rice potatoes into bowl.
6. Add to potatoes the orange pulp and a mixture of brown sugar, and salt.
7. Whip until light and fluffy. Pile lightly into orange shells. Top each with one of marshmallow halves.
8. Place filled basket on broiler rack. Place in broiler with tops of marshmallows about 4 in. from heat until marshmallows are browned and slightly melted.

6 servings

Whipped Sweet Potatoes

6 **medium (about 2 lbs.) sweet potatoes, cut in quarters**
2 **tablespoons butter or margarine**
½ **cup hot milk or cream (adding gradually)**
½ **teaspoon salt**

1. Wash, scrub and cook sweet potatoes covered in boiling salted water to cover .
2. Cook about 20 min., or until potatoes are tender when pierced with a fork. Drain and peel sweet potatoes.
3. To dry potatoes, shake pan over low heat. To heat potato masher, food mill or ricer and a mixing bowl, scald them with boiling water.
4. Mash or rice potatoes thoroughly. Whip in butter or margarine, milk or cream and salt until potatoes are fluffy.
5. Whip potatoes until light and fluffy. If necessary, keep potatoes hot over simmering water and cover with folded towel until ready to serve.

About 3 cups whipped potatoes

Mellow Sweet Potato Bake: Follow recipe for Whipped Sweet Potatoes. Grease a 1½-qt. baking dish. Substitute **orange juice** for milk or cream. Blend into whipped potatoes a mixture of **½ cup (about 2 oz.) chopped pecans, ⅓ cup firmly packed brown sugar, 1 teaspoon cinnamon** and **½ teaspoon nutmeg.** Spoon into baking dish. Cut **6 marshmallows** into halves; arrange them on top of potatoes. Put baking dish under broiler with top of food 4 in. from heat. Broil until marshmallows are delicately browned and slightly melted.

Cooked Turnips or Rutabagas

2½ **pounds turnips**
1   **cup water**
1   **teaspoon salt**

1. Pare turnips and cut into cubes.
2. Heat water and salt to boiling, add turnips, cover pan tightly to prevent escape of steam and heat again to boiling.
3. Reduce heat at once and simmer 20 to 35 minutes. Drain if necessary. (Makes about 4 cups, mashed.)
4. To serve, season with pepper and melted butter.
5. To prepare milder-flavored vegetable, cook as for Cooked Cabbage, being very careful not to overcook the turnips.
6. Diced young white turnips will cook tender in 15 to 20 minutes.

Serves 6 to 8

Mashed Turnips

4   **cups Cooked Turnips**
⅛   **teaspoon pepper**
3   **tablespoons butter**

Mash turnips and add pepper and butter. Beat over low heat until smooth and most of liquid has evaporated.

Serves 6 to 8

Baked Turnips

2   **pounds turnips**
¼   **cup butter**
1½   **teaspoons salt**
1½   **teaspoons sugar**
⅓   **cup water**

1. Pare turnips and cut into cubes.
2. Place in baking dish with remaining ingredients.
3. Cover closely and bake in moderate oven (350°F.) about 1 hour or until tender.

Serves 6 to 8

Honey-Glazed Turnips

6   **white turnips**
1   **cup chicken broth**
3   **tablespoons honey**
¼   **teaspoon salt**
¼   **teaspoon white pepper**
     Paprika

1. Pare and slice turnips.
2. Bring broth to a boil in a large saucepan. Add turnips; boil covered, 5 minutes. Remove cover and continue cooking over low heat until most of liquid has evaporated.
3. Add honey, salt, and pepper. Put into a 1½-quart casserole. Cover and refrigerate overnight.
4. Bake, covered, at 350°F 30 minutes, or until heated through. If desired, sprinkle with snipped parsley.

6 servings

Sugared Yams

2 cups water
2 cups sugar
2 tablespoons butter
  Dash nutmeg
8 uncooked yams

1. Heat water and sugar to a boil and add butter and nutmeg.
2. Pare and slice yams, drop into boiling syrup, cover and let simmer until yams are tender and transparent.

Serves 8

Candied Yams

4 medium yams
  Salt
½ cup brown sugar
3 tablespoons butter
  Cinnamon
½ cup boiling water

1. Parboil sweet potatoes or yams, pare and cut in halves, lengthwise. Arrange in casserole, sprinkling each layer with salt, paprika and brown sugar.
2. Dot with bits of butter and add a few dashes of cinnamon.
3. Add water, cover and bake in moderate oven (350°F.) for 30 minutes or until tender. When half baked, turn layers over so that top layers are at the bottom of the dish in syrup.
4. Add more water, if necessary.

Serves 4

Meat & Poultry

Baked Ham

1   **smoked ham**
    Glaze, Whole cloves

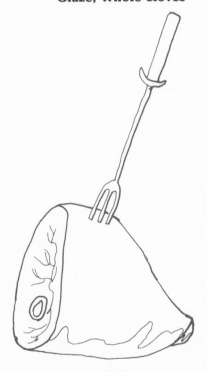

Have ham warmed to room temperature and bake according to directions given by packer, or as follows.

1. Wipe ham with clean cloth, wrap loosely in one of the papers wrapped around ham or in clean wrapping paper and place fat side up on rack of shallow pan.

2. Do not cover pan or add water. For baking allow allow 15 minutes per pound for hams, 12 pounds or over; allow 18 minutes per pound for hams, under 12 pounds; allow 22 minutes per pound for half hams; or bake to an internal temperature of 150°F., being sure bulb of thermometer is inserted into center of thickest part of meat and does not touch bone.

3. Bake in slow oven (325°F.) until within 45 minutes of total baking time. Remove paper and rind from ham, make a series of shallow cuts across fat to cut into squares or diamonds, spread with desired glaze and insert 1 clove into each square of fat. Bake uncovered in 325°F oven for remaining 45 minutes.

Glazes:

One cup brown sugar, juice and grated rind of 1 orange.

One cup brown or white sugar and ½ cup maraschino cherry juice, cider or sweet pickle juice from pickled fruit.

One cup honey.

One cup brown sugar, 1 tablespoon mustard.

One cup pureed apricots, rhubarb or applesauce.

One glass currant jelly, melted. Use maraschino cherries and mint cherries fastened with pieces of toothpicks instead of cloves.

Three-fourths cup pineapple juice, ¾ cup strained honey and ½ teaspoon mustard cooked until thick.

One-half cup maple syrup, ½ cup cider or apple juice and 2 tablespoons mustard.

One-half cup orange marmalade.

Cook ½ pound fresh cranberries with 1 cup maple syrup until skins pop open. Press mixture through sieve and spread over ham.

Decorate baked ham with golden stars of orange peel to give dinner an extra sparkle.

Foil-Baked Flavor-Glazed Ham

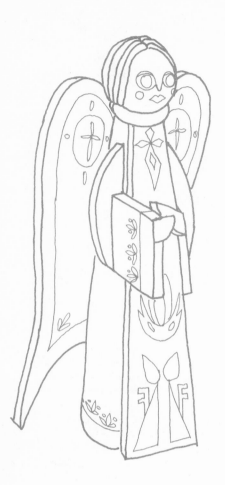

1. Arrange a large sheet of heavy-duty aluminum foil in a shallow roasting pan; place ham in center.
2. Pour one-half of the desired Flavor Blend over ham and brush it in. Bring foil up, covering ham loosely.
3. About 30 minutes before baking is finished, open and turn back foil. Spoon out melted fat; remove rind (skin). Score ham in diamond pattern.
4. Stud with cloves. Pour remaining Flavor Blend over ham. Insert meat thermometer and continue baking with foil open, basting with drippings, until browned.
5. Slip a foil frill on bone end of ham after transferring ham to serving platter. Accompany with fruit or wine sauce.

Flavor Blends for Foil-Baked Ham
Orange: Combine one-half of 1 can (6 ounces) frozen orange juice concentrate, thawed, 1 cup firmly packed brown sugar, and ½ cup bottled steak sauce.
Pineapple: Combine ¾ cup unsweetened pineapple juice with 1 cup firmly packed brown sugar. Decorate ham with pineapple slices.
Sherry Or Madeira: Pour 1 cup wine over ham before baking. To brown and glaze, sprinkle lightly with brown sugar and baste with 1 cup wine.

Sauces for Foil-Baked Ham
Orange: Blend remaining half of orange juice concentrate with 1 cup fruit juice or water.
Pineapple: Use 1 cup unsweetened pineapple juice.
Wine: Use 1 cup water. Stir in any of of the above liquids, blending with the juices and drippings in pan. To thicken, add a mixture of cornstarch and liquid (about 1 tablespoon per cup of liquid). Bring to boiling, stirring constantly, and cook 1 to 2 minutes.

Cider Roast Ham

10	lb. smoked whole ham
¾	cup firmly packed brown sugar
2	tablespoons maple syrup
½	teaspoon dry mustard
	Whole cloves
¾	cup apple cider

1. Set out a shallow roasting pan with rack.
2. Have smoked whole ham ready.
3. Follow directions on wrapper for roasting or place ham fat side up on rack. Insert roast meat thermometer in center of thickest part of lean; bulb should not rest on bone or in fat.
4. Roast, uncovered, at 300°F for 2½ hrs.
5. Meanwhile, prepare Glaze.
6. *For Glaze*—Blend brown sugar, maple syrup and dry mustard.
7. When ham has roasted 2½ hrs., remove from oven. Remove rind (if any), being careful not to remove the fat. Cut fat surface into diamond pattern or use a scalloped cutter to make a flower design. Insert whole cloves in centers of patterns.
8. Spread the glaze over ham. Return ham to oven and continue roasting about 45 min., or until internal temperature reaches 160°F. (Total roasting time is about 3 hrs., allowing 18 to 20 min. per pound.) Occasionally baste ham using apple cider.
9. Garnish as desired.

About 20 servings

Cooked Whole Country Ham

Country-style ham, 14 to 16 lbs.

1. Scrub country-style ham thoroughly with warm water, rinse and put into a large kettle with a tight-fitting cover. (If a large kettle is not available, whole ham may be cut into halves and each piece cooked separately until done.)

2. Cover ham completely with cold water, cover kettle and bring to boiling. Pour off water and again cover ham with cold water. Cover and bring to boiling. Reduce heat and simmer, covered, 4 to 6 hrs., or until internal temperature reaches 170°F. Internal temperature is obtained by inserting roast meat thermometer into center of thickest part of lean at this time, being sure bulb does not rest on bone or in fat.

3. Remove ham from kettle. Allow to stand 15 or 20 min. before slicing. This allows meat to set and become easier to slice. Serve ham either hot or cold, cut into thin slices.

4. If desired, cook only half of ham; store uncooked half in refrigerator for future use.

Baked Country Ham: Follow recipe for Cooked Whole Country Ham. Remove ham from kettle about ½ hr. before done. Remove rind (if any), being careful not to remove fat. Making diagonal cuts, score fat surface of ham to form a diamond pattern. Place **whole cloves** in centers of diamonds. Place ham, fat side up, on a rack in a shallow roasting pan. Spread glaze over ham and bake at 300°F 30 to 40 min., or until ham tests done with a meat thermometer and glaze is set.

For Glaze—Mix in a small bowl **1 cup firmly packed brown sugar, 1 tablespoon all-purpose flour** and **teaspoon dry mustard.** Blend in **2 tablespoons vinegar** until smooth. Spread on ham.

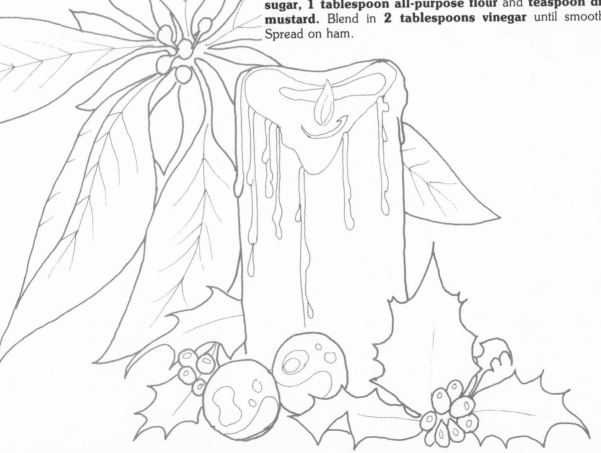

Savory Roast Ham

10   **lb. smoked whole ham**
1   **cup firmly packed brown**
     sugar
1   **tablespoon all-purpose**
     flour
1   **teaspoon dry mustard**
2   **tablespoons cider vinegar**
1   **can (8 ¼ oz.) pineapple**
     tidbits (about ⅔ cup,
     drained)
1   **orange**
8   **maraschino cherries**
1   **can (20 oz.) pineapple**
     slices
     Melted butter or margarine
     Brown sugar
     Sprigs of parsley

1. For Ham—Set out a shallow roasting pan with a rack. Follow directions on wrapper for roasting or roast as directed below.

Place ham fat side up on rack. Insert roast meat thermometer in thickest part of lean, being sure bulb does not rest on bone or in fat.

Roast uncovered at 300°F 2½ hrs.

Meanwhile, prepare Glaze and Fruit Garnish.

2. For Glaze and Fruit Garnish—Mix in a small bowl brown sugar, all purpose flour, and dry mustard.

Add and stir in cider vinegar to form a smooth paste. Set aside.

Drain (reserving syrup for use in other food preparation) pineapple tidbits and set aside.

Rinse orange.

With a sharp knife, cut away peel through colored part only (white is bitter). Cut peel into desired shapes for decorating; set aside.

Thoroughly drain maraschino cherries.

Cut two cherries into thin slices and remainder into halves. Set aside.

3. To Glaze and Garnish Ham—Remove ham from oven after it has roasted 2½ hrs. Remove rind (if any), being careful not to remove fat. Making diagonal cuts, score fat surface of ham to make diamond pattern; or use scalloped cookie cutter to make flower pattern. Spread about one half of Glaze over ham. Arrange pineapple tidbits, whole and sliced maraschino cherries, and pieces of orange peel on ham in an attractive design, and press firmly into glaze. Carefully spread remainder of Glaze over fruit. Return ham to oven and continue roasting about 45 min., or until internal temperature of ham reaches 160°F. (The total roasting time is about 3 hrs., allowing 18 to 20 min. per pound.) Remove ham from oven; remove thermometer. Keep ham hot. Allow to stand 15 to 20 min. before serving. This helps to make meat easier to carve.

4. For Pineapple Garnish—Drain pineapple slices, reserving syrup for use in other food preparation.

Place slices on broiler rack or a baking sheet. Brush tops with butter or margarine.

Sprinkle with brown sugar.

Place under broiler with tops of pineapple slices 3 in. from heat. Broil 5 to 6 min., or until brown sugar is melted and pineapple slices are lightly browned.

Garnish ham platter with the pineapple and sprigs of parsley.

About 20 servings

Savory Roast Half Ham: Follow recipe for Savory Roast Ham. Substitute **5-lb. smoked half ham** for the whole ham. Allow 22 to 25 min. per pound for roasting. Prepare and apply one half of the Glaze and Fruit Garnish.

About 10 servings

Roast Turkey I

1. Rinse bird with cold water. Drain and pat dry with absorbent paper or soft cloth.
2. Prepare cooked giblets and broth for gravy (see instructions).
3. Prepare favorite stuffing.
4. Rub body and neck cavities with salt. Fill lightly with stuffing. (Extra stuffing may be put into a greased covered baking dish or wrapped in aluminum foil and baked with turkey the last hour of roasting time.)
5. Fasten neck skin to back with skewer and bring wing tips onto back. Push drumsticks under band of skin at tail, or tie with cord. Set, breast up, on rack in shallow roasting pan. Brush with melted fat.
6. If meat thermometer is used, place it in center of inside thigh muscle or thickest part of breast meat. Be sure that tip does not touch bone. If desired, cover top and sides of turkey with cheese-cloth moistened with melted fat. Keep cloth moist during roasting by brushing occasionally with fat from the bottom of pan.
7. Roast, uncovered, at 325°F until turkey tests done (the thickest part of the drumstick feel soft when pressed with fingers and meat thermometer registers 180°F to 185°F).
8. When turkey is two thirds done, cut band of skin or cord at drumsticks. Roast until done. For easier carving, let turkey stand 20 to 30 minutes, keeping it warm. Meanwhile, if desired, prepare gravy from drippings.
9. Remove cord and skewers from turkey and place on heated platter. Garnish platter and, if desired, put paper frills on drumsticks.

Note: If desired, turkey may be roasted in heavy-duty aluminum foil. Brush bird thoroughly with melted fat; wrap securely in foil; close with a drugstore or lock fold to prevent leakage of drippings. Place, breast up, in roasting pan (omit rack). Roast a 10-to 12-pound turkey at 450°F about 3 hours. About 20 minutes before end of roasting time, remove from oven. quickly unfold foil to edge of pan. Insert meat thermometer. Return uncovered bird to oven and complete cooking. (Turkey will brown sufficiently in this time.)

Cooked Giblets And Broth: Put turkey neck and giblets (except liver) into a saucepan with 1 large onion, sliced, parsley, celery with leaves, 1 medium-sized bay leaf, 2 teaspoons salt, and 1 quart water. Cover and simmer until giblets are tender, about 2 hours; add the liver the last 15 minutes of cooking. Strain; reserve broth for gravy. Chop the giblets; set aside for gravy.

For paper frills: Select a sheet of white paper twice as wide as desired for length of frills; fold lengthwise. With fold toward you, make parallel cuts through fold 1/8 inch apart to within 1/2 inch of opposite side. Cut paper desired length; turn inside out. Wind around drumsticks. Fluff fringed ends with fingers. Fasten in place with cellulose tape.

How to Carve

Whole Ham

1. Ham is placed on platter with decorated or fat side up and shank to carver's right. Location of bones in right and left hams may be confusing so double check location of knee cap which may be on near or far side of ham. Remove two or three lengthwise slices from thin side of ham which contains knee cap.

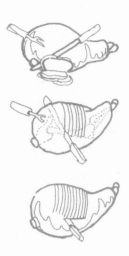

2. Make perpendicular slices down to leg bone.

3. Release slices by cutting along leg bone.

Poultry

Standard Style

1. To remove leg (drumstick and thigh), hold the drumstick firmly with fingers, pulling gently away from body of bird. At the same time cut through skin between leg and body.

2. Press leg away from body with flat side of knife. Then cut through joint joining leg to backbone and skin on the back. Hold leg on service plate with drumstick at a convenient angle to plate. Separate drumstick and thigh by cutting down through the joint to the plate.

3. Slice drumstick meat. Hold drumstick upright at a convenient angle to plate and cut down, turning drumstick to get uniform slices. Drumsticks and thighs from smaller birds are usually served whole.

4. Slice thigh meat. Hold thigh firmly on plate with a fork. Cut slices of meat parallel to the bone.

5. Cut into white meat parallel to wing. Make a cut deep into the breast to the body frame parallel to and close to the wing.

6. Slice white meat. Beginning at front, starting halfway up the breast, cut thin slices of white meat down to the cut made parallel to the wing. The slices will fall away from the bird as they are cut to this line. Continue carving until enough meat has been carved for first servings. Carve more as needed.

Side Style

1. Remove wing tip and first joint. Grasp wing tip firmly with fingers, lift up, and cut between first and second joint. Place wing tip and first joint portion on side of platter. Leave second joint attached to bird.

2. Remove the drumstick. Grasp end of drumstick and lift it up and away from the body, disjointing it from the thigh. Thigh is left attached to the bird. Place drumstick on service plate for slicing. Hold drumstick upright at an angle and cut down toward plate, parallel with bone, turning to make even slices.

3. Anchoring the fork where it is most convenient to steady the bird, cut slices of thigh meat parallel to the body until the bone is reached. Run the point of the knife around the thigh bone, lift up with fork, and remove bone. Slice the remaining thigh meat.

4. Begin at front end of bird and slice white meat until the wing socket is exposed. Remove second joint of wing. Continue slicing until enough slices have been provided, or until the breastbone is reached.

5. Remove stuffing from hole cut into cavity under thigh. Slit the thin tissue in the thigh region with tip of knife and make an opening large enough for a serving spoon. Stuffing in breast cavity may be served by laying the skin back.

Butter-Roasted Turkey

These instructions for roasting make use of an aluminum-foil tent.

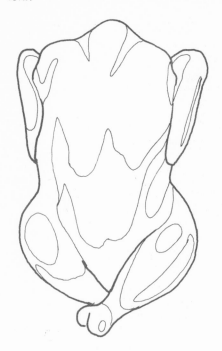

1. Rinse a ready-to-cook turkey, drain, and pat dry. Rub the body and neck cavities with salt. Fill lightly with desired stuffing. (Extra stuffing may be put into a greased covered baking dish or wrapped in aluminum foil and baked with turkey the last hour of roasting time.) Fasten neck skin to back with skewer and bring wing tips onto back. Push drumsticks under band of skin at tail, or tie with cord.

2. Place turkey, breast down, on foil band* put crosswise onto a rack in a foil-lined roasting pan. Brush turkey with softened butter. Roast at 325°F.

3. When turkey has roasted for about two-thirds the required time, remove from oven. Use the boil band to flip turkey first on the side then breast up. Brush breast with softened butter. Insert meat thermometer into the thickest part of the thigh during this final one-third of roasting time.

4. Crease a large piece of foil lengthwise to make a tent, and arrange it loosely over bird. Return to oven and continue roasting. The tent keeps turkey moist and prevents overbrowning. The turkey is done when thermometer registers 180° to 185°F, or the thickest part of drumstick feels soft when pressed with fingers protected with clean cloth or paper napkin.

5. Transfer turkey to a heated serving platter, lifting it with the foil band; remove band. Let turkey stand covered with the foil tent for about 30 minutes for easier carving; remove tent. Garnish platter with chutney filled oranges, or as desired.

*To make the band, fold a long piece of heavy-duty aluminum foil lengthwise over and over to make a 3 inch wide band.

Stuffed Turkey

1   **turkey (12 to 16 pounds)**
    Salt and pepper
    Juice of 1 lemon
    Stuffing
    Melted butter

Gravy:

    Flour
    Chicken broth
    White wine
    Salt and pepper

1. Clean turkey. Sprinkle inside and out with salt and pepper, then drizzle with lemon juice.

2. Spoon desired amount of stuffing into cavities of turkey. Secure openings with skewers and twine.

3. Put turkey, breast side up, on a rack in a shallow roasting pan. Cover bird with a double thickness of cheesecloth soaked in butter.

4. Roast in a 325°F oven 4½ to 5½ hours, or until done (180°F to 185°F on a meat thermometer inserted in inside thigh muscle or thickest part of breast); baste with drippings several times during roasting.

5. For gravy, stir a small amount of flour with pan drippings. Cook until bubbly. Stir in equal parts of broth and wine. Season to taste with salt and pepper.

6. Put turkey on a platter and garnish with watercress. Accompany with gravy.

12 to 16 servings

Roast Turkey II

1   **turkey 10 to 12 lbs. ready-to-cook weight**
     Herb Stuffing (page 88) or Oyster Stuffing (page 88)
2   **teaspoon salt**
     Melted fat

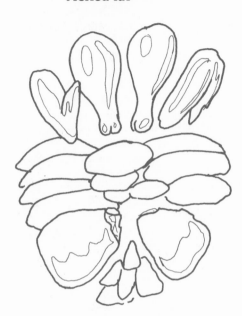

1. Set out a shallow roasting pan with rack.
2. Clean and cut off neck of turkey at body (leaving on neck skin).
3. Prepare Herb Stuffing or Oyster Stuffing.
4. Rub neck and body cavities of turkey with salt .
5. Lightly fill body and neck cavities with stuffing. To close body cavity, sew or skewer and lace with cord. Fasten neck skin to back with skewer. Push drumsticks under band of skin at tail, if present, or tie them to tail. Bring wing tips onto back. Place breast-side up on rack on roasting pan. Brush thoroughly with melted fat.
6. If meat thermometer is used, place it in center of inside thigh muscle. (When done, meat thermometer will register (180°-185°F.)
7. Roast uncovered at 325°F 3½ to 4½ hrs. When two-thirds done, cut cord of band of skin at drumsticks. Continue roasting until thickest part of drumstick feels soft when pressed with fingers; protect fingers with cloth or paper napkin. If desired, baste or brush occasionally with butter or pan drippings.
8. Remove turkey from oven. Remove roast meat thermometer and keep turkey hot. Allow to stand about 20 min. before serving.
9. Remove cord and skewers. Serve turkey on a heated platter. Garnish with parsley and serve with Spicy Cranberry Sauce (page 104). If desired, put paper frills on drumsticks.

About 16 servings

Roast Chicken: Follow recipe for Roast Turkey. For turkey, substitute **1 roasting chicken,** 3 to 4 lbs., ready-to-cook weight. For rubbing cavities, reduce salt to ¼ to ½ teaspoon. Use one third recipe of stuffing. Chicken may be placed breast-side up or down. If placed down, turn breast side up when about three-quarters done. Roast at 375°F about 2¼ to 2¾ hrs.

Roast Stuffed Turkey

1   **turkey (6 to 8 pounds)**
1   **package (7 ounces) herb-seasoned stuffing croutons**
½   **cup melted butter**
½   **cup hot water or chicken broth**
2   **tablespoons butter**
½   **cup chopped celery**
½   **cup chopped onion**
2   **tablespoons chopped parsley**
     Melted butter

1. Rinse turkey with cold water; pat dry.
2. Turn stuffing croutons into a bowl; add ½ cup melted butter and toss gently. Stir in hot water or broth.
3. Heat 2 tablespoons butter in a skillet. Add celery and onion; cook until tender. Add to bowl with stuffing; add parsley and toss to mix.
4. Spoon stuffing into cavities of bird. Place turkey, breast side up, in a large electric cooker. Insert a meat thermometer in inner thigh muscle. Brush with melted butter.
5. Cover and roast at 300°F until meat thermometer registers 180°-185°, about 6 hours.

6 to 10 servings

Note: If desired to enhance browning, place a piece of aluminum foil over turkey before covering with lid.

Roast Goose I

1 **ready-to-cook goose, 8 to 10 lbs.**
1 **tablespoon salt**
¼ **teaspoon black pepper**
1 **lb. cooking apples, pared and quartered**
¾ **lb. prunes (soaked in warm water, drained, and pitted)**
1 **tablespoon sugar**

1. Rinse goose and remove any large layers of fat from the body cavity. Pat dry with absorbent paper. Rub body and neck cavities with a mixture of the salt and pepper.
2. Mix apples, prunes, and sugar together; lightly spoon mixture into cavities. To close body cavity, sew, or skewer and lace with a cord. Fasten neck skin to back with skewer. Loop cord around legs, tighten slightly, and tie around a skewer inserted on the back above tail. Rub skin of goose with a little salt.
3. Place goose, breast down, on a rack in a shallow roasting pan.
4. Roast, uncovered, at 325°F 2½ hours, removing fat from pan several times during this period. Turn goose, breast up, and roast 45 to 60 minutes longer, or until goose tests done. To test for doneness, move leg gently by grasping end of bone. When done, drumstick-thigh joint moves easily or twists out.
5. Transfer goose to a carving board or heated serving platter while preparing Gravy, below. Garnish as desired.

About 8 servings

Gravy: Pour off all but ¼ cup of drippings from roasting pan. Add about 2 cups hot water; bring to boiling, stirring to loosen browned residue. Stir in a smooth mixture of ½ cup cold water and ¼ cup flour. Bring to boiling and boil 1 to 2 minutes, stirring constantly. Season to taste. If desired, add 2 tablespoons currant jelly and cooked giblets.

Roast Goose II

1 **goose, 10 to 12 lbs. ready-to-cook weight**
Apple Stuffing for Poultry (page 91)
2 **teaspoons salt**

1. Set out a shallow roasting pan with rack.
2. Clean goose (and cut off neck at body, leaving skin).
3. (If goose is frozen, thaw, following package directions.) Rinse and pat goose dry with absorbent paper. Set aside.
4. Prepare Apple Stuffing for Poultry and cool.
5. Rub cavity of goose with salt.
6. Lightly fill body and neck cavities with stuffing. To close body cavity, sew or skewer and lace with cord. Fasten neck skin to back with skewer. Loop cord around legs and tighten slightly. Place goose breast down on rack in roasting pan.
7. Roast at 325°F for 3¾ to 4¼ hrs. or until goose tests done. Allow about 25 min. per pound. To test for doneness, move leg gently by grasping end of bone; the thigh joint should move easily. (Protect fingers with cloth or paper.) During roasting period, spoon off fat occasionally as it accumulates. This fat may be used in other cooking.
8. Remove skewers and cord. Serve goose on heated platter. Garnish with **parsley.**

About 8 servings

Goose Oriental

3	cups cooked goose meat, cut into 2-inch pieces
1½	cups canned pineapple juice
3	tablespoons lemon juice
¼	cup cornstarch
½	cup water
1	clove garlic, put through a garlic press
2	tablespoons cooking oil
1½	teaspoons salt
1	tablespoon brown sugar
½	teaspoon ginger
¼	teaspoon pepper
½	teaspoon allspice
½	teaspoon cinnamon
½	teaspoon cloves
½	teaspoon nutmeg
2	medium oranges, peeled and cut in segments

1. Place goose meat in a 1½-quart dish. Combine all remaining ingredients except orange segments and pour over goose. Cover and chill 2 to 3 hours.
2. Turn mixture into a large wok and cover. Bring to boiling and simmer 20 minutes, or until thoroughly heated. During last 5 minutes of cooking, place orange sections over goose; cover.
3. Serve with **hot fluffy rice** and pass bowls of **salted peanuts** and **fresh flaked coconut**.

6 servings

Roast Goose With Baked Apples

8	pound goose
2	quarts bread crumbs
2	onions, chopped
2	tablespoons fat
1	teaspoon sage
2	teaspoons salt, Dash pepper
8	apples
¼	cup brown sugar
3	cooked mashed sweet-potatoes

1. Cook giblets (gizzard, heart and liver) until tender; chop and mix with bread crumbs, onion, fat, sage, salt and pepper.
2. Clean goose; remove fat from body cavity. Remove neck at body, leaving on neck skin. Rinse bird, pat dry. Rub cavities with salt. Spoon stuffing into body and neck; close cavity and fasten neck skin back with skewer.
3. Place, breast side down, on rack in roasting pan. Roast uncovered at 325°F. for 2½ hours. Drain off fat occasionally.
4. Turn goose, breast side up. Place apples in pan; bake 1 hour longer, or until goose tests done.
Baked Apples—Wash and core apples; sprinkle with brown sugar and stuff with seasoned sweet potatoes.

Serves 8

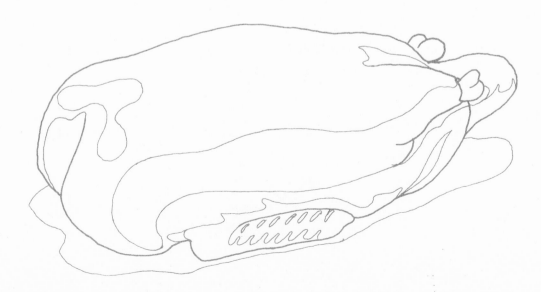

Roast Goose With Prune Apple Stuffing

2   cups pitted cooked prunes
1   goose, 10 to 12 lbs.
    ready-to-cook weight
    Salt
6   medium (about 2 lbs.) ap-
    ples

1. Set out a shallow roasting pan with rack.
2. Have ready pitted cooked prunes.
3. Reserve about 8 to 10 prunes for garnish.
4. Clean and remove any layers of fat from body cavity and opening of goose.
5. Cut of neck at body, leaving on neck skin. (If goose is frozen, thaw, following directions on package.) Rinse and pat dry with absorbent paper. (Reserve giblets for use in gravy or other food preparation.) Rub body and neck cavities of goose with salt.
6. Wash, quarter, core and pare apples.
7. Lightly fill body and neck cavities with the apples and prunes. To close body cavity, sew or skewer and lace with cord. Fasten neck skin to back with skewer. Loop cord around legs and tighten slightly. Place breast-side down on rack in roasting pan.
8. Roast uncovered at 325°F 3 hrs. Remove fat from pan is it accumulates during this period. Turn goose breast side up. Roast 1 to 2 hrs. longer, or until goose tests done. To test for doneness, move leg gently by grasping end of bone; drumstick-thigh joint should move easily. (Protect fingers with paper napkin.) Allow about 25 min. per pound to estimate total roasting time.
9. To serve, remove skewers and cord. Place goose on heated platter. Remove some of the apples from goose and arrange on the platter. Garnish with the reserved prunes and **watercress.** For an attractive garnish, place cooked **prunes** on top of cooked **apple rings** if desired.

8 servings

Roast Goose With Potato Stuffing: Follow recipe for Roast Goose With Prune Apple Stuffing. Omit apples and prunes. Prepare and lightly fill body and neck cavities with **Potato Stuffing** (page 96).

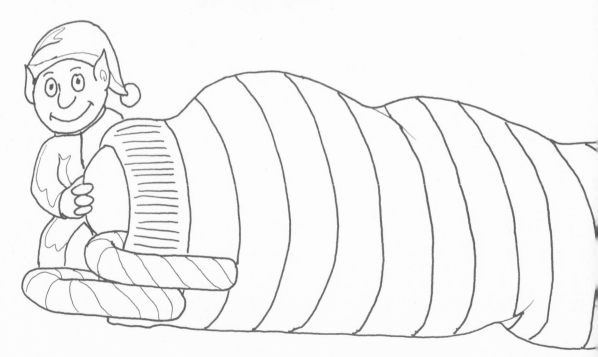

Roast Goose With Prune Stuffing

1   **goose, 10 to 12 lbs. ready-to-cook weight**
1   **cup large dried prunes**
2   **cups water**
1   **tablespoon fat**
1   **lb. lean pork, coarsely ground**
½   **cup chopped onion**
1   **teaspoon salt**
½   **teaspoon pepper**
1   **egg yolk, slightly beaten**
¼   **cup chopped green olives**
    Salt

1. Set out a shallow roasting pan with rack, a saucepan, and a skillet with cover.
2. Clean, cut off neck at body, leaving skin, and thoroughly wash in cold water, body and neck cavities of goose.
3. Drain and pat dry with absorbent paper. Set goose aside.
4. Put into the saucepan dried prunes and water.
5. Cover saucepan; bring to boiling and simmer prunes about 20 min., or until plump and tender. Slit prunes with a sharp knife and carefully remove pits. Set prunes aside.
6. Meanwhile, heat fat in the skillet.
7. Add lean pork and chopped onion.
8. Cook and stir over medium heat until meat is lightly browned. Season with salt and pepper.
9. Cover skillet and cook over low heat about 20 min.
10. Remove from heat and stir in egg yolk.
11. Remove ¼ cup of pork stuffing and combine with chopped green olives.
12. Fill prunes with this mixture and gently mix prunes with remaining stuffing.
13. Rub cavity of goose with salt.
14. Lightly fill body and neck cavities with stuffing. To close body cavity, sew or skewer and lace with cord. Fasten neck skin to back with skewer. Loop cord around legs and tighten slightly. Place breast-side down on rack in roasting pan.
15. Roast uncovered at 325°F for 3 hrs. Remove fat from pan several times during this period. Turn goose breast-side up. Roast 1 to 2 hrs. longer, or until it tests done. (Allow about 25 min. per pound for total roasting time.) To test for doneness, move leg gently by grasping end of drumstick; thigh joint should move easily.
16. Remove skewers and cord. Serve on heated platter. Garnish as desired.

8 servings

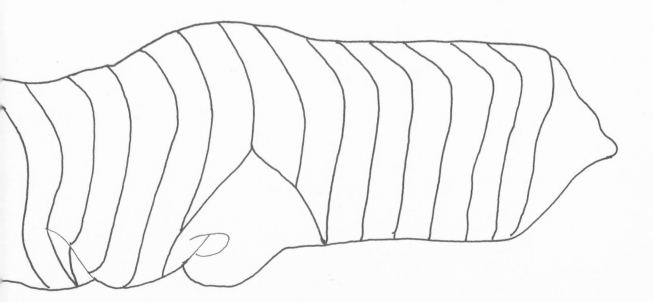

Roast Duckling A L'Orange

2   **ready-to-cook ducklings, 4 lbs. each**
2   **teaspoons salt**
     Apricot-Rice Stuffing, page 90
1   **cup orange juice**
2   **tablespoons butter or margarine**
     Orange Gravy, below

1. Rinse ducklings and pat dry with absorbent paper. Rub cavities of ducklings with salt.
2. Prepare Apricot-Rice Stuffing and set aside.
3. Heat orange juice and butter together over low heat until butter is melted. Remove from heat and, using a pastry brush, brush cavities with the mixture.
4. Lightly fill body and neck cavities with the stuffing; do not pack. To close body cavities, sew, or skewer and lace with cord; fasten neck skin to backs and wings to bodies with skewers. Place ducklings, breast up, on rack in roasting pan. Brush with juice mixture.
5. Roast, uncovered, at 325°F 2½ to 3 hours. To test doneness, move leg gently by grasping end bone; drumstick-thigh joint should move easily. Brush frequently with orange juice mixture; pour off and reserve drippings as they accumulate.
6. Place ducklings on a heated platter; remove skewers and cord. Garnish with broiled orange slices and parsley; serve with Orange Gravy.

6 to 8 servings

Orange Gravy: Leaving brown residue in roasting pan, pour drippings and fat into a bowl. Allow fat to rise to surface; skim off fat and reserve 3 tablespoons; put reserved fat into roasting pan. Blend in 3 tablespoons flour, ¼ teaspoon salt, and ⅛ teaspoon black pepper. Stirring constantly, heat until mixture bubbles. Remove from heat. Continue to stir while slowly adding 2 cups reserved drippings plus orange juice. Return to heat and cook rapidly, stirring constantly, until gravy thickens. Cook 1 to 2 minutes longer. While stirring, scrape bottom and sides of pan to blend in brown residue. Blend in ⅓ cup orange marmalade. Remove from heat; pour into gravy boat and serve hot.

Roast Duck

5   **pound duck**
     Salt, pepper, clove garlic
3   **cups pared quartered apples**
1   **cup seedless raisins**
1   **cup orange juice, if desired**

1. Wash, singe and clean duck, season, rub with garlic and fill with apples mixed with raisins; place in pan and roast uncovered in slow oven (325°F.), allowing 20 to 30 minutes per pound.
2. Baste every 10 minutes using 1 cup of orange juice, if the flavor is desired.
3. Serve with Currant or Cranberry Jelly.

Serves 5

Pineapple Duck

1   **duckling (about 3 pounds)**
2   **cups boiling water**
     Salt and pepper
2   **tablespoons soy sauce**
1   **can (20 ounces) pineapple chunks**

1. Cut duckling into serving portions. Place in a large wok and cover with boiling water. Simmer, covered, until almost tender (about 1 hour).
2. Skim off fat. Stir in salt, pepper, soy sauce, and pineapple with syrup.
3. Cook 30 minutes, or until duckling is done.

4 servings

Duckling, Southern Style

2	tablespoons butter
1	tablespoon flour
2	tablespoons chopped ham
¾	teaspoon salt
⅛	teaspoon pepper
	Paprika
2	tablespoons minced onion
½	cup chopped celery
2	tablespoons chopped green pepper
1	tablespoon chopped parsley
1½	cups bouillon or con-somme
1	whole clove
¼	teaspoon mace
2	cups diced cooked duck-ling

1. Melt butter in cooking pan of a chafing dish. Stir in flour and ham. Blend in salt, pepper, paprika, onion, celery, green pepper, and parsley.
2. Gradually stir in bouillon; add clove and mace. Simmer 15 minutes.
3. Stir in cooked duck and place over simmering water. Heat thoroughly and serve with fried hominy or mush.

4 servings

Glazed Duckling Gourmet

2	ready-to-cook ducklings, 4 lbs. each
½	teaspoons salt
¼	teaspoon nutmeg
4	tablespoons butter or margarine
1	clove garlic, minced
1½	teaspoons rosemary, crushed
1½	teaspoons thyme
1½	cups Burgundy
2	teaspoons red wine vinegar
⅓	cup currant jelly
2	tablespoons cold water
2	teaspoons cornstarch
1½	cups halved seedless green grapes

1. Rinse ducklings, pat dry and quarter.
2. Skin duckling pieces (do not use wings, necks and backs) and remove excess fat. Rub pieces with a mixture of salt and nutmeg.
3. Heat butter or margarine and garlic in a large skillet over medium heat.
4. Add duckling pieces and brown well on all sides. Sprinkle rosemary and thyme over duckling.
5. Add a blend of Burgundy, red wine vinegar and currant jelly.
6. Bring to boiling, cover skillet, lower heat and cook gently until duckling is tender, about 45 min. Remove duckling to a heated platter and keep warm.
7. Combine cold water and cornstarch, blending well.
8. Stir into liquid in skillet and bring to boiling. Cook and stir 1 to 2 min. Add seedless green grapes and mix lightly until thoroughly heated.
9. Pour the hot sauce over duckling; garnish platter with sprigs of **watercress.**

6 to 8 servings

Roast Capon I

5   to 8lb. capon
     Salt
     **Stuffing (your favorite
     recipe or a packaged stuf-
     fing mix)**
     Melted fat

1. Prepare for stuffing (see Roast Turkey).
2. Rub body and neck cavities with salt.
3. Fill cavities lightly with Stuffing.
4. Fasten neck skin to back with a skewer and bring wing tips on-to back. Push drumsticks under band or skin at tail, or tie with cord. Place breastside up on rack in shallow roasting pan. Brush with melted fat.
5. Roast at 325°F 2½ to 3½ hrs., or until thickest part of drumstick feels soft when pressed with fingers, basting frequently with melted fat or pan drippings.
6. When capon is two-thirds done, cut band of skin or cord at drumsticks. Roast until done. After removal from oven, allow capon to stand about 20 min., to make carving easier.
7. Meanwhile, prepare gravy from drippings, if desired.

1 Stuffed capon

Roast Capon II

6   **pound capon**
      Salt
4½   **pounds sweet potatoes**
¾   **cup fat**
2   **cups marrons**
      **Chopped leaves 1 bunch
      celery**
1   **tablespoon minced onion**
½   **cup heavy cream**

1. Dress capon, clean and rub inside well with salt. Boil enough sweet-potatoes to make 6 cups mashed.
2. Add salt and ½ cup fat. Mash marrons, reserving 6 for later use, and add to mashed potatoes; mix well.
3. Dice reserved marrons and stir into stuffing. Stuff capon with this mixture and close opening.
4. Rub the capon with unsalted fat.
5. Brown celery leaves and onion in remaining fat in roaster, breast up and cover with cloth.
6. Place capon on the sauteed leaves, dipped into melted fat. Bake in slow oven (325°F) 22 to 30 minutes per pound, basting frequently with melted fat. When capon is nearly tender, remove celery from pan. remove cloth and brush breast with the cream. Continue roasting until tender.
7. Prepare Gravy from the drippings in roaster, strain and serve with capon.

Serves 6 to 8

Rock Cornish Hens with Oranges and Almonds

1 Rock Cornish hen per serving

For each serving:
- **2 tablespoons butter, melted**
- **2 tablespoons orange juice**
- **Salt and pepper to taste**
- **¼ teaspoon marjoram**
- **¼ teaspoon thyme**
- **½ garlic clove, crushed in a garlic press**
- **½ navel orange with peel, cut in thin slices**
- **2 tablespoons honey (about)**
- **5 almonds, blanched, slivered, and toasted**

1. Rinse hen well. Drain and pat dry. Place in a shallow baking dish. Drizzle inside and out with butter.
2. Combine orange juice, salt, pepper, marjoram, thyme, and garlic in a small bowl. Pour over and into the bird. Marinate 2 hours; turn occasionally.
3. Set bird on a broiler rack and put under broiler about 6 inches from heat. Broil 12 minutes on each side, or until tender, basting frequently with the marinade. During the last few minutes of broiling, arrange orange slices around the birds and drizzle with honey.
4. Garnish with almonds and serve at once.

Pasta & Rice

Lasagne I

Tomato Sauce with Meat (page 101)
- 3 tablespoons olive oil
- 1 pound ground beef
- 1 pound lasagne noodles, cooked and drained
- ¾ pound mozzarella cheese, thinly sliced
- 2 hard-cooked eggs, sliced
- ¼ cup grated Parmesan cheese
- ½ teaspoon pepper
- 1 cup ricotta

1. Prepare sauce, allowing 4½ hours for cooking.
2. Heat olive oil in a skillet. Add ground beef and cook until browned, separating into small pieces.
3. Spread ½ cup sauce in a 2-quart baking dish. Top with a layer of noodles and half the mozzarella cheese. Spread half the ground beef and half the egg slices on top. Sprinkle on half the Parmesan cheese and ¼ teaspoon pepper. Top with ½ cup ricotta.
4. Beginning with sauce, repeat layering, ending with ricotta. Top ricotta with ½ cup sauce. Arrange over this the remaining lasagne noodles. Top with more sauce.
5. Bake at 350°F about 30 minutes, or until mixture is bubbling. Let stand 5 to 10 minutes to set the layers. Cut in squares and serve topped with remaining sauce.

6 to 8 servings

Lasagne II

Tomato Sauce with Meat (page 101)
- 1 pound lasagne noodles, cooked, drained, and rinsed
- 2 pounds ricotta
- 1 pound mozzarella or scamorze cheese, shredded
- 1 cup shredded Parmesan cheese

1. Prepare Tomato Sauce with Meat.
2. Spread about 1 cup tomato sauce in a buttered 13x9x2-inch baking dish. Using a fourth of each, add a layer of noodles and then one of tomato sauce. Using a third of each, top evenly with 3 cheeses. Repeat layering and end with sauce.
3. Heat in a 375°F oven about 30 minutes, or until bubbly. Allow to stand 10 to 15 minutes to set layers before serving. Cut into squares.

12 to 15 servings

Lasagnette

Tomato Meat Sauce (half recipe, page 101)
Basic Noodle Dough
8   quarts water
¼   cup salt
1   tablespoon olive oil
1   cup (8 ounces) ricotta
2   tablespoons grated Parmesan cheese
¼   teaspoon salt
⅛   teaspoon pepper

1. Prepare Tomato Meat Sauce.
2. Prepare noodle dough. Roll lightly ⅛ inch thick to form a rectangle about 12 inches long. Cut dough lengthwise with pastry cutter into strips ½ to ¾ inch wide.
3. Bring water to boiling in a large saucepot. Add ¼ cup salt, then noodles. Boil rapidly, uncovered, about 15 minutes, or until tender. Drain by pouring into a colander or large sieve; keep warm.
4. Put ½ cup meat sauce into a saucepan. Mix in ricotta, Parmesan cheese, ¼ teaspoon salt, and pepper. Cook over low heat until thoroughly heated.
5. Put noodles on a warm serving platter and pour cheese sauce over them. Cover with meat sauce. Serve immediately.

About 8 servings

Lasagne Bolognese

3   tablespoons butter or margarine
3   tablespoons flour
1   cup milk
1   cup whipping cream
¼   teaspoon salt
    Dash of pepper
½   pound lasagne noodles
    Meat Sauce Bolognese II (page 102)
1   cup (4 ounces) grated Parmesan cheese

1. Melt butter in saucepan; blend in flour. Gradually add milk and cream, stirring until thickened and smooth. Add salt and pepper.
2. Cook lasagne noodles in **boiling salted water** according to package directions. Drain, rinse, and spread on a damp towel.
3. Spread a thin layer of Meat Sauce Bolognese in a 13x9-inch baking dish. Top with a layer of half the lasagne noodles, half the Meat Sauce Bolognese, half the white sauce, and half the cheese; repeat layers.
4. Bake, uncovered, at 375°F 35 to 40 minutes, or until mixture is bubbly and top is golden brown. Let stand 10 minutes. Cut into squares to serve.

8 servings

Manicotti Tuscan Style

Egg Pasta Dough for Manicotti (page 96)
Tomato Sauce (page 101)
3   tablespoons butter
1   tablespoon olive oil
1   clove garlic, minced
6   mushrooms, minced
1   pound ground beef round
1   pound ground beef round
1   teaspoon salt
¼   teaspoon pepper
½   pound ricotta
¼   pound Parmesan cheese, grated

1. Prepare pasta dough and Tomato Sauce.
2. Heat butter and oil in a skillet. Add garlic; saute until soft. Stir in mushrooms, beef, salt, and pepper. Cook until meat is brown, stirring often. Add ricotta and half the Parmesan cheese, blending well.
3. When dough squares are dry, spread ½ tablespoon of the beef mixture on each square and roll up tightly. Press edges together to seal, moistening edges with water if necessary. Filling mush be sealed in completely, or it will fall out during the cooking in boiling water.
4. Cook manicotti in gently boiling salted water until just tender. Remove with a slotted spoon and drain. Arrange a layer of manicotti (about 30) in a buttered 3-quart casserole. Cover with Tomato Sauce and sprinkle with half of remaining Parmesan cheese. Arrange remaining manicotti crosswise in another layer, cover with Tomato Sauce, and sprinkle with remaining Parmesan cheese.
5. Bake at 350°F 25 minutes, or until cheese browns and sauce bubbles.

About 60 manicotti

Meat-Stuffed Manicotti

2 tablespoons olive oil
½ pound fresh spinach, washed, dried, and finely chopped
2 tablespoons chopped onion
½ teaspoon salt
½ teaspoon oregano
½ pound ground beef
2 tablespoons fine dry bread crumbs
1 egg, slightly beaten
1 can (6 ounces) tomato paste
8 manicotti shells (two thirds of a 5½-ounce package), cooked and drained
1½ tablespoons butter, softened (optional)
2 tablespoons grated Parmesan or Romano cheese (optional)
Mozzarella cheese, shredded

1. Heat olive oil in a skillet. Add spinach, onion, salt, oregano, and meat. Mix well, separating meat into small pieces. Cook, stirring frequently, until meat is no longer pink.
2. Set aside to cool slightly. Add bread crumbs, egg, and 2 tablespoons tomato paste; mix well. Stuff manicotti with mixture. Put side by side in a greased 2-quart baking dish. If desired, spread butter over stuffed manicotti and sprinkle with the grated cheese.
3. Spoon remaining tomato paste on top of the manicotti down the center of the dish. Sprinkle mozzarella cheese on top of tomato paste. Cover baking dish.
4. Bake at 425°F 12 to 15 minutes, or until mozzarella melts.

4 servings

Ravioli

Tomato Meat Sauce (page 101)
3 cups (about 1½ pounds) ricotta
1½ tablespoons chopped parsley
2 eggs, well beaten
1 tablespoon grated Parmesan cheese
¾ teaspoon salt
¼ teaspoon pepper
Basic Noodle Dough (page 85)
7 quarts water
2 tablespoons salt
Grated Parmesan or Romano cheese

1. Prepare Tomato Meat Sauce.
2. Mix ricotta, parsley, eggs, 1 tablespoon grated Parmesan, ¾ teaspoon salt, and pepper.
3. Prepare noodle dough. Divide dough in fourths. Lightly roll each fourth ⅛ inch thick to form a rectangle. Cut dough lengthwise with pastry cutter into strips 5 inches wide. Put 2 teaspoons filling 1½ inches from narrow end in center of each strip. Continuing along strip, put 2 teaspoons filling at 3½-inch intervals.
4. Fold each strip in half lengthwise, covering mounds of filling. To seal, press the edges together with the tines of a fork. Press gently between mounds to form rectangles about 3½ inches long. Cut apart with a pastry cutter and press cut edges of rectangles with tines of fork to seal.
5. Bring water to boiling in a large saucepot. Add 2 tablespoons salt. Add ravioli gradually; cook about half of ravioli at one time. Boil, uncovered, about 20 minutes, or until tender. Remove with slotted spoon and drain. Put on a warm platter and top with Tomato Meat Sauce. Sprinkle with grated cheese.

About 3 dozen ravioli

Egg Noodles with Poppy Seed

1½   quarts boiling water
1   teaspoon salt
3   cups egg noodles
½   cup milk
½   cup poppy seed, ground
3   tablespoons sugar or 2 tablespoons honey

1. Combine boiling water and salt in a large saucepan. Add noodles and cook until tender. Drain.
2. Meanwhile, scald milk; mix in poppy seed and sugar. Cook 5 minutes.
3. Combine poppy seed mixture with the noodles. Serve hot.

4 to 6 servings

Noodles with Poppy Seed and Raisins

2   cups cooked egg noodles
2   tablespoons butter, melted
1   can (12 ounces) poppy seed cake and pastry filling
1   teaspoon vanilla extract
1   teaspoon lemon juice
1½   teaspoons grated lemon peel
⅓   cup raisins

1. Toss noodles with butter in a saucepan.
2. Combine poppy seed filling with vanilla extract, lemon juice and peel, and raisins. Add to noodles and mix well. Cook just until heated through.

About 6 servings

Basic Noodle Dough

4   cups sifted all-purpose flour
½   teaspoon salt
4   eggs
6   tablespoons cold water

1. Sift flour and salt together into a large bowl.
2. Make a well in center of flour. Add eggs , one at a time, mixing slightly after each addition.
3. Add cold water gradually.
4. Mix well to make a stiff dough. Turn dough onto a lightly floured surface and knead. Proceed as directed in recipes.

Egg Pasta Dough for Manicotti

4   cups all-purpose flour
4   eggs, beaten
1½ teaspoons salt
2   teaspoons olive oil
    Warm water (about ½ cup)

1. Put flour onto a board, make a well in center, and add eggs, salt, and olive oil. Mix until a soft dough is formed, adding warm water as needed.
2. Knead about 10 minutes until dough is smooth and elastic. Add more flour if dough is too soft.
3. Divide dough in quarters. Roll each quarter into as thin a sheet as possible. Cut the sheets into 3-inch squares. Dry on cloth or cloth-covered board for 1 hour before using.

About 1¾ pounds dough

Perfection Boiled Rice

2 qts. water
1 tablespoon salt
1 cup uncooked rice

1. Bring water and salt to boiling in a deep saucepan.
2. Add uncooked rice gradually to water so boiling will not stop.
3. (The Rice Industry no longer considers it necessary to wash rice before cooking.) Boil rapidly, uncovered, 15 to 20 min., or until a kernel is entirely soft when pressed between thumb and finger.
4. Drain in colander or sieve and rinse with hot water to remove loose starch. Cover colander and rice with clean towel and set over hot water until kernels are dry and fluffy.

About 3½ cups cooked rice

Peas in Rice Ring

1 package (6 or 6¾ ounces) seasoned wild and white rice mix
3 pounds fresh peas Butter

1. Cook rice mix according to package directions.
2. Meanwhile, rinse and shell peas just before cooking to retain their delicate flavor. Cook covered in boiling salted water to cover for 15 to 20 minutes, or until peas are tender. Drain and add just enough butter so peas glisten.
3. Butter a 1-quart ring mold. When rice is done, turn into mold, packing down gently with spoon. Invert onto a warm serving platter and lift off mold.
4. Spoon hot peas into rice ring just before serving.

About 6 servings

Turkey Stuffing

4   slices toasted bread, crumbled
1   medium-sized pan cornbread, crumbled
     Turkey stock
6   eggs
1   stalk celery, chopped
3   large onions, chopped
¼   cup butter

1. Mix toast and cornbread crumbs with enough turkey stock so that mixture will not be stiff.
2. Add the eggs, celery, onion, and butter. Season to taste with salt, pepper, and sage.
3. Bake at 325°F about 1 hour.

8 servings

Stuffing for a Small Turkey

½   cup butter
1   onion, minced
1   medium cooking apple, pared, cored, and diced
1   pound mushrooms, sliced
2   medium potatoes, boiled, peeled, and diced
½   cup pine nuts
½   cup dried black currants
1   cup blanched almonds, sliced
2   pounds chestnuts, boiled and cleaned
4   cups prepared bread stuffing
2   cups or more chicken stock to make a moist stuffing
1   can (4½ ounces) pate de foie gras
     Salt and pepper to taste

1. Melt butter in a large deep skillet. Add onion, apple, and mushrooms; cook until tender.
2. Add potatoes, pine nuts, currants, almonds, chestnuts, stuffing, and stock. Heat thoroughly over low heat, adding more liquid if necessary.
3. Stir in pate. Season with salt and pepper.
4. Cool completely. Stuff bird.

Stuffing for a small turkey or 2 capons

Bread Stuffing

1½ pound loaf bread, dried
1   cup fat, melted
1   teaspoon salt
¼   teaspoon white pepper
¼   cup minced onion
2   tablespoons poultry
      seasoning

1. Remove crusts from bread and cut bread into 1-inch cubes. Toss all ingredients together lightly. Will fill a 6-pound fowl.
2. Stuffing does not necessarily need to be baked in the fowl or meat. If the bird is small or if there is some stuffing left over it may be baked or steamed in a greased ring mold, loaf or individual molds.
3. Fill center of ring with vegetables. Croquettes of stuffing may be served around bird.

Celery—Add 2 cups chopped celery, parboiled or uncooked.

Chestnut—Add 1 pound chestnuts, cooked and chopped.

Giblet—Add chopped, cooked giblets.

Mushroom—Add ¼ to ½ pound mushrooms, chopped and sauteed in 1 tablespoon butter for 5 minutes.

Olive—Add 1 cup or more coarsely chopped olives.

Oyster—Add 1 pint oysters, chopped, and heated in 2 tablespoons butter.

Herb Stuffing

¾   cup melted butter
2   teaspoons salt
1   teaspoon sage (or ½ teaspoon each of thyme, rosemary and marjoram)
¼   teaspoon pepper
2   qts. soft bread cubes
¾   cup milk
⅓   cup chopped celery with leaves
⅓   cup chopped onion

1. Mix butter, salt, sage and pepper.
2. In a large bowl, lightly toss mixture with bread cubes, milk, chopped celery with leaves, and chopped onion.
3. Spoon stuffing into neck and body cavities of turkey—do not pack. Stuff the turkey just before roasting. Extra stuffing may be place in greased, covered baking dish or wrapped in aluminum foil and baked with turkey the last hour of roasting time.
Stuffing for 10-lb. turkey

Note: Immediately after meal is served, remove stuffing from turkey. Store stuffing in a covered dish in refrigerator. If only one side of turkey has been carved, wrap remainder in waxed paper or aluminum foil. If more than one half of the meat has been carved off, remove remainder of meat from bone. Store covered in refrigerator.
This stuffing may also be used for chicken, goose or duckling. Allow about 1 cup bread cubes per pound of ready-to-cook weight of birds; if weight is 10-lbs. or less, subtract 1 cup from total; if weight is more than 10 lbs., subtract 2 cups from total. Proportionately decrease or increase the remaining ingredients in recipe. Mix diced apple with the stuffing before filling cavity of goose or duckling. Use ½ teaspoon marjoram instead of sage.

Old-Fashioned Cornbread Stuffing

1   cup dark or golden
     seedless raisins
1½   cups thinly sliced celery
8   cups soft white-bread
     crumbs
6   cups cornbread crumbs
1   cup coarsely chopped
     salted toasted almonds
½   cup chopped parsley
1   teaspoon poultry season-
     ing
1   teaspoon ground nutmeg
1   teaspoon salt
½   teaspoon pepper
⅔   cup giblet broth
½   cup instant minced onion
¾   cup butter or margarine,
     melted
2   eggs, beaten

1. Combine raisins, celery, crumbs, almonds, and parsley. Sprinkle with a mixture of the poultry seasoning, nutmeg, salt, and pepper.
2. Add broth and onion to butter; add butter mixture and eggs to crumb mixture, mixing lightly.
3. Spoon mixture lightly into turkey; or shape into stuffing balls, place on greased baking sheet, and bake at 350°F 20 minutes, or until lightly browned.

Stuffing for a 15-pound Turkey or 20 Balls

Wild Rice Stuffing

1   cup wild rice, cooked
½   lb. fresh mushrooms, sliced
2   tablespoons chopped
     onion
½   cup butter or margarine
½   teaspoon crushed sage
     leaves (optional)
     Dash thyme (optional)

1. While wild rice is cooking, lightly brown the mushrooms with onion in ¼ cup heated butter in a skillet. Toss gently with the wild rice and herbs.
2. Add remaining ¼ cup butter, melted, and continue tossing until thoroughly mixed. Add salt and pepper to taste.

About 4 cups stuffing

Wine Stuffing For Turkey

3   qts. bread cubes
2   cups chopped blanched
     almonds
4   cups diced celery
2   cups chopped celery
     leaves
¼   cup butter or margarine
½   cup finely chopped green
     onion
2   cloves garlic, minced
3   eggs, slightly beaten
1   tablespoon salt
¼   teaspoon cracked black
     pepper
½   teaspoon ground nutmeg
½   teaspoon ground mace
½   cup dry red wine

1. Combine the bread cubes, almonds, celery, and celery leaves; toss lightly until well mixed.
2. Heat the butter in a skillet. Add the green onion and garlic and cook, stirring occasionally, until lightly browned. Add contents of skillet to bread mixture.
3. Combine the eggs, salt, pepper, nutmeg, and mace. Pour egg mixture and wine over bread cubes; toss lightly to mix thoroughly.
4. Lightly spoon into body and neck cavities of turkey (do not pack).

About 16 cups stuffing

Apricot-Rice Stuffing

¼ cup orange juice
¼ cup butter or margarine, melted
½ teaspoon salt
¼ teaspoon pepper
⅛ teaspoon thyme
⅛ teaspoon ground nutmeg
⅛ teaspoon ground cloves
3½ cups cooked rice
1 cup finely chopped dried apricots
¼ cup finely chopped onion
¼ cup finely chopped celery
2 tablespoons finely chopped parsley

Combine all ingredients in a large bowl. Toss lightly until thoroughly mixed.

About 5 cups stuffing

Cran-Prune Stuffing For Turkey

2 pkgs. (8 oz. each) herb-seasoned stuffing croutons
1½ cups fresh cranberries, rinsed and drained
1 cup diced pitted prunes
1 cup diced celery
1 large onion, chopped
½ cup butter or margarine, melted
1½ cups orange juice

1. Combine in a large mixing bowl herb-seasoned stuffing croutons, cranberries, prunes, celery, onion, butter or margarine and orange juice.
2. Toss ingredients lightly but thoroughly.

Stuffing for 12 to 15-lb. turkey

Cranberry Stuffing

1 lb. fresh cranberries
¾ cup sugar
1 cup butter or margarine, melted
6 qts. bread cubes
2 cups seedless raisins, plumped
2 teaspoons salt
1 teaspoon ground cinnamon
Grated peel of 3 lemons
1 cup water or giblet broth

Coarsely chop cranberries and mix with the sugar. Toss butter with bread cubes in a large bowl; add cranberry mixture and remaining ingredients. Mix lightly.

Stuffing for a 14 to 16-pound turkey

Apricot-Prune Stuffing

1 pkg. (8 oz.) stuffing mix
2/3 cup finely cut dried apricots
1/2 cup finely cut dried prunes
1/4 cup finely chopped onion

1. Prepare stuffing mix according to directions on package for moist stuffing.
2. Add apricots, prunes, and onion; toss. Lightly spoon stuffing into body and neck cavities of bird (do not pack).

About 5½ cups stuffing

Apple Stuffing

2 medium-sized apples, pared and diced (about 2 cups, diced)
1/3 cup chopped celery with leaves
1/3 cup chopped onion
8 cups soft bread cubes
3/4 cup melted butter
2 teaspoons salt
1/4 teaspoon pepper
1 teaspoon marjoram
3/4 cup apple cider

1. Combine apple, celery, and onion with bread cubes in a large bowl. Toss with butter, salt, pepper, and marjoram.
2. Pour cider over bread mixture and toss until thoroughly mixed. Spoon the stuffing lightly into neck and body cavities of bird (do not pack).

Stuffing for three 4-pound Ducklings

Apricot Stuffing

Perfection Boiled Rice (page 86)
1 cup (about 5 oz.) finely chopped dried apricots
1/4 cup Cointreau
1/4 cup butter, melted
1/2 teaspoon salt
1/4 teaspoon pepper
1/8 teaspoon thyme
1/8 teaspoon nutmeg
1/8 teaspoon cloves
1/4 cup finely chopped onion
1/4 cup finely chopped celery
2 tablespoons finely chopped parsley

1. Prepare Perfection Boiled Rice.
2. Meanwhile, finely chop dried apricots.
3. Set aside.
4. Mix in a large bowl Cointreau, butter, salt, pepper, thyme, nutmeg and cloves.
5. Add the rice, apricots, onion, celery and parsley.
6. Toss lightly until thoroughly combined.

About 5 cups stuffing

Orange Filbert Stuffing

4	cups white bread cubes
2	cups chopped pared apple
1	cup chopped celery
½	cup chopped onion
2	cups chopped toasted filberts
2	teaspoons finely shredded orange peel
1½	teaspoons finely shredded lemon peel
¼	cup butter or margarine, melted
2	eggs
½	cup orange juice
2	tablespoons lemon juice
1	teaspoon seasoned salt
½	teaspoon pepper
½	teaspoon thyme
¼	teaspoon nutmeg

1. Have bread cubes ready.
2. Prepare apple, celery, onion, filberts, orange peel and lemon peel.
3. Put bread cubes, apples, celery, onion and filberts into a large bowl with the shredded peels. Drizzle with butter or margarine.
4. Toss lightly.
5. Beat eggs until frothy.
6. Stir in orange juice, lemon juice, seasoned salt, pepper, thyme and nutmeg.
7. Pour over mixture in bowl and toss lightly.
8. Spoon into body cavities of poultry or into a greased 2-qt. casserole. Truss poultry and roast at 325°F, or cover casserole and bake stuffing at 325° 1 hr.

About 2 qts. stuffing

Pineapple Nut Stuffing

4	cups dry bread, ½-inch cubes
¾	cup finely chopped celery
¾	cup pineapple wedges
½	cup walnut meats, chopped fine
1	canned pimiento, chopped
	Dash cayenne
1	teaspoon paprika
1½	teaspoons salt
¼	cup butter
2	eggs

1. Combine bread, celery, pineapple, walnut, meats, pimiento and seasonings.
2. Melt butter, remove from heat, stir in unbeaten eggs and add to bread mixture. Toss lightly. Use as stuffing for turkey, chicken or duck.
3. Use chopped cooked bacon instead of nuts, reduce salt to ½ teaspoon and add grated onion or use red or green pepper instead of pimiento.

Walnut Poultry Stuffing

	Giblets from 1 fowl
1	onion, sliced
1	bay leaf
1	cup boiling water
½	pound dry bread
1	tablespoon salt
2	tablespoons poultry seasoning or sage
2	cups chopped walnuts
4	tablespoons fat, melted

1. Cook giblets, onion and bay leaf in boiling water until tender.
2. Remove bay leaf, drain giblets and chop fine. Remove crusts from bread and break into fine crumbs.
3. Combine all ingredients and toss together lightly. Moisten with giblet stock. Will fill a 12 to 14 pound fowl.

Fruit Stuffing For Goose

3	cups bread cubes
½	cup fat, melted
1	cup chopped apples
½	cup chopped cooked prunes
½	cup chopped nuts
1	teaspoon salt
¼	teaspoon pepper
1	tablespoon lemon juice

Mix all ingredients lightly. Will fill a 4 to 5 pound goose.

Filbert Stuffing For Turkey

4	qts. bread cubes
2	cups coarsely chopped filberts, toasted*
¾	cup snipped parsley
¼	cup chopped celery
1	turkey liver, cut in small pieces
½	cup milk
¾	cup chopped onion
1	cup butter or margarine

1. Put all ingredients except onion and butter into a large bowl; set aside.
2. Cook onion about 3 minutes in hot butter in a skillet. Add to ingredients in bowl; toss lightly to mix. Lightly spoon into body and neck cavities of turkey (do not pack).

Stuffing for a 14-to 16-pound turkey

*To toast filberts, spread nuts in a shallow baking pan and set in a 400°F oven 10 minutes, or until browned, stirring occasionally.

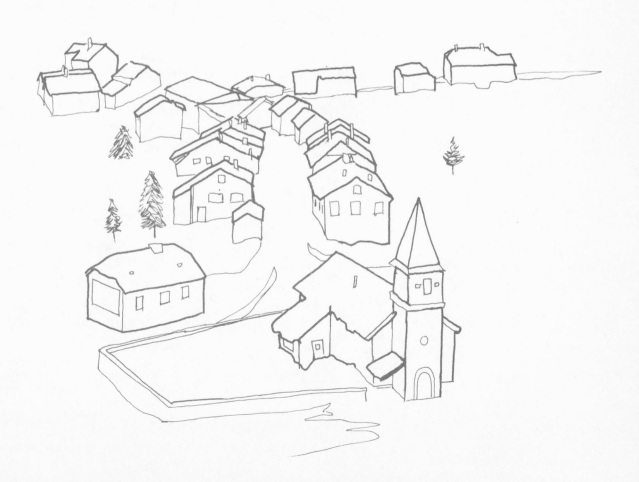

Walnut Stuffing

2   pkgs. (7 to 8 oz. each) herb-seasoned stuffing mix
¾   cup butter or margarine, melted
2   cups chicken broth
1   can (6 oz.) broiled sliced mushrooms, undrained
1½   cups chopped toasted walnuts

Toss stuffing mix with the melted butter in a bowl. Lightly mix in remaining ingredients.

Stuffing for a 14 to 16-pound turkey

Chestnut Stuffing

¼   cup butter
1   small onion, chopped
½   cup chopped celery
1   cup soft bread crumbs
1   tablespoon chopped parsley
1   teaspoon salt
⅛   teaspoon pepper
2   lbs. chestnuts, cooked and cut in pieces
½   cup cream

1. Heat butter in a skillet; add onion and celery; cook until onion is transparent and celery tender.
2. Remove skillet from heat. Add bread crumbs, parsley, salt, and pepper; mix well.
3. Put half of the chestnuts through a ricer or food mill; coarsely chop remaining ones.
4. Combine the chestnuts with bread mixture; drizzle cream over stuffing and toss lightly.
5. Lightly spoon stuffing into neck and body cavities of bird (do not pack).

About 3⅓ cups stuffing

*Roast chestnuts as directed on page 44. Put shelled chestnuts into boiling salted water to cover and boil 20 minutes, or until tender. Cool.

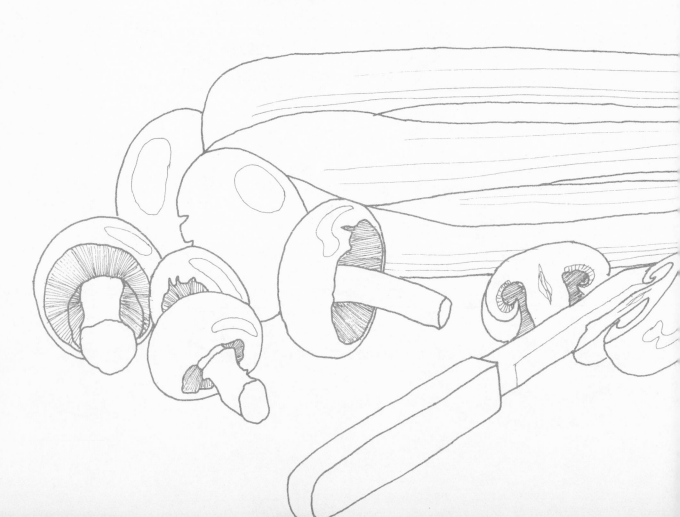

Water Chestnut-Celery Stuffing

1 pkg. (8 oz.) stuffing mix
1 cup diced celery
¼ cup finely chopped onion
1 can (8 oz.) water chestnuts, drained and sliced
2 tablespoons dried parsley flakes

1. Prepare stuffing mix according to directions on package for moist stuffing.
2. Add celery, onion, water chestnuts, and parsley flakes; toss lightly to mix. Lightly spoon stuffing into body and neck cavities of bird (do not pack).

About 5⅓ cups stuffing

Oyster-Mushroom Stuffing

½ cup butter or margarine
1 lb. mushrooms, coarsely chopped
1 cup chopped onion
1 cup chopped celery with leaves
1 qt. oysters, cut in halves (reserve liquor)
2 qts. bread cubes
2 tablespoons chopped parsley
2 teaspoons salt
¼ teaspoon pepper
1½ teaspoons poultry seasoning
3 eggs, beaten

1. Heat butter in a large skillet. Add mushrooms, onion and celery; cook 5 to 8 minutes over medium heat, stirring occasionally. Set aside.
2. In a large bowl, mix the oysters, bread cubes, parsley, and a mixture of the salt, pepper, and poultry seasoning. Add vegetables, the reserved oyster liquor, and the beaten eggs; toss lightly to mix.

Stuffing for a 14 to 16-pound turkey

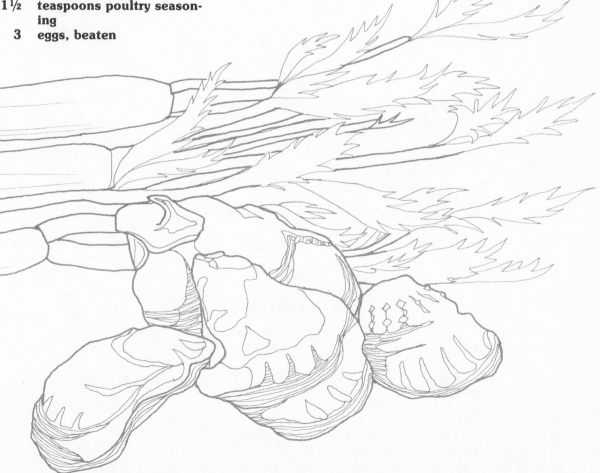

Potato Stuffing I

3⅓ lbs. (about 10 medium potatoes)
1 cup (about 2 medium) chopped onion
⅔ cup chopped celery
½ cup fat
4 cups (about 6 slices) soft bread crumbs
2 eggs, beaten
1 tablespoon poultry seasoning
2 teaspoons salt
¼ teaspoon pepper

1. Wash, pare and cook potatoes.
2. Cook about 30 min., or until potatoes are tender when pierced with a fork. Drain. Dry potatoes by shaking pan over low heat.
3. Meanwhile, prepare onion and celery.
4. Heat fat in a skillet.
5. Add the onion and celery and cook over medium heat until vegetables are tender, occasionally moving and turning them with spoon. Remove skillet from heat; set aside.
6. Force potatoes through a food mill or ricer into a large bowl. Add cooked vegetables and bread crumbs.
7. Mix thoroughly; toss with a mixture of eggs, poultry seasoning, salt, and pepper.
8. Spoon stuffing into neck and body cavities of goose; do not pack. Stuff the goose just before roasting. Extra stuffing may be placed in greased baking dish and baked with goose the last hour of baking.

Stuffing for a 10 to 12-lb. goose

Potato Stuffing II

2 tablespoons onion
¼ cup salt pork cubes
2 cups hot mashed potatoes
1 teaspoon poultry seasoning
Salt and pepper
1 cup cooked sausages, chopped

1. Cook onion and pork until brown.
2. Add remaining ingredients and mix well.
3. Use for stuffing chicken, turkey and goose. Makes enough stuffing for 1 3-pound fowl.

Bohemian Potato Stuffing

5 large potatoes
1 onion, grated
1 teaspoon caraway seeds
1 teaspoon minced parsley
1 tablespoon melted butter

1. Boil potatoes in their skins until tender.
2. Drain, peel and mash. Add remaining ingredients and mix well.

Makes 4 to 5 cups

Irish Potato Stuffing

8 potatoes
4 tablespoons melted goose fat or butter
1 cup chopped onions
½ cup chopped celery
1 cup bread crumbs
½ teaspoon sage
1 teaspoon celery salt
½ teaspoon summer savory
1 teaspoon salt
¼ teaspoon pepper
2 eggs, beaten

1. Pare potatoes and cook until tender.
2. Drain and rice. Add remaining ingredients and mix well.
3. Will fill 10-pound goose.
4. Save potato water for basting goose during roasting.

Potato And Celery Stuffing

2 onions
2 tablespoons melted butter
½ cup pork sausage
¼ cup chopped celery leaves
5 large uncooked potatoes
2 stalks celery
1 teaspoon salt
½ teaspoon paprika

1. Dice 1 onion and saute in butter until golden brown.
2. Add sausage and celery leaves and cook 2 minutes.
3. Pare potatoes and put through food chopper with celery stalks and remaining onion. Add to cooked mixture wsith salt and paprika and mix well. Will fill a 3 to 4-pound fowl.

Country Potato Stuffing—Use 3 cups hot mashed potatoes instead of uncooked potatoes. Use only 1 onion; omit butter. Dice celery and onion and mix all ingredients together without sauteing. Add ½ cup bread crumbs; 1 egg, beaten; ¼ cup cream and ½ teaspoon mustard. Mix together thoroughly and use to stuff poultry or crown roast of lamb or pork.

Dressings & Sauces

Lime French Dressing

½   cup olive or salad oil
¼   cup lime juice
¼   cup lemon juice
½   teaspoon salt
     Few grains cayenne
2   tablespoons sugar or honey

1. Combine all ingredients.
2. Shake well before using.

Makes 1 cup

Whipped Cream Dressing

⅔   cup sugar
2   tablespoons flour
2   eggs, beaten
2   tablespoons salad oil
3   tablespoons lemon juice
4   tablespoons orange juice
1   cup pineapple juice
½   cup heavy cream, whipped

1. Combine sugar and flour in top of double boiler.
2. Add remaining ingredients except cream and cook until thickened, stirring constantly.
3. When cool, fold in whipped cream.

Makes 2 cups

Medium White Sauce

2 tablespoons butter
2 tablespoons flour
1 cup milk
¼ teaspoon salt
⅛ teaspoon pepper

Method 1—Melt butter and blend in flour. Add milk gradually, stirring constantly. Reduce heat and cook 3 minutes longer; add seasonings.

Method 2—Blend butter and flour together and add to hot milk, stirring constantly until mixture thickens. Cook 3 minutes longer; add seasonings.

Cream Sauce: Use cream for milk.

Thin White Sauce: Use 1 tablespoon butter and 1 tablespoon flour.

French Dresing

1 cup olive or salad oil
¼ cup vinegar
½ teaspoon salt
Few grains cayenne
¼ teaspoon white pepper
2 tablespoons chopped parsley

1. Combine all ingredients.
2. Beat or shake thoroughly before using.

Makes 1¼ cups

Cheese Sauce

2 tablespoons butter, melted
1 tablespoon flour
1 cup milk
Dash salt and pepper
¾ cup American cheese, grated

1. Blend butter and flour together.
2. Add milk and boil until thickened.
3. Add seasonings and cheese and continue to heat, stirring constantly until cheese is melted.

Makes 1¾ cups

Bearnaise Sauce

4 egg yolks
1 cup butter
1 tablespoon lemon juice
1 tablespoon tarragon vinegar
¼ teaspoon salt
1 teaspoon chopped parsley
1 teaspoon onion juice
Dash cayenne

1. Place egg yolks with ⅓ of butter in top of double boiler.
2. Keep water in bottom of boiler hot but not boiling.
3. Add remaining butter as sauce thickens, stirring constantly.
4. Remove from heat and add remaining ingredients.
5. Serve with broiled meat.

Makes 1 cup

Cooked Pineapple Salad Dressing

½ cup butter or margarine
2 tablespoons flour
2 tablespoons sugar
Few grains salt
1 cup unsweetened pine-
apple juice
1 egg, slightly beaten
2 tablespoons lemon juice

1. Melt the butter in a heavy saucepan. Blend in flour, sugar, and salt; heat until mixture bubbles.
2. Add pineapple juice gradually, stirring constantly. Bring to boiling; stir and cook 3 minutes.
3. Stir about 3 tablespoons of the hot mixture into the beaten egg. Immediately blend into the mixture in saucepan and cook 3 minutes, stirring constantly.
4. Remove from heat and stir in lemon juice. Cool; chill. Store in a covered jar.

About 1½ cups dressing

Tomato Sauce

1   clove garlic
2   tablespoons olive oil
3   pounds fully ripe plum tomatoes, peeled, seeded, and diced; or use 9 cups, canned peeled plum tomatoes, sieved
1   teaspoon salt
¼   teaspoon freshly ground black pepper
1   tablespoon dried basil

1. Peel garlic and cut in thirds. Put into a deep skillet with olive oil. Heat until garlic is browned. Flatten garlic and move it around in the oil. Discard garlic.
2. Add tomatoes all at one time to skillet. Mix in salt, pepper, and basil. Cook over low heat, stirring occasionally, about 10 minutes. Continue cooking, stirring occasionally, until sauce thickens (about 20 minutes).

About 6 cups sauce

Tomato Sauce with Meat

1   cup chopped onion
1   clove garlic, minced
3   tablespoons olive oil
½   pound ground beef
½   pound ground pork
1   can (28 ounces) Italian-style tomatoes, drained
3   cans (6 ounces each) tomato paste
2   cups water
2½   teaspoons salt
½   teaspoon pepper
1   teaspoon oregano

1. Add the onion and garlic to hot oil in a large, deep skillet and cook until onion is soft.
2. Add the ground meat, separate it into small pieces, and cook until lightly browned. Stir in tomatoes, tomato paste, water, and a mixture of salt, pepper, and oregano. Cook, uncovered, over low heat about 1 hour, stirring occasionally.

About 7½ cups sauce

Tomato Sauce with Ground Meat

¼   cup plus 3 tablespoons olive oil
½   cup (about 1 medium) chopped onion
½   lb. beef chuck
½   lb. pork shoulder
½   lb. ground beef
7   cups canned tomatoes, sieved
1   tablespoon salt
1   bay leaf
¾   cup (6-oz. can) tomato paste

1. Set out a large saucepot with a tight-fitting cover.
2. Heat ¼ cup olive oil in sauceppot.
3. Add chopped onion and cook until lightly browned.
4. Add beef chuck and pork shoulder to skillet and cook, turning occasionally, until browned.
5. Add slowly a mixture of tomatoes, salt and bay leaf. Cover saucepot and simmer over very low heat, about 2½ hrs.
6. Simmer uncovered over very low heat, stirring occasionally, about 2 hrs., or until thickened. If sauce becomes too thick, add ½ cup water.
7. Meanwhile, brown ground beef in 3 tablespoons olive oil, separating beef into small pieces with fork or spoon.
8. Remove beef chuck, pork shoulder and bay leaf from sauce.
9. Add ground beef to sauce and simmer 10 min. longer. Serve over cooked spaghetti.

About 4 cups sauce

Tomato Sauce with Mushrooms: Follow recipe for Tomato Sauce with Ground Meat. Clean and slice ½ **lb. mushrooms.** Cook slowly in **3 tablespoons melted butter** until lightly browned. After removing meat from sauce, add mushrooms and cook 10 min longer.

Meat Sauce Bolognese I

6	bacon slices, diced
1	medium onion, chopped
½	cup chopped celery
½	cup chopped carrot
6	tablespoons butter or margarine
¼	pound chicken livers, diced
1	pound ground beef round
1	teaspoon salt
½	teaspoon oregano
¼	teaspoon nutmeg
1	bay leaf
2	tablespoons vinegar
1	can (8 ounces) tomato sauce
1	cup beef bouillon
1	cup sliced fresh mushrooms
½	cup dry white wine

1. Saute bacon in a skillet; drain off all but 2 tablespoons fat. Add onion, celery, and carrot; cook until tender.
2. Add 2 tablespoons butter and the chicken livers. Brown lightly; add ground beef round. Cook 10 to 15 minutes, or until well browned.
3. Stir in salt, oregano, nutmeg, bay leaf, vinegar, tomato sauce, and bouillon. Cover and simmer ½ hour.
4. Saute mushrooms in remaining 4 tablespoons butter. Add to meat sauce along with wine. Remove bay leaf. Simmer ½ hour longer.

1 quart

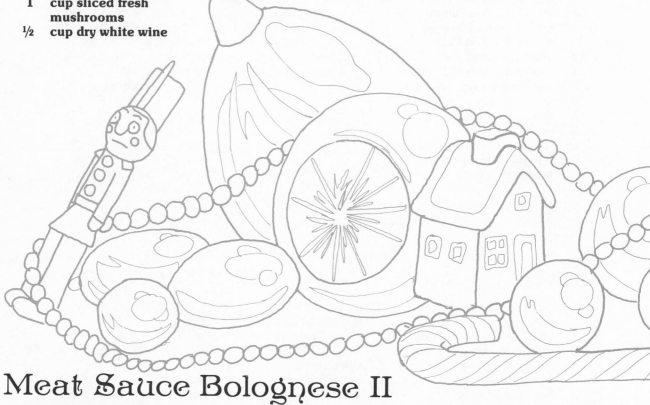

Meat Sauce Bolognese II

2	tablespoons butter
1	medium onion, finely chopped
1	small carrot, finely chopped
1	small stalk celery, finely chopped
¾	pound ground beef
¼	pound ground lean pork
¼	cup tomato sauce or tomato paste
½	cup white wine
1	cup beef broth or stock
½	teaspoon salt
¼	teaspoon pepper

1. Melt butter in a skillet. Stir in onion, carrot, and celery. Cook until tender. Add meat and cook over low heat 10 to 15 minutes.
2. Add tomato sauce, wine, ¼ cup broth, salt, and pepper; mix well. Simmer about 1¼ hours. Stir in remaining broth, a small amount at a time, while the sauce is simmering. Sauce should be thick.

About 2½ cups sauce

Marinara Sauce

2 medium cloves garlic, sliced
½ cup olive oil
1 can (28 ounces) tomatoes, sieved
1¼ teaspoons salt
⅛ teaspoon pepper
1 teaspoon oregano
¼ teaspoon chopped parsley

1. Brown garlic in hot olive oil in a large, deep skillet. Add gradually, stirring constantly, a mixture of the tomatoes, salt, pepper, oregano, and parsley. Cook rapidly uncovered about 15 minutes, or until sauce is thickened; stir occasionally. If sauce becomes too thick, stir in ¼ to ½ **cup water.**
2. Serve sauce hot on **cooked spaghetti.**

4 cups sauce

White Clam Sauce

¼ cup olive oil
1 clove garlic, thinly sliced
¼ cup water
½ teaspoon chopped parsley
½ teaspoon salt
¼ teaspoon oregano
¼ teaspoon pepper
1 cup (8-ounce can) whole littleneck clams with juice

1. Heat oil and garlic in a skillet until garlic is lightly browned.
2. Remove from heat. Add water, parsley, and dry seasonings, mix well. Stir in clams with juice. Heat thoroughly.
3. Serve hot on **cooked spaghetti** or **macaroni.**

About 1½ cups sauce

Red Clam Sauce: Follow recipe for White Clam Sauce. Sieve **3½ cups canned tomatoes,** stir in with water and seasonings, and simmer about 10 minutes. Add clams.

About 5 cups sauce

Clam Sauce

¼ cup finely chopped onion
3 tablespoons butter
2 tablespoons flour
¼ teaspoon salt
⅛ teaspoon white pepper
1 can (12 ounces) clam juice
3 tablespoons finely chopped parsley
½ teaspoon thyme
1 jar (7½ ounces) whole clams, drained and cut in pieces
1 can (2½ ounces) minced clams, drained

1. Add onion to hot butter in a saucepan and cook until soft. Blend in a mixture of flour, salt and pepper. Heat until bubbly.
2. Remove from heat and add the clam juice gradually, stirring constantly. Mix in parsley and thyme. Bring to boiling; stir and cook 1 to 2 minutes. Stir in the clams; heat thoroughly.

About 2¼ cups sauce

Spicy Cranberry Sauce

2   **cups (about ½ lb.) cranberries**
1   **cup sugar**
1   **cup water**
1   **piece (3 in.) stick cinnamon**
⅛   **teaspoon salt**

1. Sort and wash cranberries.
2. Combine sugar, water, cinnamon stick, and salt in a 1-qt. saucepan and stir over low heat until sugar is dissolved.
3. Bring to boiling; boil uncovered for 5 min. Add the cranberries. Continue to boil uncovered without stirring, about 5 min., or until skins pop. Cool and remove cinnamon stick.
4. Serve with meat or poultry.

About 2 cups sauce

Cakes & Pies

Old Williamsburg-Style Fruitcake

1	cup butter or margarine
2⅓	cups sugar
4	egg yolks
4	cups sifted all-purpose flour
½	cup sherry
1	lb. walnuts, chopped
1	pkg. (15 oz.) golden raisins
8	oz. (1 cup) finely chopped candied red cherries
8	oz. (1⅓ cups) diced candied pineapple
8	oz. (1 cup) diced candied citron
2	cups flaked coconut, finely chopped
4	egg whites, beaten to stiff, not dry, peaks
	Almond Paste, below
	Icing, below

1. Cream butter. Gradually add sugar, beating thoroughly after each addition. Add egg yolks, one at a time, beating until light and fluffy after each addition. Blend in 1 cup flour, then the sherry.
2. Mix the remaining flour, walnuts, the fruits, and coconut. Stir into mixture in bowl. Fold in beaten egg whites. Turn batter into a greased 10-inch tubed pan lined with greased brown paper or baking parchment. Spread evenly in pan.
3. Bake at 300°F 2¾ hours, or until cake tests done.
4. Cool completely on wire rack before removing the cake from the pan.
5. Brush cake with *sherry*. Wrap tightly in aluminum foil. Store in a cool place.
6. The day before the cake is to be served, brush top and sides of cake with a slightly beaten *egg white*. Place the round of Almond Paste on top of the cake and arrange pieces on sides; press edges to seal. Let dry at room temperature about 8 hours.
7. Reserving about 1 cup, spread Icing over sides and top of cake. Using a pastry bag and tube, decorate with reserved icing. Garnish with *flaked coconut* and *candied red and green cherries*. Let dry at room temperature about 4 hours.

One 10-Pound Decorated Fruitcake

Almond Paste: Blend *1 pound (about 4 cups) ground blanched almonds, 1 pound confectioners' sugar, 3 egg whites, 1 tablespoon lemon juice, ½ teaspoon orange extract,* and *⅛ teaspoon almond extract*. Press into a ball. Roll out about one third of the ball into an 8-inch round on waxed paper dusted with *confectioners' sugar*. Roll remainder of ball into a 28x4-inch strip; cut into 4 pieces.

Icing: Add *3 cups confectioners' sugar* to *2 egg whites* and beat with electric mixer at high speed about 5 minutes. Blend in *2 tablespoons lemon juice*. Add *3 cups confectioners' sugar* gradually, beating the mixture well.

Pecan Fruitcake

1 lb. (about 2½ cups) candied red cherries, cut in pieces
1 lb. (about 3 cups) golden raisins
1 lb. (about 4 cups) pecans, coarsely chopped
4 cups sifted all-purpose flour
2 teaspoons baking powder
2 cups butter or margarine
4 teaspoons lemon juice
2¼ cups sugar
6 large eggs

1. Combine cherries, raisins, pecans, and 1 cup of the flour. Blend the remaining flour and baking powder; set aside.
2. Cream butter with lemon juice. Add sugar gradually, creaming until fluffy after each addition. Add eggs, one at a time, beating thoroughly after each addition.
3. Beating only until smooth after each addition, add dry ingredients in fourths to creamed mixture. Blend in the fruit mixture. Turn batter into a well greased 10-inch tubed pan and spread evenly.
4. Place a shallow pan containing water on bottom rack of oven during baking time.
5. Bake at 275°F about 4½ hours, or until cake tests done.
6. Remove from oven to wire rack. Remove from pan before entirely cooled. Cool completely.

About 7 Pounds Fruitcake

Unbaked Fruitcake

8 oz. (1½ cups) raisins
1 cup chopped figs
1 cup chopped dried pears
1 cup chopped walnuts
6 oz. (1 cup) chopped candied pineapple
6 oz. (1 cup) chopped candied cherries
4 oz. (½ cup) chopped candied citron
8 oz. (1 cup) chopped candied orange peel
¾ cup butter or margarine
1 tablespoon grated orange peel
¾ cup confectioners' sugar
3 doz. vanilla wafers finely crushed (about 7 cups crumbs)
¼ teaspoon salt
1 cup honey

1. Pour 2 cups boiling water over dried fruits; bring to boiling and drain. Mix with walnuts and candied fruits.
2. Cream butter with orange peel; gradually add confectioners' sugar, creaming well. Blend in crumbs, salt and honey. Mix with fruit-nut mixture. Press into a well-greased 2-quart fluted mold.
3. Refrigerate 2 to 3 days before unmolding to serve.

About 5 Pounds Fruitcake

Holiday Fruitcake

1½	cups sifted all-purpose flour
1	teaspoon baking powder
1	teaspoon cinnamon
½	teaspoon ginger
½	teaspoon nutmeg
⅛	teasppoon salt
1	cup chopped mixed candied fruit (6 ounces)
1	cup raisins (5 ounces)
¾	cup chopped walnuts
½	cup butter or margarine
¾	cup packed brown sugar
1	egg
½	cup beer
	Halved candied cherries (optional)

1. Sift together dry ingredients. Mix a little with fruits and nuts.
2. Cream butter and brown sugar. Add egg; beat well.
3. Add remaining dry ingredients alternately with beer; beat until smooth.
4. Add fruits and nuts; stir by hand.
5. Turn into greased and waxed-paper-lined pans: three 5½x3x2-inch fruitcake pans, or one 9x5x3-inch loaf pan. Decorate tops with candied cherries, if desired.
6. Bake at 275°F 1¼ hours for small pans, or 1¾ to 2 hours for a 9x5-inch pan, or until done. Cool 20 minutes in pans. Turn out on wire racks.
7. Wrap each fruitcake in cheesecloth soaked in additional beer, then wrap in foil. Age in refrigerator at least 2 weeks, basting occasionally with beer.

3 small or 1 large

Dark Fruitcake

2	pounds seeded raisins, chopped
1¾	pounds sultana raisins, chopped
¾	pound citron, chopped
1	pound currants
½	pound candied pineapple
¼	cup chopped candied lemon peel
½	pound candied cherries, halved
¼	cup chopped candied orange peel
1	cup grape juice
2	cups chopped nut meats
1	pound cake flour
2	cups shortening
1	pound brown sugar
12	eggs
1	cup molasses
4	teaspoons cinnamon
4	teaspoons allspice
1½	teaspoons mace
½	teaspoon nutmeg
½	teaspoon baking soda
½	teaspoon salt
4	ounces (squares) chocolate, melted
2	tablespoons hot water

1. Combine fruit. Pour grape juice over fruit and let stand overnight.
2. Dredge fruit and nuts with half of the flour.
3. Cream shortening and sugar until fluffy.
4. Add eggs, 1 at a time, to the creamed mixture and continue creaming. Add molasses.
5. Combine remaining flour with other dry ingredients and sift 3 times. Add alternately with grape juice and fruit mixture to creamed sugar and egg mixture.
6. Add chocolate and hot water. Blend thoroughly.
7. Pour into greased loaf pans lined with brown paper.
8. Steam for 2 hours and bake in slow oven 300°F for an additional 1½ hours.
9. Cakes may be decorated with pieces of fruit before placing in oven.
10. Peel paper from cakes while warm.

8 10x2x3-inch loaves

Helpful Hints About Cakes

• Use fluted paper baking cups when preparing cupcakes. They save greasing of pans and eliminate sticking. They also make pan washing easy.

• Line cake pans with baking parchment or waxed paper for easy removal of cakes after baking. Grease pans (bottoms only) before lining with paper and grease the paper. Cut several pieces at one time to fit pans and keep on hand for future use. (Cut the circles for layer cake pans about ¼ inch smaller than size of pan.) After baked cakes are removed from pans, peel off paper immediately.

• For baking fruitcake, line the pan with heavy brown paper extending 1 inch above top of pan. When cake is baked, place on wire rack. When completely cooled, lift cake from pan and peel off paper.

• When baking an upside-down cake, line cake pan with aluminum foil, folding foil over the edges of pan. After cake is baked, let cool on rack about 5 minutes. Then place serving plate on top of cake, turn cake upside down and remove the pan. Carefully lift off the foil. Cake comes out of pan easily and pan is easy to clean.

• When making cakes (or cookies) which use shortening and call for flavoring extracts and/or ground spices, add them to the shortening before creaming with the sugar. The fat "carries" the extract and spice flavors through the batter.

• To make a lace-like decoration on a sponge or angel food cake or other unfrosted cake, place a sheer, lace paper doily on top of cake; sift confectioners' sugar over top; then carefully lift off doily.

• To make your own cinnamon sugar to be used for sprinkling over warm, not-to-be-frosted cakes and cupcakes, combine *½ cup fine granulated sugar* with *1 tablespoon ground cinnamon*. Keep the mixture on hand stored in a covered jar.

• If cooked white frosting has "sugared" somewhat, beat in a small amount of *lemon juice* until frosting is smooth.

• To make marshmallow flowers for cake decorating, use large white or colored *marshmallows*. With kitchen shears dipped in water, cut off strips about 1/8 inch thick. Place strips between 2 pieces of waxed paper and roll with rolling pin to make thin "petals." Arrange petals on frosted cake to simulate flowers.

Light Fruitcake

5	cups white raisins
2	cups chopped dried white figs
5	cups sliced citron
2	cups halved candied cherries
½	cup fruit juice
2	teaspoons cardamom seeds
3	teaspoons nutmeg
4	teaspoons mace
1	teaspoon cinnamon
1½	cups thick Orange Marmalade
4½	cups sifted flour
3	teaspoons baking powder
1½	teaspoons salt
2	cups shortening
2½	cups sugar
8	eggs
1	teaspoon vanilla
2	teaspoons lemon extract
1½	cups chopped Brazil nuts
2	cups broken walnut meats

1. Rinse fruits, drain and dry on towel. (If figs are very dry, let stand in hot water about 5 minutes.) Cut figs into thin strips.
2. Combine fruit juice and spices; mix and pour over combined fruit.
3. Add marmalade and mix well. Cover and let stand overnight.
4. Sift flour, baking powder and salt together.
5. Cream shortening and sugar until fluffy.
6. Add beaten eggs and mix.
7. Add flour, fruit mixture, flavoring and nuts and stir until fruit is well distributed.
8. Pour into 2 9-inch tube-cake pans which have been lined with 2 thicknesses of greased brown paper.
9. Smooth tops and decorate if desired.
10. Bake in very slow oven 275°F 3¾ to 4 hours.
11. Test with toothpick or cake tester before removing from oven.
12. May be used as soon as cool or ripened. Baked weight is approximately 9¾ pounds.

Bite-Size Fruitcakes: Follow and prepare one-half recipe from Light Fruitcake. Brush about 6 doz. 1¼-in. paper souffle cups with **salad oil** or **melted shortening.** Fill with about 1 tablespoon of batter. Decorate with bits of **red or green candied cherries.** Arrange, with space between cups, on baking sheet on which double thickness of wet paper toweling has been placed. Bake at 300°F about 30 min., or until cakes test done. Glaze before serving.

Cherry Fruitcake

1½	cups sifted all-purpose flour
1½	cups sugar
1	teaspoon baking powder
1	teaspoon salt
2	pkgs. (7¼ oz. each) pitted dates
1	lb. diced candied pineapple
2	jars (16 oz. each) red maraschino cherries, drained
18	oz. (about 5½ cups) pecan halves
6	eggs
½	cup dark rum
½	cup light corn syrup

1. Grease two 9x5x3-in. loaf pans; line with aluminum foil, allowing a 2-in. overhang; grease the foil.
2. Sift flour, sugar, baking powder and salt, into a large mixing bowl.
3. Add pitted dates, pineapple, maraschino cherries and pecan halves to flour mixture and toss until coated.
4. Beat eggs in a bowl until thick.
5. Blend in rum.
6. Pour over fruit mixture and toss until thoroughly mixed. Turn into prepared loaf pans, pressing mixture with spatula to pack tightly.
7. Bake at 300°F about 1¾ hrs., or until wooden pick inserted in center of loaves comes out clean.
8. Remove from oven to cooling rack and allow to cool 15 min. before removing loaves from pans. Peel off foil and while still warm brush loaves with corn syrup.
9. Cool thoroughly before serving or storing.

2 loaves fruitcake

Pecan Date Fruitcake

¾ **cup sifted all-purpose flour**
¾ **cup sugar**
½ **teaspoon baking powder**
1 **oz. (1 sq.) unsweetened chocolate**
3 **cups (about ¾ lb.) salted pecan halves**
2 **cups (about 14 oz.) pitted dates**
1 **cup (about 8 oz.) maraschino cherries well drained**
3 **eggs**
1¼ **teaspoons vanilla extract**
¼ **teaspoon almond extract**
¼ **teaspoon orange extract**

1. Prepare 9x5x3-in. loaf pan.
2. Sift flour, sugar and baking powder together.
3. Grate chocolate. Mix with dry ingredients and set aside.
4. Place pecan halves, pitted dates and maraschino cherries in a large bowl.
5. Add dry ingredients to mixture in bowl; mix lightly until fruit and nuts are well coated.
6. Beat eggs, vanilla extract, almond extract and orange extract until thick and piled softly.
7. Blend beaten eggs into fruit-nut mixture until well mixed. Turn batter into pan and spread batter to corners.
8. Bake at 300°F 1 hr. and 45 min., or until cake tests done. Cool cake in pan on cooling rack 15 min. before removing from pan.
9. Wrap in aluminium foil or moisture-vapor proof material and store in refrigerator.

One 9x5-in. fruitcake

Hazelnut Fruitcake: Follow recipe for Pecan Date Fruitcake. Omit chocolate. Substitute **3 cups unblanched whole hazelnuts** for salted pecan halves.

Regal Fruitcake

2 **cups (about 8 oz.) walnuts**
1 **cup (about 7 oz.) date pieces**
1 **cup (about 8 oz.) maraschino cherries**
1½ **cups sifted all-purpose flour**
1 **teaspoon baking powder**
½ **teaspoon salt**
3 **eggs**
¾ **cup sugar**
1 **pkg. (6 oz.) semisweet chocolate pieces**

1. Lightly grease bottom of 9x5x3-in. loaf pan. Line bottom and sides with parchment paper cut to fit pan. Lightly grease paper.
2. Coarsely chop walnuts and set aside.
3. Cut dates into small pieces and set aside.
4. Drain maraschino cherries, slice and set aside on absorbent paper. (A few pats with the paper will absorb the excess moisture from cherries.)
5. Sift all-purpose flour, baking powder and salt together and set aside.
6. Beat eggs until thick and piled softly.
7. Add sugar gradually, beating well after each addition.
8. Thoroughly blend in fruits, nuts and chocolate.
9. Mixing only until blended after each addition, add dry ingredients in thirds to egg-fruit mixture. Finally, mix only until blended. Turn batter into pan, spreading to edges.
10. Place a shallow pan containing 2 cups water on bottom rack of oven during baking period.
11. Bake at 300°F 1 hr. 45 min., or until cake test done.
12. Cool cake on cooling rack 10 min. before removing from pan. Run spatula gently around sides of pan. Cover with cooling rack. Invert. Turn right side up immediately after peeling off parchment paper.
13. Using a pastry brush, paint cake with brandy or apple cider. Cool thoroughly and wrap tightly in waxed paper, aluminum foil or moisture-vaporproof material. Store in cool place to age for 10 days before serving.

One 9x5-in. fruitcake

Chocolate Fruitcake

½ lb. (about 1¼ cups) diced assorted candied fruits

½ lb. candied red cherries, cut in quarters; about 1¼ cups, quartered

5 oz. (about 1 cup) golden raisins

⅓ cup water

⅓ cup rum

2¼ cups (about ¾ lb.) toasted salted almonds

4 oz. (4 sq.) unsweetened chocolate

2 cups sifted all-purpose flour

1 teaspoon baking powder

6 egg yolks

¾ cup butter

1½ cups sugar

6 egg whites

1. Two 1½-qt. molds will be needed.
2. Mix assorted candied fruits, cherries and raisins in a bowl.
3. Pour over the fruit a mixture of water and rum.
4. Cover tightly and allow to stand 8 hrs. or overnight.
5. Thoroughly grease molds and set aside.
6. Coarsely chop almonds and set aside.
7. Melt chocolate and set aside to cool.
8. Sift flour and baking powder together and set aside.
9. Beat egg yolks until thick and lemon-colored and set aside.
10. Cream butter until softened.
11. Add 1 cup sugar gradually, creaming until fluffy after each addition.
12. Add the beaten egg yolks in thirds, beating thoroughly after each addition.
13. Stir melted chocolate into creamed mixture. Alternately add dry ingredients in fourths and fruit mixture in thirds to creamed mixture. After each addition, beat only until batter is blended. Finally, beat only until batter is well blended (do not overbeat). Then mix in the chopped nuts.
14. Beat egg whites until frothy.
15. Add ½ cup sugar gradually.
16. Continue beating until rounded peaks are formed. Spread beaten egg whites over batter and gently fold together. Turn into prepared molds.
17. Bake at 250°F 2 hrs. to 2 hrs. 15 min., or until cake tests don. Cool completely on cooling rack before removing from pans. Wrap tightly in aluminum foil and store in cool place to age for several weeks before serving. Once or twice a week, using a pastry brush, paint cakes with rum and store again.

Two 2½-lb. Fruitcakes

Christmas Fruitcake

2	cups seeded raisins
4	cups seedless raisins
2	cups uncooked prunes
2	cups halved candied cherries
4	cups sliced citron
1	cup sliced candied pineapple
½	cup ground candied lemon peel
1	cup ground candied orange peel
3	cups broken walnut meats
1	tablespoon grated orange rind
½	cup fruit juice
5	cups sifted flour
1½	teaspoons salt
3	teaspoons baking powder
1	pound shortening
2	cups white sugar
1	cup brown sugar
3	teaspoons cinnamon
2	teaspoons cloves
1	teaspoon allspice
2	teaspoons mace
10	eggs, well beaten
1	tablespoon vanilla

1. Rinse raisins, drain, dry on a towel and slice seeded raisins.
2. Pour boiling water over prunes, cover and let stand 10 minutes; drain, dry and cut from pits into very small pieces.
3. Rinse, drain and dry cherries and citron before slicing.
4. Combine fruit, nuts and orange rind. Pour fruit juice over combined fruits.
5. Sift flour, salt and baking powder together.
6. Cream shortening, sugars and spices until fluffy. Add beaten eggs and mix thoroughly.
7. Add flour, prepared fruit mixture and flavoring and stir until fruits are well distributed. Pour into 1 10-inch tube pan and 1 loaf pan (about 10x5x3 inches) lined with 2 thicknesses of greased brown paper.
8. Smooth tops and decorate if desired.
9. Bake in very slow oven 275°F to 285°F.
10. Cake in tube pan will require from 3¾ to 4 hours baking time; in loaf pan, bout 3 to 3¼ hours.
11. Test with toothpick or cake tester before removing from oven. Baked weight approximately 10 pounds. May be served as soon as cool but improves if ripened a few days longer.

Crockery Fruitcake

¾ cup (about 4½ ounces) snipped dried figs
½ cup (about 3 ounces) snipped pitted dates
½ cup (about 2½ ounces) dark seedless raisins
½ cup (about 2½ ounces) golden raisins
½ cup (about 2½ ounces) diced candied citron
½ cup (about 2½ ounces) diced candied lemon peel
½ cup (about 2½ ounces) diced candied orange peel
¼ cup (about 1½ ounces) diced candied pineapple
¼ cup (about 1½ ounces) halved red candied cherries
¼ cup (about 1 ounce) currants
¼ cup sherry
¼ cup orange juice
½ cup (about 2 ounces) pecan halves
2 cups all-purpose flour
1 teaspoon baking powder
¼ teaspoon salt
½ teaspoon cinnamon
¼ teaspoon nutmeg
½ cup butter or margarine
½ teaspoon orange extract
1 cup sugar
3 eggs

1. Combine fruit, sherry, and orange juice in a large bowl. Cover tightly and set aside for 24 hours; stir occasionally.
2. Add nuts to fruit. Mix flour, baking powder, salt, cinnamon, and nutmeg; add to fruit and nuts; toss until pieces are well coated.
3. Cream butter with extract and sugar in a bowl; beat until light and fluffy. Add eggs, one at a time, beating thoroughly after each addition. (Mixture may be slightly curdled, but this will not affect the final product.) Using a spoon, thoroughly combine the creamed and fruit-nut mixtures.
4. Spoon batter into a greased and floured 2-pound coffee can. If desired, top with candied fruit and/or blanched almonds. Cover with 6 layers of paper toweling. Set can in an electric cooker.
5. Cover and cook on High 4 to 5 hours. Cooker lid should be slightly raised during cooking to allow release of excess moisture.
6. Set can on wire rack to cool.

One 3-pound fruitcake

Holly Wreath Coffee Cake

1 pkg. active dry yeast
¼ cup milk, scalded and cooled to warm
3¾ cups all-purpose flour
½ teaspoon salt
6 tablespoons sugar
3 eggs, well beaten
½ cup butter or margarine, melted and cooled
½ cup warm milk
2 teaspoons vanilla extract
2 cups filberts, finely ground
¼ cup red candied cherry pieces
½ cup sugar
½ cup heavy cream
⅓ cup apricot preserves

1. Soften yeast in the cooled milk.
2. Blend 2 cups of the flour, the salt, and 6 tablespoons sugar in a large bowl. Beat in a mixture of the beaten eggs, melted butter, warm milk, and extract until batter is smooth. Beat in the yeast and then the remaining flour.
3. Turn dough onto a lightly floured surface and knead until smooth and elastic. Put into a greased deep bowl and turn dough to bring greased surface to top. Cover; let rise in warm place until doubled.
4. For filling, mix filberts, cherries, ½ cup sugar, cream, and two thirds of the egg. Cover remaining egg and set aside.
5. Roll out dough into a 25x21-inch rectangle; cut into three 25x7-inch strips. Spread each with preserves and the nut filling. Turn edges of dough about one half over filling and press to seal. Starting with a long edge, roll up each portion; seal.
6. Gently braid the three long rolls. Form a wreath and press ends together. Carefully fit into a greased 9-inch tubed pan. Cover; let rise again until doubled. Brush top with the reserved egg.
7. Place in a 400°F oven; reduce oven temperature to 350°F, and bake about 30 minutes. Check cake for browning. If top is sufficiently browned, cover loosely with a piece of aluminum foil. Continue baking 15 to 20 minutes. Remove from oven; cool 5 to 10 minutes in pan on wire rack.
8. Using a holly-leaf pattern, cut shapes from green candied pineapple slices (thin crosswise slices).
9. Blend ¼ cup confectioners' sugar and 1 teaspoon water. Spread over top of warm coffee cake. Press leaf shapes and re-candied cherry pieces on glaze at intervals to resemble a holly wreath.

One 9-inch tubed Coffee Cake

Berlin Wreaths

3¾ to 4 cups sifted all-purpose flour
½ teaspoon baking soda
⅛ teaspoon salt
1 cup butter or margarine
4 egg yolks
1 cup sugar
½ cup dairy sour cream
1 teaspoon vanilla or almond extract
Egg white, slightly beaten
Crushed loaf sugar

1. Lightly grease cookie sheets.
2. Sift flour, baking soda and salt together into a large bowl.
3. Cut butter or margarine in with a pastry blender or two knives until pieces are size of small peas. Set aside.
4. Beat egg yolks until thick and lemon-colored.
5. Add sugar gradually, beating well after each addition.
6. Blend sour cream and extract into the egg mixture.
7. Add the sour cream mixture to the flour mixture and mix well. Chill dough until firm enough to handle.
8. Break off small pieces of dough. Roll with hands on a lightly floured surface into rolls about 6 in. long and ¼ in. thick. Form into wreaths or bowknots, or twist into pretzels. Brush top of each bookie with egg white.
9. Dip each cookie into crushed loaf sugar.
10. Bake at 350°F about 10 min., or until firm and very lightly browned. Remove to cooling racks.

About 8 doz. cookies

Bohemian Christmas Twist

1 cake yeast
¼ cup lukewarm water
1 cup milk
½ cup sugar
¼ cup butter
2 eggs or 4 yolks
Grated rind of 1 lemon
⅛ teaspoon mace
1 teaspoon salt
4¼ cups sifted flour
½ cup raisins
½ cup chopped blanched almonds
Coffee Cake Icing (below)

1. Soften yeast in lukewarm water.
2. Scald milk and add sugar and butter. Cool to lukewarm.
3. Add softened yeast, beaten eggs, lemon rind, mace, salt and 2 cups flour. Beat well to make smooth batter. Cover and let rise until light.
3. Add raisins, nuts and remaining flour to make a dough just firm enough to be handled easily. Knead until smooth. Cover and let rise until doubled in bulk.
4. Punch down and divide dough into 3 large portions and 5 smaller ones.
5. Roll each portion into a long roll.
6. Braid the 3 larger rolls loosely and place on greased baking shett.
7. Then braid 3 of the smaller portions and place on top of the large braid.
8. Twist the last 2 portions together and place on top. Cover and let rise until light.
9. Brush with sweetened milk and bake in hot oven 400°F 45 minutes.
10. When cool, spread with icing and sprinkle with chopped nuts.

1 loaf

Coffee-Cake Icing

1 cup confectioners' sugar
2 tablespoons warm milk
½ teaspoon vanilla

Combine ingredients and mix thoroughly. Frosting for 1 (12-inch) coffee cake.

Christmas Wreath Ring

¼ cup softened butter
½ cup granulated sugar
2 tablespoons water
¼ cup candied cherries, halved
¼ cup citron, cut into strips
2 cups sifted flour
3 teaspoons baking powder
¾ teaspoon salt
4 tablespoons cold shortening
⅔ to ¾ cup milk
2 tablespoons melted butter
½ cup brown sugar
Cinnamon
¼ cup currants

1. Spread softened butter in ring mold and pat granulated sugar over bottom and sides. Sprinkle water in mold.
2. Arrange cherries and citron in bottom to resemble holly.
3. Sift flour, baking powder and salt together. Cut in shortening.
4. Add milk to make a soft dough.
5. Turn out on lightly floured board and knead gently ½ minute.
6. Roll out in rectangle, 6 inches wide and ¼ inch thick.
7. Brush lightly with melted butter, and sprinkle with brown sugar, cinnamon and currants.
8. Roll like jelly roll and cut into 1½-inch slices. Place cut side down in mold.
9. Bake in hot oven 400°F 30 minutes.
10. Let stand in pan 1 minute after removing from oven.
11. Serve hot or cold.

1 9-inch ring or 12 rolls

Filled Holiday Coffee Cake

2   **pkgs. active dry yeast**
1   **cup milk, scalded and cooled to warm**
4   **cups all-purpose flour**
½   **cup sugar**
1   **teaspoon salt**
1   **cup firm butter**
2   **eggs, beaten**
1   **teaspoon vanilla extract**
    Vanilla-Butter Filling, above
1   **cup chopped nuts**
    Confectioners' Sugar Icing

1. Soften yeast in the cooled milk.
2. Mix flour, sugar, and salt in a large bowl. Cut in the butter with a pastry blender until particles are the size of rice kernels. Mixing well after each addition, add the yeast, then the mixture of eggs and extract.
3. Cover bowl with moisture-vaporproof material. Chill several hours or overnight.
4. Before removing dough from refrigerator, prepare Vanilla-Butter Filling. Spread 2 tablespoons filling over bottom and sides of each of two 9x5x3-inch loaf pans.
5. Divide dough into halves. On a lightly floured surface, roll each portion into an 18x10-inch rectangle. Spread each with half of remaining filling and sprinkle with half of nuts. Cut rectangle into three 10x6-inch strips. Starting with long side, roll up each strip and twist slightly. Braid three rolls together and place one braid in each pan, being sure to tuck ends under. Brush tops with *melted butter*.
6. Cover; let rise in a warm place until doubled, about 1½ hours.
7. Bake at 350°F 45 to 50 minutes. Immediately remove from pans and cool on wire racks.
8. Spread coffee cakes with Confectioners' Sugar Icing II. Before icing is set, decorate top with *marzipan fruit, glazed dried apricots,* and *preserved kumquats.*

2 Filled Coffee Cakes

Confectioners' Sugar Icing: Blend 1 cup confectioners' sugar, 1 tablespoon softened butter, 1 teaspoon light corn syrup, and 1 tablespoon hot water.

Black Forest Torte

1½ cups toasted filberts, grated*
¼ cup flour
½ cup butter or margarine
1 cup sugar
6 egg yolks
4 oz. (4 sq.) semisweet chocolate, melted and cooled
6 tablespoons kirsch
6 eggs whites
   Cherry Filling, below
3 cups chilled heavy cream
⅓ cup confectioners' sugar
   Chocolate curls

1. Grease and lightly flour an 8-inch springform pan; set aside.
2. Blend grated filberts and flour; set aside.
3. Cream butter until softened. Beat in sugar gradually until mixture is light and fluffy. Add egg yolks, one at a time, beating thoroughly after each addition.
4. Blend in the chocolate and 2 tablespoons of the kirsch. Stir in nut-flour mixture until blended.
5. Beat egg whites until stiff, not dry, peaks are formed. Formed. Fold into batter and turn into the pan.
6. Bake at 375°F about 1 hour, or until torte tests done. (Torte should be about 1½ inches high and top may have slight crack.)
7. Cool 10 minutes in pan on a wire rack; remove from pan and cool.
8. Using a long sharp knife, carefully cut torte into 3 layers. Place top layer inverted on a cake plate; spread with Cherry Filling.
9. Whip cream (1½ cups at a time) until soft peaks are formed, gradually adding half of the confectioners' sugar and 2 tablespoons of the kirsch to each portion.
10. Generously spread some of the whipped cream over the Cherry Filling. Cover with second layer and remaining Cherry Filling. Spread generously with more whipped cream and top with third torte layer. Frost entire torte with remaining whipped cream.
11. Decorate torte with reserved cherries and chocolate curls.

One 8-inch Torte

*To grate nuts, use a rotary-type grater with hand-operated crank.

Cherry Filling: Drain 1 jar (16 ounces) red maraschino cherries, reserving ½ cup syrup. Set aside 13 cherries for decoration; slice remaining cherries. Set aside. Combine reserved syrup and 4 tablespoons kirsch. In a saucepan, gradually blend syrup mixture into 1½ tablespoons cornstarch. Mix in 1 tablespoon lemon juice. Stir over medium heat until mixture boils ½ minute. Mix in sliced cherries and cool.

1⅓ Cups Filling

Pumpkin Cake

2¼ cups sifted cake flour
3 teaspoons baking powder
½ teaspoon baking soda
½ teaspoon salt
1½ teaspoons ground cinnamon
½ teaspoon ground allspice
½ teaspoon ground ginger
½ cup butter or margarine
½ cup sugar
1 cup lightly packed dark brown sugar
2 eggs
¾ cup buttermilk
¾ cup canned pumpkin
½ cup finely snipped or chopped golden raisins

1. Sift the flour, baking powder, baking soda, salt, and spices together and blend thoroughly; set aside.
2. Cream butter; gradually add sugars, creaming until fluffy. Add eggs, one at a time, beating thoroughly after each addition.
3. Beating only until smooth after each addition, alternately add dry ingredients in fourths and a mixture of the buttermilk, pumpkin, and raisins in thirds to creamed mixture. Turn batter into 2 prepared 9-inch layer cake pans and spread evenly.
4. Bake at 350°F about 30 minutes, or until cake tests done.
5. Cool and remove from pans as directed for butter-type cakes.

Two 9-Inch Cake Layers

Pumpkin Miniatures: Follow recipe for Pumpkin Cake. Spoon batter into 1¾-inch muffin-pan wells lined with paper baking cups, half filling each. Bake at 375°F about 13 minutes, or until cupcakes test done. Remove from pans and cool on racks. Frost with *butter cream frosting.*

6½ Dozen Cupcakes

Ribbon Cakes

1   cup butter or margarine, softened
1   teaspoon vanilla extract
1   cup sugar
4   eggs
2   cups all-purpose flour
1   teaspoon salt
1½   cups dairy sour cream
½   cup finely chopped pecans
6   tablespoons red raspberry jam
¼   cup apricot jam

1. Invert a 15x10x1-inch jelly roll pan; grease and flour the bottom.
2. Cream the butter with extract. Gradually add the sugar, creaming until fluffy. Add eggs, one at a time, beating well after each addition. Mix in the flour and salt.
3. Spread one third of the batter on the prepared pan. Spread evenly to ½ inch from edge of pan.
4. Bake at 350°F about 10 minutes. Remove from oven and carefully cut layer in half crosswise, forming two layers; remove to wire rack.
5. Repeat twice with the remaining batter, making a total of 6 thin layers. (Wash, grease, and flour pan before each baking.)
6. Mix the sour cream and pecans. Place one cake layer, top side up, on a cutting board. Spread evenly with about ¼ cup of the sour cream mixture. Then spread with about 2 tablespoons raspberry jam.
7. Add a second cake layer and spread with ¼ cup sour cream mixture and 2 tablespoons apricot jam. Repeat with remaining layers, leaving the top plain. Place a board on top to compress the layers; chill overnight or 24 hours.
8. Trim off crust edges and spread top with a *creamy butter frosting*. Lightly sprinkle with *colored decorators' sugar*. Cut crosswise into 12 strips, about ¾ inch wide; cut each strip into fourths.

48 Ribbon Cakes

Miniature Fruitcakes: Brush 2½-inch paper baking cups with cooking or salad oil and place in muffin-pan wells. Fill each two thirds full with your favorite *fruitcake batter*. Decorate tops with whole *candied cherries or almond halves*. Bake at 300°F about 45 minutes, placing shallow pan containing water on bottom rack of oven while baking. Glaze before serving.

Refrigerator Christmas Cake

2   tablespoons unflavored gelatin
1   quart milk
2   eggs, separated
¾   cup sugar
¼   teaspoon salt
¾   cup chopped maraschino cherries
⅓   cup maraschino juice
1   teaspoon vanilla
1½   cups heavy cream
2   dozen vanilla wafers

1. Soften gelatin in ½ cup milk.
2. Scald remaining milk and pour onto beaten egg yolks.
3. Add sugar, salt and softened gelatin; return to double boiler; cook until mixture coats a spoon. Cool.
4. Add cherries, juice and vanilla. Chill until mixture begins to thicken.
5. Fold in beaten egg whites and half the cream, whipped.
6. Butter a cake pan and arrange vanilla wafers around it.
7. Pour in fillng and cover top with remaining vanilla wafers.
8. Chill overnight.
9. Unmold and frost sides and top of cake with remaining cream, whipped.

Serves 12

Mincemeat Cake Roll

1   cup sifted cake flour
¼   teaspoon salt
4   egg yolks
1   cup sugar
¼   cup water
1½   teaspoons vanilla extract
4   egg whites
½   teaspoon cream of tartar
     sifted confectioners' sugar
1¾   cups Mincemeat (½ recipe, page 125)

1. Grease bottom of a 15x10x1-in. pan; line with waxed paper cut to fit bottom of pan; grease again.
2. Sift flour and salt together and set aside.
3. Beat egg yolks, ½ cup sugar, water and vanilla extract until very thick and lemon-colored. Gently fold in dry ingredients until well blended. Set aside.
4. Beat egg whites until frothy.
5. Add cream of tartar and beat slightly.
6. Add ½ cup sugar gradually, beating thoroughly after each addition.
7. Continue beating until very stiff peaks are formed. Gently spread egg yolk mixture over egg whites and carefully fold together until blended. Turn batter into pan and spread evenly to edges.
8. Bake at 350°F 20 to 25 min., or until a wooden pick or cake tester inserted in center of cake comes out clean.
9. Immediately loosen edges of cake with a sharp knife; turn onto clean towel sprinkled with sifted Confectioners' sugar.
10. Carefully remove paper and cut off any crisp edges of cake. To roll, begin rolling nearest edge of cake. Using towel as a guide, tightly grasp nearest edge of towel and quickly pull it over beyond opposite edge. Cake will roll itself as you pull. Wrap cake in towel and set on cooling rack to cool (about ½ hr.).
11. Shortly before ready to serve, unroll cake and spread with Mincemeat.
12. Carefully reroll cake. Cut filled cake roll into crosswise pieces and serve.

1 cake roll

Cream-Filled Chestnut Cake

1   pound chestnuts in the shell; or use 1¼ cups pecans, chopped
¾   cup butter
1   cup sugar
½   teaspoon vanilla extract
6   eggs, separated
1¼   cups all-purpose flour
1   teaspoon baking powder
½   cup milk
     Chestnut Cream

1. Prepare chestnuts (see Note).
2. Cream butter with sugar and vanilla extract until fluffy. Mixing well after each addition, add the chestnut puree, then the egg yolks, one at a time.
3. Mix flour with baking powder, and add alternately with milk to the chestnut mixture, mixing well after each addition. Beat egg whites until stiff, but not dry. Fold into batter.
4. Turn mixture into 2 greased and floured 9-inch round layer cake pans.
5. Bake at 350°F about 25 minutes, or until done.
6. Let cool, then put layers together and decorate cake with chestnut cream.

One 9-Inch Layer Cake

Note: To prepare chestnuts, rinse chestnuts and make a slit on two sides of each shell. Put into a saucepan; cover with boiling water and boil about 20 minutes. Remove shells and skins; return chestnuts to saucepan and cover with boiling salted water. Cover and simmer until chestnuts are tender (10 to 20 minutes). Drain and finely chop.

Chestnut Cream: Prepare **¾ pound chestnuts** in the shell (see Note above); or use **1 cup pecans,** chopped. Whip **1 cup whipping cream** until thickened. Mix in **⅔ cup confectioners' sugar** and **½ teaspoon vanilla extract,** then chestnuts.

Holiday Refrigerator Cake

½   **pound marshmallows, quartered**
1   **cup cream**
1   **cup graham cracker crumbs**
1   **cup chopped candied cherries**
1   **cup chopped candied pineapple**
1   **cup chopped dates**
1   **cup chopped salted pecan meats**
2   **teaspoons grated orange rind**
2   **teaspoons sherry or lemon juice**

1. Heat marshmallows and cream over low heat, folding over and over until marshmallows are half melted.
2. Remove from heat and continue folding until mixture is smooth and fluffy. Cool.
3. Sprinkle buttered loaf pan with ¼ cup graham cracker crumbs.
4. Add remaining crumbs, fruit, nut meats, orange rind and sherry to marshmallows, then pour over crumbs.
5. Chill thoroughly.
6. Slice and serve plain or with whipped cream.

Serves 12

Star Cake

2¼   **cups sifted cake flour**
3   **teaspoons baking powder**
¼   **teaspoon salt**
½   **cup shortening**
1½   **cups sugar**
2   **eggs, separated**
1   **cup milk**
¾   **teaspoon lemon extract**
1¼   **cups tart red jelly**
1   **cup heavy cream, whipped**

1. Sift flour, baking powder and salt together.
2. Cream shortening with 1¼ cups of the sugar until fluffy.
3. Add egg yolks and beat vigorously.
4. Add sifted dry ingredients and milk alternately in small amounts, beating well after each addition.
5. Beat egg whites until nearly stiff, add remaining sugar and beat until stiff, then fold into cake with flavoring.
6. Turn into 2 greased 8-inch pans and bake in moderate oven 350°F 30 minutes.
7. When cooled, melt jelly over warm water and spread between layers and over top and sides of cake.
8. Chill until set.
9. Just before serving, pipe whipped cream in star shape on top and serve with more whipped cream.

Serves 10

Christmas Cake

3	cups all-purpose flour
2	cups sugar
2	teaspoons baking soda
1	teaspoon allspice
1	teaspoon cinnamon
1	teaspoon nutmeg
1	teaspoon cloves
1	teaspoon salt
2/3	cup butter or margarine
2	cups buttermilk
1	cup chopped dates, raisins, or mixed candied fruits
1/2	cup chopped almonds or walnuts

1. Combine flour, sugar, baking soda, spices, and salt in a bowl. Cut in butter with pastry blender or two knives until particles resemble rice kernels. Add buttermilk; mix thoroughly. Mix in dates and nuts.
2. Turn batter into a generously greased and floured (bottom only) 9-inch tube pan or into two 8x4x3-inch loaf pans.
3. Bake at 350°F about 1 hour, or until a wooden pick comes out clean.
4. Cool in pan on wire rack 15 minutes. Remove from pan and cool completely on wire rack.

1 tube cake

Holiday Delight

1/2	cup butter
3/4	cup sugar
2	eggs, unbeaten
2	cups, sifted cake flour
1/4	teaspoon salt
4	teaspoons baking powder
1 1/2	cups raspberry jam
1/2	cup blanched almonds, chopped
1/2	pint heavy cream, whipped

1. Cream butter and sugar together until fluffy. Add eggs.
2. Sift flour, salt and baking powder together and add to first mixture.
3. Form into balls.
4. Place in buttered muffin pans and press around edges of pans. Fill center with mixture of jam and nuts and bake in hot oven (450°F) about 10 minutes.
5. Cool and serve with whipped cream.

Serves 8

Plain Pastry

2   cups sifted flour
¾   teaspoon salt
⅔   cup shortening
4   to 6 tablespoons cold water

1. Sift flour and salt together and cut in shortening with 2 knives or pastry blender.
2. Add water, using only a small portion at a time, until mixture will hold together.
3. Divide dough into 2 parts.
4. Roll out on floured board to desired size.
5. Line the piepan with one piece of dough, being careful not to stretch dough.
6. After filling is placed in pastry, dampen edges of lower crust with cold water and cover with remaining dough which has been rolled out and slashed in several places to allow steam to escape while baking.
7. Press edges together with prongs of fork and bake according to recipe for filling selected.

2 9-inch shells for one 2-crust 9-inch pie

Christmas Tree: Mark to suggest branches and decorate with green sugar.

Santa Claus: Mark to suggest features and decorate with red sugar.

Southern Pastry

2   cups sifted flour
½   teaspoon salt
1   cup shortening
6   tablespoons ice water

1. Mix flour and salt.
2. Cut shortening into flour; add water a tablespoon at a time, using only enough to make a workable paste; too little will leave it crumbly.
3. This pastry, being exceedingly rich, must be handled deftly.
4. Roll out pastry and line piepan.

2 9-inch pastry shells or 1 two-crust 9-inch pie

Note: Thorough chilling before rolling makes pastry easier to handle.

Christmas Tree: Mark to suggest branches and decorate with green sugar.

Santa Claus: Mark to suggest features and decorate with red sugar.

Hot Water Pastry

2   cups sifted flour
½   teaspoon baking powder
1   teaspoon salt
⅓   cup boiling water
⅔   cup shortening

1. Sift flour, baking powder and salt together.
2. Pour water over shortening and mix with fork until creamy, add flour mixture and mix into a dough.
3. Chill thoroughly and proceed as for Plain Pastry.

1 9-inch dough crust pie or 2 9-inch single crust pies

Christmas Tree: Mark to suggest branches and decorate with green sugar.

Santa Claus: Mark to suggest features and decorate wit red sugar.

Pastry For 1-Crust Pie

1   **cup sifted all-purpose flour**
½   **teaspoon salt**
⅓   **cup lard, vegetable shortening, or all-purpose shortening**
3   **tablespoons cold water**

1. Sift and salt together into a bowl. Cut in shortening with pastry blender or two knives until pieces are the size of small peas.
2. Sprinkle the water over mixture, a teaspoonful at a time, mixing lightly with a fork after each addition. Add only enough water to hold pastry together. Work quickly; do not overhandle. Shape into a ball and flatten on a lightly floured surface.
3. Roll from center to edge into a round about ⅛ inch thick and about 1 inch larger than overall size of pan.
4. Loosen pastry from surface with spatula and fold in quarters. Gently lay pastry in pan and unfold it, fitting it to pan so it is not stretched.
5. Trim edge with scissors or sharp knife so pastry extends about ½ inch beyond of pie pan. Fold extra pastry under at edge, and flute.
6. Thoroughly prick bottom and sides of shell with a fork. (Omit pricking if filling is to be baked in shell.)
7. Bake at 450°F 10 to 15 minutes, or until crust is light golden brown.
8. Cool on rack.

One 8 or 9-inch Pie Shell

Pastry For 2-Crust Pie: Double recipe for Pastry For 1-Crust Pie. Divide pastry into halves and shape into a ball. Roll each ball as above. For top crust, roll out one ball of pastry and cut 1 inch larger than pie pan. Slit pastry with knife in several places to allow steam to escape during baking. Gently fold in half and set aside while rolling bottom crust. Roll second ball of pastry and gently fit pastry into pie pan; avoid stretching. Trim pastry with scissors or sharp knife around edge of pan. Do not prick. Fill as directed in specific recipe. Moisten edge with water for a tight seal. Carefully arrange top crust over filling. Gently press edges to seal. Fold extra top pastry under bottom pastry. Flute.

Pastry For Little Pies And Tarts: Follow recipe for Pastry for 1-Crust Pie. Roll pastry ⅛ inch thick and cut about ½ inch larger than overall size of pans. Carefully fit rounds into pans without stretching. Fold excess pastry under at edge. Flute. Prick bottom and sides of shell with fork. (Omit pricking if filling is to be baked in shell.) Bake at 450°F 8 to 10 minutes, or until light golden brown. Cool on wire rack.

Three 6-inch pies, six 3½ inch tarts, or nine 1½-inch tarts

Mincemeat Pie

3½   cups Mincemeat (page 125; if using packaged condensed mincemeat, prepare according to package directions)

1   teaspoon grated lemon peel

1   tablespoon lemon juice
    Pastry for 2-Crust Pie (page 123; use a 9-in. pie pan)

1. Mix Mincemeat, lemon peel and lemon juice in a saucepan.
2. Heat mixture thoroughly. Set aside to cool slightly.
3. Meanwhile prepare Pastry for 2-Crust Pie.
4. Fill pastry shell with mincemeat mixture. Complete as in Pastry for 2-Crust Pie.
5. Bake at 450°F 10 min. Reduce heat and bake at 350°F 40 min. longer, or until crust is light golden brown.
6. Cool on cooling rack.

One 9-in. pie

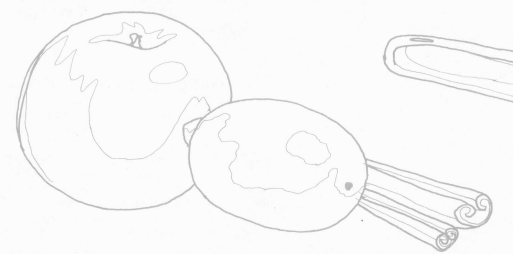

Mince Pie I

1   recipe Plain Pastry (page 122)

2½   cups mincemeat

1. Line piepan with pastry, fill with mincemeat and cover with top crust.
2. Bake in hot oven 400°F about 35 minutes or until pastry is browned.
3. Serve hot.

1 9-inch pie.

Mince Pie II

Pastry for a 2-crust pie (page 123)

3½   cups moist mincemeat

1¼   cups chopped apple

1   teaspoon grated lemon peel

1   tablespoon lemon juice

1. Prepare a 9-inch pie shell; roll out remaining pastry for top crust. Set aside.
2. Blend mincemeat and remaining ingredients in a saucepan; heat thoroughly. Cool slightly.
3. Turn filling into unbaked pie shell. Complete as directed for 2-crust pie.
4. Bake at 425°F 35 minutes. Cool on wire rack.

One 9-Inch Pie

Mincemeat

¼	lb. suet
1½	cups ground cooked lean beef
4	medium apples (about 3 cups, chopped)
1	cup firmly packed brown sugar
1	cup apple cider
½	cup fruit jelly
½	cup raisins, chopped
½	cup currants
2	tablespoons molasses
1	teaspoon salt
1	teaspoon cinnamon
½	teaspoon cloves
½	teaspoon nutmeg
¼	teaspoon mace
1	tablespoon grated lemon peel
1	tablespoon lemon juice

·1. Set out a large heavy skillet.
2. Put suet through medium blade of food chopper and add to ground meat. Set aside.
3. Wash, quarter, core, pare and chop apples.
4. Put apples and meat into skillet; add and mix brown sugar, apple cider, fruit jelly, raisins, currants and molasses.
5. Add mixture of salt, cinnamon, cloves, nutmeg and mace.
6. Stirring occasionally, simmer uncovered 1 hr., or until almost all of liquid is absorbed. Add lemon peel and lemon juice.
7. Blend thoroughly.

3½ cups Mincemeat

Homemade Mincemeat

1	pound cooked lean roast beef, cut in pieces
½	pound suet
5	pounds tart apples
½	pound seedless raisins, chopped
1	pound dried currants
¼	pound candied citron, chopped
¼	pound candied orange peel, chopped
2	tablespoons grated orange peel
1	tablespoon grated lemon peel
¼	cup orange juice
2	tablespoon lemon juice
2	cups sugar
1	teaspoon cinnamon
½	teaspoon cloves
½	teaspoon nutmeg
½	teaspoon mace
½	teaspoon powdered coriander seed
1	teaspoon salt
½	teaspoon pepper
2	cups apple cider
1	can (16 ounces) tart red cherries (undrained)
½	pound walnuts, coarsely chopped
1	cup brandy

1. Finely chop meat and beef suet or put through coarse blade of food chopper, and put into a large electric cooker.
2. Wash, quarter, core, and pare the apples; coarsely chop or put through coarse blade of a food chopper (there should be about 6 cups chopped).
3. Add apples and all other ingredients, except nuts and brandy, to cooker; stir.
4. Cover and cook on High 4 to 6 hours, stirring occasionally.
5. Stir in nuts.
6. Cover and cook on High 15 to 30 minutes.
7. Stir in brandy. Quickly ladle the mincemeat into hot, sterilized jars; seal.

About 7 (1-pint) jars

Cranberry Pie

4	cups cranberries
1½	cups sugar
2	tablespoons flour
¼	teaspoon salt
3	tablespoons water
1	tablespoon melted butter
1	recipe Plain Pastry (page 122)

1. Wash berries, chop and mix with sugar, flour, salt, water, and melted butter.
2. Line piepan with pastry, pour in filling and arrange strips of pastry over top in lattice design.
3. Bake in very hot oven 450°F 15 minutes; reduce to moderate 350°F and bake about 30 minutes longer.

1 9-inch pie

Chocolate Eggnog Pie

9   in. pastry shell (page 123)
1   cup finely chopped
    toasted walnuts (see note)
½   cup sugar
1   env. unflavored gelatin
⅛   teaspoon salt
⅛   teaspoon mace or nutmeg
1   cup milk
1   oz. (1 sq.) unsweetened
    chocolate, cut fine
4   eggs
1   cup heavy cream, chilled
2   tablespoons brandy or
    light rum

1. Set out a double boiler and a 9-in. pie pan.
2. Prepare 9-in. pastry shell and bake.
3. Prepare toasted walnuts and set aside.
4. Combine in top of double boiler, ¼ cup of sugar, unflavored gelatin, salt and mace or nutmeg, mixing thoroughly.
5. Stir in milk and chocolate. Heat over hot water until chocolate is melted.
6. Separate eggs. Beat egg yolks slightly. Using same beater, beat milk-chocolate mixture until smooth. Blend in the egg yolks and continue cooking over simmering water until slightly thickened, stirring occasionally. Remove from heat and cool.
7. When mixture is completely cold and begins to gel, beat egg whites until foamy. Beating constantly, add ¼ cup of sugar gradually.
8. Continue beating meringue until very stiff peaks are formed. Using same beater, beat ½ cup heavy cream until soft peaks are formed.
9. Fold the meringue, whipped cream, and walnuts into gelatin mixture along with brandy or light rum.
10. Continue folding gently until well mixed and turn into baked pie shell. Refrigerate several hours to chill thoroughly.
11. When ready to serve, whip ½ cup heavy cream. Swirl over pie and decorate with walnut halves, chocolate candies and cherries.

One 9-in. pie

Note: To toast walnuts, drop kernels into rapidly boiling water; boil 2 min. and drain. Spread in shallow baking pan and heat in 350°F oven 15 min., or until golden, stirring often.

Holiday Pear and Cranberry Pie

    Pastry for 2-crust pie
    (page 123)
3   fresh winter pears, cored
    (do not pare) and sliced
1½   cups fresh cranberries,
    rinsed and sorted
1   cup sugar
2   teaspoons grated orange
    peel
⅛   teaspoon salt
2   tablespoons quick-cooking
    tapioca

1. Using one half the pastry, line a 9-inch pie pan and flute the pastry edge. Roll out remaining pastry. Using a paper cutout of a pear tree with pears and a partridge, cut the tree from the pastry.
2. Combine pears and cranberries with remaining ingredients; mix well and spoon into pie shell. Carefully place the pear tree cutout over the pie filling.
3. Bake at 400°F about 40 minutes, or until fruit is tender and pie crust is light golden brown.

One 9-Inch Pie

Pecan-Topped Pumpkin Pie

1   unbaked 9-in. pie shell
1   can (16 oz.) pumpkin, about 2 cups
⅔   cup firmly packed light brown sugar
1   teaspoon ground cinnamon
½   teaspoon ground ginger
½   teaspoon ground nutmeg
⅛   teaspoon ground cloves
½   teaspoon salt
2   eggs, slightly beaten
2   cups cream, scalded
3   tablespoons butter or margarine
1   cup pecan halves
¼   cup firmly packed light brown sugar

1. Prepare pie shell; set aside.
2. For filling, combine pumpkin, ⅔ cup brown sugar, and a mixture of spices and salt in a bowl. Add the eggs and mix well. Gradually add the scalded cream, stirring until mixture is smooth. Pour filling into unbaked pie shell.
3. Bake at 400°F about 50 minutes, or until a knife inserted near center comes out clean. Cool on rack.
4. For topping, melt the butter in a small skillet. Add pecans; turn them with a spoon until coated with butter. Turn nuts into a bowl containing ¼ cup brown sugar; toss to coat thoroughly.
5. When pie is cool, arrange coated pecans, rounded side up, over the top in an attractive design. Place under broiler about 3 inches from source of heat. Broil 1 to 2 minutes.

One 9-Inch Pie

Pecan Pie

¼   cup butter
⅔   cup brown sugar, firmly packed
¼   teaspoon salt
¾   cup dark corn syrup
3   eggs, beaten
1   teaspoon vanilla
½   recipe Plain Pastry (page 122)
1   cup pecan halves

1. Cream butter and sugar together until fluffy.
2. Add salt, corn syrup, eggs, and vanilla.
3. Line piepan with pastry and sprinkle with pecans; pour the filling over pecans.
4. Bake in very hot oven 450°F 10 minutes, reduce temperature to moderate 350°F and bake 35 minutes longer or until knife inserted in center comes out clean.

1 8-inch pie

Plum Pie

3   cups pitted fresh plums
1¼   cups sugar
2   tablespoons flour
2   tablespoons lemon juice
⅛   teaspoon salt
1   recipe Plain Pastry (page 122)
1   tablespoon butter

1. Combine plums, sugar, flour, lemon juice and salt.
2. Line piepan with pastry, add filling, dot with butter and cover with top crust.
3. Bake in very hot oven 450°F 10 minutes; reduce temperature to moderate 350°F and bake 35 minutes longer until plums are tender.

1 9-inch pie

Pumpkin Pie

⅛	teaspoon salt
⅔	cup sugar
2	teaspoons pumpkin pie spice
2	eggs, slightly beaten
1⅔	cups milk
1½	cups mashed cooked pumpkin
½	recipe Plain Pastry (page 122)

1. Sift dry ingredients together and stir into eggs.
2. Add milk and pumpkin.
3. Line piepan with pastry and pour in filling.
4. Bake in very hot oven 450°F 10 minutes; reduce temperature to slow 325°F and bake 35 minutes longer or until knife inserted in center comes out clean. Cool.

1 9-inch pie

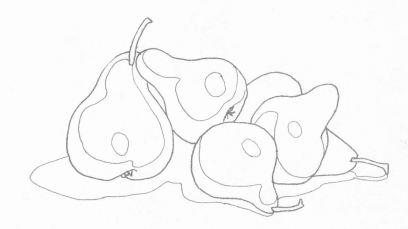

Cookies

Melting Snowflakes

⅓	cup butter, chilled
1	cup sifted all-purpose flour
2	egg yolks
1	teaspoon cream
½	teaspoon almond extract
	Egg white, slightly beaten

1. Cut butter into flour until particles are the size of rice kernels.
2. Beat egg yolks, cream, and extract until very thick. Using a fork, blend into flour mixture in halves, mixing well after each addition. Chill dough thoroughly.
3. Roll dough ¼ inch thick on a floured surface; fold lengthwise in half, then crosswise in half; chill 1 hour.
4. Again roll dough ¼ inch thick. Cut with 1¼-inch round cutter. Transfer to ungreased cookie sheets. Brush rounds with egg white.
5. Bake at 350°F about 20 minutes.
6. Remove cookies to wire racks and sift with *Vanilla Confectioners' Sugar, page 148.*

About 2 dozen cookies

Swedish Gingersnaps

1½	cups sifted all-purpose flour
1	teaspoon baking soda
1½	teaspoons ground ginger
1	teaspoon ground cinnamon
¼	teaspoon ground cloves
½	cup butter
¾	cup sugar
1	egg
1½	teaspoons dark corn syrup
	Whole blanched almonds, cut in small pieces

1. Sift flour, baking soda, and spices together; set aside.
2. Cream butter; add sugar gradually, beating until fluffy. Add egg and corn syrup and beat thoroughly.
3. Blend in dry ingredients in fourths, mixing thoroughly after each addition. Refrigerate dough several hours.
4. Using a portion of the dough at a time, roll about 1/16 inch thick on a lightly floured surface. Cut with lightly floured cookie cutters into various shapes. Transfer to ungreased cookie sheets. Place one almond piece in the center of each.
5. Bake at 375°F 6 to 8 minutes.

About 7 dozen cookies

Scotch Shortbread

1 cup shortening
2/3 cup brown sugar
2 2/3 cups cake flour
Egg
Milk

1. Cream shortening and sifted sugar together and work into the flour. Chill.
2. Roll out 1/3 inch thick on a pastry cloth.
3. Cut with small fancy cutters and brush tops with a mixture of egg and milk for a glaze.

60 cookies

Note: If desired, roll out in a large sheet 1/3 to 1/2 inch thick and cut lengthwise in strips 1 1/2 inches wide, then diagonally 1 1/2 inches apart to form diamond shapes. Bake in a slow oven 325°F 30 minutes or until slightly browned. Store in cool place.

Sand Tarts I

1/2 cup shortening
1 cup sugar
1 egg, beaten
2 cups cake flour
2 teaspoons baking powder
1/4 teaspoon salt
1/2 cup almonds, blanched
1 egg white
1 tablespoon sugar
1/4 teaspoon cinnamon

1. Cream shortening and sugar thoroughly.
2. Add beaten egg and dry ingredients which have been sifted together.
3. Chill dought until stiff.
4. Roll out 1/8 inch thick and cut with various shaped cutters.
5. Press 1/2 almond in the center of each, brush tops of cookies with egg white and sprinkle with cinnamon and sugar mixture.
6. Bake in moderate oven 375°F 10 minutes.

76 cookies 2 1/2-inch diameter
A crisp cookie which keeps well

Variation—Roll thin, cut with tiny bridge-set cutters, bake 5 minutes, remove from oven and cool. Frost with Peppermint Spread and while moist outline each with candy beads.

Sand Tarts II

2 cups butter
2 1/2 cups sugar
2 eggs
4 cups sifted all-purpose flour
1 egg white, slightly beaten

1. Cream butter; add sugar gradually, beating until fluffy. Add eggs one at a time, beating thoroughly after each addition.
2. Add flour in fourths, mixing until well blended after each addition. Chill dough overnight.
3. Removing from refrigerator only amount needed for a single rolling, roll dough about 1/16 inch thick on a floured surface; cut with 2-inch round or fancy cutter. Brush tops with egg white; sprinkle with a mixture of *1/2 cup sugar* and *2 teaspoons ground cinnamon*.
4. Transfer to ungreased cookie sheets; press a quarter of *pecan* onto center of each cookie.
5. Bake at 350°F about 9 minutes.

About 17 1/2 dozen cookies

Norwegian Christmas Cookies

1¾	cups sifted all-purpose flour
½	cup cornstarch
2	teaspoons baking powder
½	teaspoon salt
¼	to ½ teaspoon pepper
½	teaspoon ground cardamom
½	teaspoon ground cinnamon
½	teaspoon ground cloves
1	cup butter or margarine
¼	teaspoon vanilla extract
1	cup sugar
¼	cup cream
⅔	cup finely chopped blanched almonds

1. Sift flour, cornstarch, baking powder, salt, and spices together; set aside.
2. Cream butter with extract. Add sugar gradually, beating until light and fluffy.
3. Add dry ingredients alternately with cream, mixing after each addition. Stir in almonds.
4. Shape dough into ¾-inch balls; place 1 inch apart on ungreased cookie sheets.
5. Bake at 350°F about 15 minutes.

About 6 dozen cookies

Fig Cookies

2¼	cups sifted cake flour
½	teaspoon cinnamon
1	teaspoon soda
½	cup shortening
1	cup brown sugar
2	eggs, beaten
2	tablespoons sour cream
1	cup chopped figs

1. Sift flour, cinnamon and soda together.
2. Cream shortening with sugar until fluffy; add eggs, cream and figs.
3. Add sifted dry ingredients with more flour if necessary. Chill thoroughly.
4. Roll out on lightly floured board to ⅛-inch thickness, cut with cookie cutter and bake on greased cookie sheet in moderate oven 350°F 10 to 12 minutes or until browned.

5 dozen cookies

Christmas Cut Outs

½	cup shortening
1	cup sugar
1	egg
2	teaspoons baking powder
2½	cups cake flour
½	teaspoon salt
½	cup milk
1	teaspoon vanilla

1. Cream shortening well.
2. Add sugar and egg and blend together.
3. Sift baking powder, flour and salt together and add to creamed mixture alternately with the milk.
4. Stir in vanilla. Chill.
5. Roll out 1/16 inch thick on pastry cloth, cut in Christmas designs, brush with egg white, decorate and bake at 350°F 10 to 12 minutes.

100 2-inch cookies

Decoration—Cut cookies in the shape of Santa Claus, frost with red Confectioners' Icing. Using pastry tube, trim with white frosting making a white beard, fur collar and cuffs on pants, hat and jacket. Use raisins for eyes, nose and mouth.

Pfeffernusse

5	eggs, beaten
2	cups sugar
	Grated rind 1 lemon
3	tablespoons lemon juice
½	cup citron or other candied fruit or fruit peel, chopped
6	cups cake flour
2	teaspoons baking powder
½	teaspoon salt
½	teaspoon cloves
½	teaspoon nutmeg
½	teaspoon mace
1	tablespoon cinnamon
½	cup chopped nuts

1. Beat eggs well. Add sugar about two tablespoons at a time and beat thoroughly with each addition.

2. Add lemon rind and juice, finely chopped citron, the dry ingredients which have been mixed and sifted together, and the finely chopped nuts.

3. Chill at least an hour, roll ½ inch thick and cut out with a pfeffernusse cutter, a round cutter about ⅞ of an inch in diameter.

4. Place pfeffernusse on a cookie sheet and let stand overnight in a cool place to dry.

5. The next morning before baking, invert each cookie and put a drop of fruit juice or brandy on the moist spot on the bottom of the cookie and bake upside down.

6. This tends to make the pfeffernusse "pop". Bake in a slow oven 300°F 8 minutes.

Note: If a pfeffernusse cutter is not available, a narrow bottle top or round tin bouillon cube box will do very nicely.

NORTH POLE

Weiser Lebkuchen

5	eggs, beaten
2	cups sugar
1	cup finely shredded citron
1/4	cup finely chopped candied cherries
3/4	cup almonds, finely chopped
4 1/2	cups cake flour
1/2	teaspoon cinnamon
1/2	teaspoon cloves
1/2	teaspoon nutmeg
1/2	teaspoon salt

1. Beat eggs till thick.
2. Add sugar gradually and beat well.
3. Add citron, cherries, almonds and the flour which has been sifted with the spices and the salt.
4. Roll and cut in squares.
5. Let stand overnight and bake in a moderate oven 350°F 15 to 20 minutes until a very light brown.

96 squares

Christmas Trees: Omit citron, cherries and almonds and proceed as in Weiser Lebkuchen recipe. Cut trees with a knife and cut away the edges of the tree with a corrugated cutter. Sprinkle liberally with green sugar. Ornament with colored candies and bake.

Christmas Wreaths: Omit citron, cherries and almonds and proceed as in Weiser Lebkuchen recipe. Cut with doughnut cutter. Sprinkle liberally with green sugar. Dot with tiny red candies and bake.

Cinnamon Stars

6	egg whites
2	teaspoons cinnamon
2 3/4	cups confectioners' sugar
1	pound almonds, not blanched
	Confectioners' sugar

1. Mix egg whites, cinnamon and sugar until well blended. 2. Set aside 1/4 cup for frosting.
3. Add finely ground almonds.
4. Roll out mixture on sugar-flour dusted board to 1/8 inch thick.
5. Cut with star cutter, frost with egg mixture stiffened with additional confectioners' sugar.
6. Bake at 300°F 20 minutes.

60 cookies

Swiss Christmas Cookies

1 1/4	cups strained honey
3/4	cup shortening
2	cups sugar
1/4	cup fruit juice
	Grated rind of 1 orange
	Grated rind of 1 lemon
2	cups unblanched almonds, chopped
10	cups cake flour
1	teaspoon salt
1	teaspoon cinnamon
2	teaspoons nutmeg
1	teaspoon cloves
4	teaspoons baking powder

1. Melt honey and shortening together over hot water.
2. Add sugar and fruit juice and stir until dissolved.
3. Add grated rinds of orange and lemon, chopped almonds, and the dry ingredients which have been sifted together. Chill in refrigerator.
4. The dough may be kept several days to ripen or used at once. Roll about 1/8 of an inch thick and cut in strips about 2 by 2 1/2 inches in size.
5. Bake in a slow oven 300°F 20 minutes. While still warm frost with Confectioners' Icing.

180 cookies

Cheese Cookies

3	ounces cream cheese
½	cup butter
½	cup sugar
1	egg yolk
½	teaspoon vanilla
1	cup sifted flour
¼	teaspoon salt
⅛	teaspoon nutmeg

1. Blend cheese and butter together, add sugar and egg yolk and cream together thoroughly.
2. Add vanilla.
3. Sift remaining ingredients together and add to cream mixture.
4. Chill until firm enough to roll.
5. Roll out on lightly floured board, cut with cookie cutter and place on greased baking sheet.
6. Bake in moderate oven 375°F about 10 minutes.

24 cookies

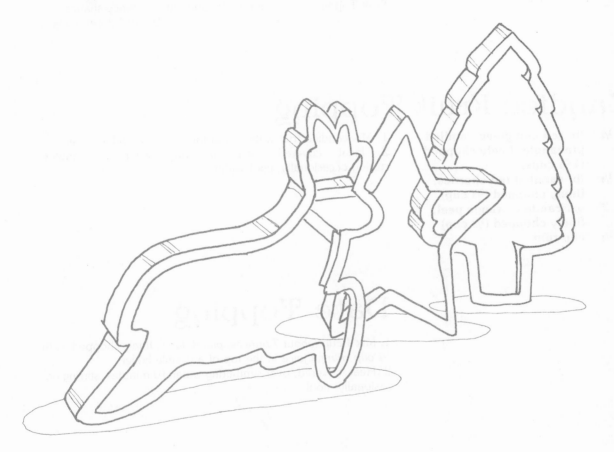

Snowball Meltaways

1	cup butter
½	cup confectioners' sugar
1	teaspoon vanilla extract
2½	cups sifted all-purpose flour
½	cup finely chopped pecans

1. In a heavy saucepan over low heat, melt and heat butter until light brown in color. Pour into a small mixing bowl; chill until firm.
2. Cream browned butter with confectioners' sugar and extract until light and fluffy. Gradually add flour, mixing until blended. Stir in the pecans. Chill several hours for ease in handling.
3. Shape into 1-inch balls. Place on ungreased cookie sheets.
4. Bake at 350°F about 20 minutes.
5. Remove to wire racks. While still hot, dust with *confectioners' sugar*.

About 4 dozen cookies

Crown Jewels

Topping, (below)
1 cup butter or margarine
½ teaspoon grated orange peel
½ cup sugar
2 hard-cooked egg yolks, sieved
2 cups sifted all-purpose flour

1. Prepare Topping.
2. Cream butter with orange peel. Gradually add sugar, beating until fluffy.
3. Blend in sieved hard-cooked egg yolks. Add flour in fourths, mixing well after each addition.
4. Press dough firmly onto bottom of ungreased 15x10x1-inch jelly roll pan.
5. Bake at 350°F 20 minutes.
6. While still warm, spread with Date Topping and then Candied Fruit Topping. Cool thoroughly and cut into fancy shapes.

About 3 dozen cookies

Candied Fruit Topping

½ lb. red and green candied pineapple, finely chopped (1⅔ cups)
¼ lb. candied red cherries, finely chopped (⅔ cup)
2 oz. candied orange peel, finely chopped (⅓ cup)
⅓ cup rum

1. Mix candied fruit with rum in the top of a double boiler.
2. Heat, covered, over simmering water 30 minutes, stirring occasionally; cool slightly.

Date Topping

1. Mix *1 cup (about 7 ounces) pitted dates,* finely chopped, with *¼ cup orange juice* in the top of a double boiler.
2. Heat, covered, over simmering water 10 minutes, stirring occasionally; cool.

Cherry Jewels

½ cup butter
1 teaspoon vanilla extract
¼ cup sugar
1 egg
1 teaspoon grated lemon peel
1 tablespoon lemon juice
1¼ cups sifted all-purpose flour
¾ cup finely chopped pecans
18 candied cherries, halved

1. Cream butter with extract and sugar until light and fluffy. Add the egg and lemon peel and juice; beat thoroughly. Gradually add flour, mixing until blended. Chill.
2. Shape dough into 1-inch balls, roll in chopped pecans and place on greased cookie sheets. Press a cherry half onto center of each ball.
3. Bake at 350°F 10 to 12 minutes.
4. Cool on wire racks.

3 dozen cookies

Lemon Sugar Cookies

¾ cup butter
1 teaspoon grated lemon peel
1 tablespoon lemon juice
1¼ cups sugar
2 eggs
2 cups sifted all-purpose flour
1½ teaspoons baking powder
½ teaspoon salt

1. Cream butter with lemon peel and juice; add the sugar gradually, creaming until fluffy. Add the eggs, one at a time, beating thoroughly after each addition.
2. Sift flour, baking powder, and salt together; add in fourths to creamed mixture, mixing until blended after each addition. Chill dough thoroughly.
3. Roll a third of dough at a time ⅛ inch thick; cut with 2¼-inch round or fancy cutter. Transfer to ungreased cookie sheets.
4. Bake at 325°F 15 to 18 minutes.

About 4½ dozen cookies

Note: If desired, add sugar sparkle by evenly sprinkling *granulated sugar* over the rolled dough. Roll lightly to press sugar into dough. Or, add decorations by brushing rolled dough with slightly beaten *egg white* (or egg yolk beaten with 1 tablespoon water or milk); top with pieces of *angelica, citron,* or *candied cherries* or sprinkle with *colored sugar* or crushed *rock candy.*

Brown Sugar Cookies: Follow recipe for Lemon Sugar Cookies. Omit lemon peel and juice; add *1 teaspoon vanilla extract.* Substitute *1 cup firmly packed brown sugar* for granulated sugar.

Brown Moravian Cookies

4 cups sifted all-purpose flour
¼ teaspoon baking soda
¼ teaspoon salt
1 teaspoon ground cin-namon
½ teaspoon ground cloves
¼ teaspoon ground ginger
1 cup firmly packed light brown sugar
½ cup butter
½ cup lard*
1½ cups light molasses
½ teaspoon cider vinegar

1. Sift flour, baking soda, salt, and spices together into a large bowl. Add brown sugar; mix well.
2. Cut in butter and lard. Add molasses and vinegar gradually, mixing well. Chill dough thoroughly.
3. Using a small amount of dough at a time, roll out about ⅛-inch thick on a lightly floured surface. Cut with fancy cookie cutters. Transfer to greased cookie sheets.
4. Bake at 350°F 8 to 10 minutes.

About 6 dozen cookies

Note: *Use butter, if desired, but then cookie will not be authentic.

Decorated Sugar Cookies

2½ cups sifted all-purpose flour
¼ teaspoon baking powder
¼ teaspoon salt
1 cup butter or margarine
1¼ teaspoons vanilla extract
1 cup confectioners' sugar
1 egg yolk
2 teaspoons cream
Sugar, colored sugar, chocolate sprinkles or finely chopped nuts

1. Set out cookie sheets and cookie cutters.
2. Sift flour, baking powder and salt together and set aside.
3. Cream butter or margarine and vanilla extract until butter is softened. Add confectioners' sugar gradually, creaming until fluffy after each addition.
4. Mixing until well blended after each addition, add dry ingredients in fourths to creamed mixture.
5. Put one third of the dough on a lightly floured surface. Roll about ¼ in. thick. Cut out cookies with lightly floured cookie cutters. Transfer cookies to cookie sheets. Repeat for remaining dough. Set aside.
6. Beat egg yolk and cream together until blended. Brush over cookies. Sprinkle with sugar, colored sugar, chocolate sprinkles or finely chopped nuts.
7. Bake at 350°F 12 to 15 min. With spatula remove cookies to cooling racks.

4 to 5 doz. cookies

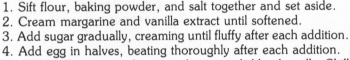

Big Fellow Sugar Cookies

2	cups sifted all-purpose flour
1	teaspoon baking powder
½	teaspoon salt
⅔	cup butter or margarine
1	teaspoon vanilla extract
¾	cup sugar
1	egg, well beaten

1. Sift flour, baking powder, and salt together and set aside.
2. Cream margarine and vanilla extract until softened.
3. Add sugar gradually, creaming until fluffy after each addition.
4. Add egg in halves, beating thoroughly after each addition.
5. Gradually stir in dry ingredients and blend well. Chill thoroughly in refrigerator.
6. Lightly grease cookie sheets.
7. Roll dough ⅛ in. thick on lightly floured surface. Cut dough with a floured large cookie cutter. Sprinkle tops of cookies with **sugar.** Place cookies on cookie sheets.
8. Bake at 375°F 10 to 12 min. Remove immediately to rack to cool.

1½ doz. large cookies

Ginger Cookies: Follow recipe for Big Fellow Sugar Cookies. Reduce baking powder to ½ teaspoon. Sift **¼ teaspoon baking soda, 1½ teaspoons ginger, ½ teaspoon cinnamon** and **¼ teaspoon allspice** with flour mixture. Decrease sugar to ½ cup and blend **6 tablespoons molasses** into creamed mixture. Omit vanilla extract.

Butterscotch Cookies: Follow recipe for Big Fellow Sugar Cookies. Reduce sugar to ¼ cup. Add **½ cup firmly packed brown sugar.** Increase shortening 2 tablespoons.

Spiced Sugar Cookies: Follow recipe for Big Fellow Sugar Cookies. Sift **½ teaspoon cinnamon, ¼ teaspoon mace** and **¼ teaspoon nutmeg** with flour.

Chocolate Sugar Cookies: Follow recipe for Big Fellow Sugar Cookies. Melt **2 oz. (2 sq.) unsweetened chocolate** and set aside to cool. Blend in after addition of egg.

Lemon or Orange Sugar Cookies: Follow recipe for Big Fellow Sugar Cookies. Substitute **1½ teaspoons lemon or orange juice** for vanilla extract. Add **1 tablespoon grated lemon peel** or **2 tablespoons grated orange peel.**

Coconut Sugar Cookies: Follow recipe for Big Fellow Sugar Cookies. Blend in **1 cup (4 oz.) moist shredded coconut** after addition of dry ingredients.

Gingerbread Men

4½	cups sifted all-purpose flour
1	tablespoon cinnamon
1	teaspoon salt
1	teaspoon baking soda
1	teaspoon ginger
½	teaspoon cloves
½	cup butter or margarine
½	cup firmly packed brown sugar
1	egg
1	cup molasses
2	teaspoons vinegar

1. Sift flour, cinnamon, salt, baking soda , ginger, and cloves together and set aside.
2. Cream butter or margarine until softened.
3. Add brown sugar gradually, creaming until light and fluffy after each addition.
4. Add egg and beat thoroughly.
5. Add molasses and vinegar gradually while beating.
6. Stir in dry ingredients.
7. Wrap dough in moisture-vaporproof material and chill in refrigerator 8 hrs. or overnight. Lightly grease cookie sheets.
8. Roll one portion of chilled dough at a time, ¼ in. thick, on lightly floured surface. Cut dough with gingerbread-man cookie cutter, or lay a cardboard pattern over dough and cut with sharp knife carefully around pattern. Using pancake turner, transfer cookies to cookie sheets.
9. Bake at 350°F about 10 minutes. When cool, add fancy decorations with frosting or candies.

About 1½ doz. Gingerbread Men or 2½ doz. round cookies

Linzer Wreath Cookies

- ¼ cup (about 1 oz.) finely chopped walnuts
- ¼ cup sugar
- 2 cups sifted all-purpose flour
- ½ cup confectioners' sugar
- ¼ teaspoon baking soda
- ½ cup unsalted butter, chilled and cut in pieces
- 2 egg yolks, slightly beaten
- ¼ teaspoon vanilla extract
- ¼ teaspoon grated lemon peel
  Egg, slightly beaten
- ¼ cup thick jam, such as apricot or strawberry
- 2 tablespoons confectioners' sugar

1. Lightly grease cookie sheets.
2. Mix walnuts and sugar and set aside.
3. Sift flour, ½ cup confectioners' sugar and baking soda together into a large bowl.
4. Work butter into the dry ingredients by pressing against bottom and sides of bowl with a fork.
5. Gradually add to the ingredients in the bowl, mixing with a fork after each addition, a mixture of egg yolks, vanilla extract and lemon peel. (Mixture will be crumbly.) Gather dough into a ball. Turn dough out onto lightly floured surface. Work with hands, squeezing dough until well blended. Shape into smooth ball with palms of hands. If dough becomes too soft, chill slightly in refrigerator.
6. Roll dough ⅛ to ¼ in. thick. With lightly floured 2-in. scalloped cookie cutter, cut dough into rounds. Place one half of the rounds onto cookie sheets. Using a thimble dipped in flour, cut ½-in. holes in centers of remaining rounds, forming rings. Brush all the rounds and rings with egg.
7. Dip top surface of rings into the nut-sugar mixture. Place rings, coated-side up, on cookie sheets (not on top of cookie rounds).
8. Bake at 350°F 15 to 20 min., or until lightly browned. Remove cookies to cooling racks.
9. Set out jam. Spread ½ to ¾ teaspoon of the jam onto each plain cookie round. Top each with a nut-topped cookie ring. Sprinkle confectioner's sugar onto cookies.

About 1½ doz. cookies

Poor Man's Cookies

- 5 cups sifted all-purpose flour
- 1 teaspoon cardamom
- 10 egg yolks
- 2 egg whites
- ¾ cup sugar
- 3 tablespoons brandy
- 1 cup heavy cream
  Lard

1. A deep saucepan or automatic deep fryer will be needed.
2. Sift flour and cardamom together and set aside.
3. Beat egg yolks, egg whites, sugar and brandy until mixture is thick and lemon-colored.
4. Add heavy cream slowly.
5. Blend in flour mixture, about ½ cup at a time, to make a soft dough. Wrap dough in waxed paper and chill overnight in refrigerator.
6. Set out a deep saucepan or automatic deep fryer and heat lard to 365°F to 370°F.
7. Meanwhile, roll dough, a small portion at a time, to ¹⁄₁₆-in. thickness on a lightly floured surface. Cut into diamond shapes, 5x2-in. (A pattern may be used as a guide around which to cut with a floured knife.) Make a lengthwise slit in the center of the diamond and pull one tip end through it and tuck back under itself.
8. Deep-fry only as many cookies at one time as will float uncrowded one layer deep in fat. Deep-fry 1 to 2 min., or until golden brown, turning once during deep-frying time. Drain over fat a few seconds before removing to absorbent paper. Sprinkle with confectioners' sugar.
9. Store in tightly covered containers.

About 6 doz. cookies

Short'nin' Bread

1 cup firmly packed light brown sugar
4 cups sifted all-purpose flour
1 lb. softened butter

1. Set out cookie sheets.
2. Press brown sugar through a sieve. Mix thoroughly with all-purpose flour.
3. Add butter and work in until a smooth dough is formed.
4. Turn onto a lightly floured surface and pat to ½-in. thickness. (If necessary, chill dough for easier handling.) Cut into desired shapes and transfer to cookie sheets.
5. Bake at 325°F about 25 min., until very delicately browned.
6. Remove sheets to cooling racks 5 min. before transferring cookies to racks to cool thoroughly.

3 to 4 doz. cookies

English Toffee Bars

1 cup butter
1 cup sugar
1 egg yolk
2 cups sifted all-purpose flour
1 teaspoon ground cinnamon
1 egg white, slightly beaten
1 cup chopped pecans
2 oz. (2 sq.) semisweet chocolate, melted

1. Cream butter; add sugar gradually, beating until fluffy. Beat in egg yolk.
2. Sift the flour and cinnamon together; gradually add to creamed mixture, beating until blended.
3. Turn into a greased 15x10x1-inch jelly roll pan and press evenly. Brush top with egg white. Sprinkle with pecans and press lightly into dough.
4. Bake at 275°F 1 hour.
5. While still hot, cut into 1½-inch squares. Drizzle with melted chocolate. Cool on wire rack.

5 to 6 Dozen Cookies

Moji Pearls

¾ cup butter
½ teaspoon vanilla extract
⅓ cup sugar
1½ cups sifted all-purpose flour
⅛ teaspoon salt

1. Cream butter with extract; add sugar gradually, beating until fluffy.
2. Blend flour and salt; add in thirds to creamed mixture, mixing until blended after each addition. Chill dough until easy to handle.
3. Shape into 1-inch balls or into crescents (if desired, roll in sesame seed). Place about 2 inches apart on ungreased cookie sheets.
4. Bake at 325°F 20 minutes.

About 3 Dozen Cookies

Pecan Poofs: Follow recipe for Moji Pearls. Substitute ¼ *cup confectioners' sugar* for sugar. Decrease flour to 1 cup. Mix in *1 cup pecans*, finely chopped. Shape dough into balls or pyramids.

Anise Cookies

1 package active dry yeast
½ cup warm water
2 teaspoons salt
5 cups all-purpose flour
3 tablespoons sugar
1 cup each butter and
vegetable shortening (at
room temperature)
4 teaspoons anise extract
1 teaspoon baking powder
Red and green decorating
sugar

1. Dissolve yeast in water in a large bowl. Add salt and about 1 cup flour; mix very well. Add all other ingredients except the remaining flour and baking powder; mix thoroughly. Add remaining flour and baking powder; mix well.
2. Make 6 or 8 balls; with the palm of your hand, make long, thin rolls (about the size of the ring finger) and cut them into squares.
3. Place pieces, leaving space between them, on a cookie sheet. Make a cut on top of each.
4. Bake at 350°F about 25 minutes, or until golden brown.
5. Remove from cookie sheets and coat with red and green sugar. Cool on wire racks.

About 10 dozen

Mexican Christmas Cookies

1 cup vegetable shortening
2 teaspoons grated orange
peel
1¼ cups sugar
1 egg
⅓ cup fresh orange juice
3¾ cups all-purpose flour
¼ teaspoon salt
1 teaspoon cinnamon
½ teaspoon ground cloves
½ cup finely chopped pecans
Very fine sugar

1. Cream shortening, orange peel, and sugar until light. Beat in egg, then orange juice.
2. Blend flour, salt, and spices. Stir into creamed mixture. Mix in pecans.
3. Wrap dough and chill overnight.
4. Next day, roll out a small amount at a time on lightly floured surface to ⅛-inch thickness. Cut in desired shapes with fancy cookie cutter.
5. Put on lightly greased cookie sheets.
6. Bake at 375°F 8 to 10 minutes, or until golden brown.
7. Sprinkle with sugar while still warm.

About 10 dozen

Italian Butter Cookies

4 cups sifted all-purpose flour
1 cup sugar
2½ teaspoons grated lemon peel
1 tablespoon rum
4 egg yolks, beaten
1 cup firm unsalted butter, cut in pieces
1 egg white, slightly beaten

1. Combine flour, sugar, and lemon peel in a large bowl; mix thoroughly. Add rum and then egg yolks in fourths, mixing thoroughly after each addition.
2. Cut butter into flour mixture with pastry blender until particles are fine. Work with fingertips until a dough is formed.
3. Roll one half of dough at a time about ¼ inch thick on a lightly floured surface. Cut into desired shapes. Brush tops with egg white. Transfer to lightly greased cookie sheets.
4. Bake at 350°F. about 15 minutes.

About 6 dozen cookies

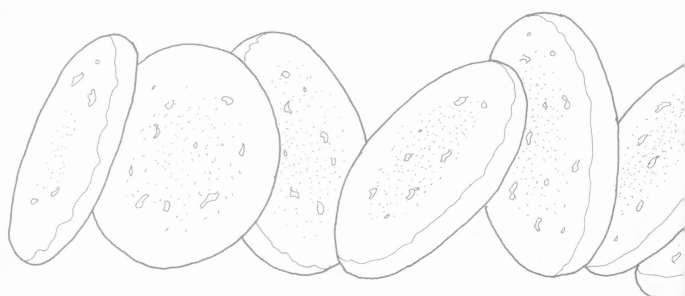

Honey Clusters

2 cups sifted all-purpose flour
¼ teaspoon salt
3 eggs
½ teaspoon vanilla extract
1 cup honey
1 tablespoon sugar
1 tablespoon tiny multicolored candies

1. Set out deep saucepan or automatic deep fryer for deep-frying and heat fat to 365°F.
2. Meanwhile, place flour and salt in a large bowl.
3. Make a well in center of flour. Add eggs, one at a time, mixing slightly after each addition.
4. Add vanilla extract. Mix well to make a soft dough.
5. Turn dough onto a lightly floured surface and knead. Divide dough into halves. Lightly roll each half ¼ in. thick to form a rectangle. Cut dough with a pastry cutter into strips ¼ in. wide. Use palm of hand to roll strips to pencil thickness. Cut into pieces about ¼ to ½ in. long.
6. Fry only as many pieces of dough as will float uncrowded, one layer deep in the fat. Fry 3 to 5 min., or until lightly browned, turning occasionally during frying time. Drain over fat before removing to absorbent paper.
7. Meanwhile, cook honey and sugar in skillet over low heat about 5 min.
8. Remove from heat and add deep-fried pieces. Stir constantly until all pieces are coated with honey-sugar mixture. Remove Strufoli with a slotted spoon and set in refrigerator to chill slightly. Remove to a large serving platter and arrange in a cone-shape mound.
9. Sprinkle with multicolored candies.
10. Chill in refrigerator. Serve by breaking off individual pieces.

8 to 10 servings

Norwegian Cones

1½	cups sifted all-purpose flour
½	cup cornstarch
1½	teaspoons ground cardamom
1	cup butter
1¼	cups sugar
3	egg yolks
3	egg whites
⅛	teaspoon salt

1. Blend flour, cornstarch, and cardamom.
2. Cream butter; add sugar gradually, beating until fluffy. Add egg yolks, one at a time, beating thoroughly after each addition.
3. Add dry ingredients in fourths, mixing until blended after each addition.
4. Beat egg whites and salt until stiff peaks are formed; gently fold into batter.
5. Heat krumkake iron (usually available in the housewares section of department stores) following manufacturer's instructions, until a drop of water "sputters" on hot surface.
6. For each, spoon 1½ to 2 teaspoons batter onto hot iron; close the iron and bake on each side for a few minutes, or until lightly browned.
7. Using a spatula, immediately remove wafer and roll into cone. Cool completely.

About 4 dozen cookies

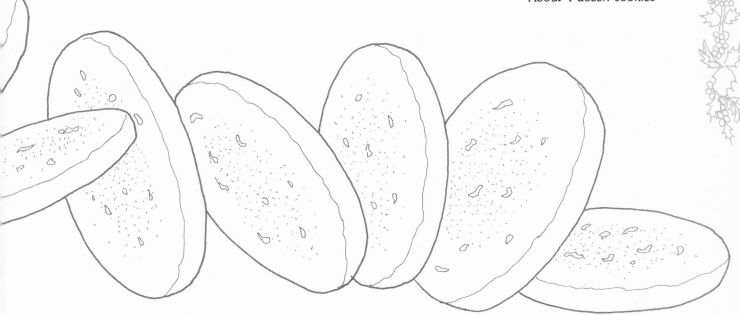

Belgian Christmas Cookies

⅔	cup butter
1	teaspoon almond extract
1	cup firmly packed dark brown sugar
2	eggs
1⅔	cups sifted all-purpose flour
1½	teaspoons baking powder
½	teaspoon salt
½	cup finely chopped unblanched almonds
½	teaspoon ground cinnamon
2	teaspoons red sugar
2	teaspoons green sugar

1. Cream butter with extract; add brown sugar gradually, creaming until fluffy. Add eggs, one at a time, beating thoroughly after each addition.
2. Sift flour, baking powder, and salt together; add in thirds to creamed mixture, mixing until blended after each addition. Turn into a greased 15x10x1-inch jelly roll pan and spread evenly to edges.
3. Sprinkle a mixture of almonds and cinnamon over batter, then sprinkle with a mixture of red and green sugars.
4. Bake at 375°F 10 to 12 minutes.
5. Cut into bars while still warm.

About 5 dozen cookies

Jan Hagel

1 cup butter
1 cup sugar
1 egg yolk
2 cups sifted all-purpose flour
¼ teaspoon salt
1 egg white
4 pieces loaf sugar, finely crushed
½ teaspoon ground cinnamon
½ cup finely chopped nuts

1. Cream butter; add sugar gradually, beating until fluffy. Add egg yolk and beat well.
2. Blend flour and salt; add in fourths to creamed mixture, mixing until blended after each addition.
3. Divide dough into halves and roll each on an ungreased cookie sheet into a 12x10-inch rectangle.
4. Beat egg white slightly with a small amount of water; brush lightly over dough. Mix crushed sugar with cinnamon and nuts; sprinkle over each rectangle.
5. Bake at 375°F 15 minutes.
6. Trim the edges and cut into bars while warm.

About 4 dozen cookies

Currant Cakes

2 cups butter
2 teaspoons grated lemon peel
2 tablespoons lemon juice
2¼ cups sugar
6 eggs, well beaten
3¼ cups sifted all-purpose flour
¼ teaspoon salt
½ lb. (1½ cups) currants

1. Cream butter with lemon peel and juice; add sugar gradually, beating until fluffy. Add eggs in thirds, beating thoroughly after each addition.
2. Blend flour and salt; add to creamed mixture in thirds, mixing until blended after each addition. Mix in the currants.
3. Drop by teaspoonfuls onto large well-greased cookie sheets, spreading batter for each cookie very thinly.
4. Bake at 350°F 10 minutes.

About 7½ dozen cookies

Danish Christmas Crullers I

5 egg yolks
1 egg
1 cup sugar
5 teaspoons finely shredded lemon peel
3¾ cups sifted all-purpose flour
½ cup heavy cream
Lard for deep frying

1. Combine egg yolks, egg, sugar, and lemon peel. Beat until very thick. Beating only until smooth after each addition, alternately add flour in thirds and cream in halves. Chill thoroughly.
2. About 20 minutes before ready to deep fry, start heating lard to 365°F.
3. Working with a small amount of dough at a time (keep remainder of dough chilled) on a floured surface, knead dough until smooth and roll it out thin. Cut into 3x1½-inch strips, slanting the ends. Cut a slit about 1½ inches long in center of each strip and draw one end through the slit.
4. Fry in the hot fat until golden brown, turning once.
5. Remove to absorbent paper and drain thoroughly before serving or storing.

8 to 12 cookies
(depending on thickness)

Danish Christmas Crullers II: Follow recipe for Danish Christmas Crullers I. Omit lemon peel and blend **½ to 1 teaspoon ground cardamom** with the flour.

Holly Cheese Cakes

Filling:
- 3   packages (8 ounces each) cream cheese
- 1½   teaspoons vanilla extract
- 1   cup sugar
- 5   eggs

Topping:
- 1   pint dairy sour cream
- ¼   cup sugar
- 1   teaspoon vanilla extract

Decoration:
- Red and green candied cherries, cut in pieces

1. Line 1½-inch muffin pan wells with fluted paper cups.
2. For filling, cream the cheese with vanilla extract. Add sugar and eggs; beat well. Spoon about 1 tablespoon mixture into each paper cup.
3. Bake at 350°F about 20 minutes, or until top cracks slightly.
4. Meanwhile, for topping, combine sour cream, sugar, and vanilla extract.
5. Spoon a small amount of topping onto each cake. Bake 5 minutes. Cool on racks.
6. Decorate with red and green cherry pieces to resemble holly. Refrigerate until ready to serve.

6½ to 7 dozen cakes

Fattigmann

- 10   egg yolks
- 2   egg whites
- ¾   cup sugar
- ¼   cup brandy
- 1   cup heavy cream
- 5   cups sifted all-purpose flour
- 2   teaspoons ground cardamom
- Lard for deep frying

1. Beat egg yolks, egg whites, sugar, and brandy until very thick. Add cream slowly, stirring well.
2. Sift flour and cardamom together; add about ½ cup at a time to egg mixture, mixing thoroughly after each addition. Wrap and chill overnight.
3. Heat lard to 365°F in a deep saucepan.
4. Roll dough, a small portion at a time, 1/16 inch thick on a floured surface.
5. Using a floured knife or pastry wheel, cut into diamond shapes, 5x2 inches; make a lengthwise slit in the center of each diamond. Pull the tip of one end through each slit and tuck back under itself.
6. Deep fry 1 to 2 minutes, or until golden brown, turning once. Drain and cool.
7. Sprinkle cookies with **confectioners' sugar.** Store in tightly covered containers.

About 6 dozen cookies

Cinnamon Stars

- ⅓   cup plus 1 tablespoon egg whites
- 1   cup confectioners' sugar
- 1   teaspoon grated lemon peel
- ¾   teaspoon ground cinnamon
- 2   cups unblanched almonds, grated

1. Lightly grease 2 cookie sheets, sprinkle with **flour,** and shake off excess; set aside.
2. Using an electric beater, beat egg whites until stiff, not dry, peaks are formed. Add confectioners' sugar gradually, beating 5 minutes at medium speed. Remove ⅓ cup of meringue and set aside.
3. Into remaining meringue, beat the lemon peel and cinnamon. Fold in the almonds.
4. Turn almond mixture onto a pastry canvas sprinkled with **confectioners'** or **granulated sugar.** Gently roll ¼ to ⅜ inch thick. Lightly sprinkle with sugar. Cut with a 2-inch star-shaped cookie cutter dipped in confectioners' sugar.
5. Transfer to cookie sheets; drop about ½ teaspoonful of reserved meringue onto each star and spread out evenly onto points. Set aside in a warm place (about 80°F) 1½ hours.
6. Bake at 375°F 5 minutes.

About 3 dozen cookies

Swedish Sand Tarts

1	cup butter
¼	teaspoon almond extract
¾	cup sugar
1	egg
2	cups sifted all-purpose flour
⅓	cup blanched almonds, finely chopped

1. Cream butter with extract; add sugar gradually, beating until fluffy. Add egg and beat thoroughly.
2. Add flour in fourths, mixing until blended after each addition. Stir in almonds. Chill dough thoroughly.
3. Remove a small portion of dough at a time from refrigerator and, depending upon size of mold, place 1 or 2 teaspoonfuls in each sandbakelse mold (usually available in the housewares section of department stores); press firmly to cover bottom and sides of mold evenly. Set lined molds on cookie sheets.
4. Bake at 375°F 6 to 8 minutes.
5. Immediately invert molds onto a smooth surface; cool slightly.
6. To remove sand tart, hold mold and tap lightly but sharply with back of spoon. Remove molds and cool cookies. Invert and sift Vanilla Confectioners' Sugar (below) over cookies.

About 5 dozen cookies

Vanilla Confectioners' Sugar: Cut a vanilla bean lengthwise, then crosswise, into pieces. Poke pieces into *1 to 2 pounds confectioners' sugar* at irregular intervals. Cover tightly and store. (The longer sugar stands, the richer the flavor.) When necessary, add more sugar. Replace vanilla bean when aroma is gone. Flavor *granulated sugar* this way, also.

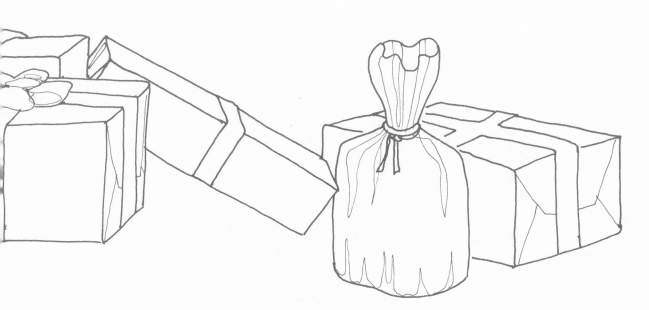

Pepparkakor

1	cup butter
1½	cups sugar
1	egg
1	tablespoon dark corn syrup
2¾	cups all-purpose flour
2	teaspoons baking soda
1	tablespoon cinnamon
2	teaspoons ginger
1	teaspoon ground cloves
	Blanched almonds
	Icing

1. Beat butter in a bowl until softened. Add sugar gradually, creaming well. Add egg and beat thoroughly. Blend in corn syrup.

2. Blend flour, baking soda, and spices; add to creamed mixture gradually, mixing until blended.

3. Chill dough until easy to handle.

4. Using a portion of the chilled dough at a time, roll dough on a lightly floured surface to ⅛-inch thickness. Cut with floured cookie cutters.

5. Transfer cookies to cookie sheets and decorate some with almonds.

6. Bake at 400°F 5 to 7 minutes. Remove immediately to wire racks.

7. Decorate cooled cookies with icing.

About 6 dozen cookies

Icing: Put **1 egg white** and ⅛ **teaspoon almond extract** into a small bowl. Add **2 cups sifted confectioners' sugar** gradually to egg white while mixing; beat until smooth and glossy.

Almond Wreaths

¾ cup butter
½ cup sugar
1 egg
2 cups sifted all-purpose flour
  Egg yolk, slightly beaten
½ cup blanched almonds, finely chopped

1. Cream butter; add sugar gradually, beating until fluffy. Add egg and beat thoroughly.
2. Add flour in fourths, mixing until well blended after each addition. Chill dough thoroughly.
3. Roll one half of dough at a time ¼ inch-thick on a floured surface; cut with 1¾-inch round cutter and cut out centers with a ¾-inch round cutter. (Bake centers for samplers.)
4. Transfer rounds and rings to ungreased cookie sheets. Brush tops with egg yolk and sprinkle with almonds.
5. Bake at 350°F 10 to 15 minutes.

About 6 dozen cookies

Basler Brunsli

1 lb. unblanched almonds, grated* (5 cups)
4 to 4½ oz. (4 to 4½ sq.) unsweetened chocolate, grated*
2½ cups sugar
1 teaspoon ground cinnamon
1 tablespoon kirsch
4 egg whites (about ⅔ cup)

1. Thoroughly blend almonds and chocolate with a mixture of sugar and cinnamon. Drizzle with the kirsch.
2. Beat the egg whites until stiff, not dry, peaks are formed. Blend into nut mixture. Chill thoroughly.
3. Roll a fourth of the mixture at a time ½ inch thick on a lightly sugared surface. Cut with 1¼-inch round cutter. Place on lightly greased cookie sheets.
4. Bake at 300°F 15 minutes. Cool on wire racks.

About 10 dozen cookies

*Blender grating speeds the job.

Brandied Apricot Teacakes

8 ounces dried apricots, chopped
1 package (11 ounces) currants
½ cup boiling water
1 cup apricot brandy
½ cup butter
1½ cups firmly packed light brown sugar
3 eggs
2 cups all-purpose flour
½ teaspoon baking soda
½ teaspoon salt
1 teaspoon allspice
1 teaspoon cinnamon
1 teaspoon cloves
  Confectioners' sugar

1. Put apricots and currants into a bowl; add water and brandy and mix well. Cover and let stand overnight.
2. Beat butter in a large bowl until softened. Add brown sugar gradually, creaming well. Add eggs, one at a time, and beat thoroughly after each addition.
3. Blend flour, baking soda, salt, and spices; add to creamed mixture gradually, mixing well. Blend in fruit mixture.
4. Set midget foil baking cups on baking sheets. Spoon a rounded tablespoonful of mixture into each cup.
5. Bake at 325°F about 30 minutes, or until a wooden pick inserted in cake comes out clean. Remove to wire rack to cool.
6. Before serving, sift confectioners' sugar over cakes.

About 5 dozen teacakes

Note: For smaller teacakes without baking cups, use well-buttered 1¾-inch muffin pan wells. Spoon 1 tablespoon mixture into each well. Bake at 325°F about 20 minutes.

About 7 dozen teacakes.

Anise Form Cookies

2 eggs
1 cup sugar
½ teaspoon grated lemon peel
8 drops anise oil
2 cups sifted all-purpose flour
¼ teaspoon crushed ammonium carbonate (available at your pharmacy)

1. Beat eggs, sugar, lemon peel, and anise oil until very thick.
2. Blend flour and ammonium carbonate; add in fourths to egg-sugar mixture, mixing until blended after each addition.
3. Cover with a clean towel and let stand at room temperature 1 hour.
4. Shape dough into a ball and, on a floured surface, knead lightly with fingertips; roll ¼ inch thick.
5. Press lightly floured springerle rolling pin or mold firmly into dough to make clear designs.
6. Brush dough surface gently with soft brush to remove excess flour; cut the frames apart; cover and let stand 24 hours.
7. Lightly grease cookie sheets; sprinkle entire surface with **anise seed.**
8. Lightly brush back of each frame with water and set on anise seed.
9. Bake at 325°F 8 minutes.
10. When thoroughly cool, store in a tightly covered container 1 to 2 weeks before serving. To soften cookies, store for several days with a piece of apple or orange.

About 4 dozen cookies

Holiday String-Ups

1 cup butter
2 teaspoons vanilla extract
1½ cups sugar
2 eggs
3¼ cups sifted all-purpose flour
1 teaspoon baking powder
½ teaspoon salt
Confectioners' Sugar Icing, page 148

1. Cream butter with extract; add sugar gradually, beating until fluffy. Add eggs, one at a time, beating thoroughly after each addition.
2. Sift flour, baking powder, and salt together; add to creamed mixture in fourths, mixing until blended after each addition. Chill dough thoroughly.
3. Roll a small amount of dough at a time ¼ inch thick on a floured surface; cut into a variety of shapes with cutters. Transfer to ungreased cookie sheets.
4. Insert 1-inch long pieces of paper straws or macaroni into top of each cutout, or press both ends of a piece of colored cord into the dough on the underside of each cutout.
5. Bake at 400°F 6 to 8 minutes.
6. Cool; gently twist out straws, leaving holes for ribbons or cord to be pulled through after decorating.
7. Prepare icing. Color with desired amount of **red** or **green food coloring.** Sprinkle with **decorative sugar.**

About 5 dozen cookies

Note: This versatile dough may be thinly rolled and baked cookies sandwiched together with filling.

Chocolate String-Ups: Follow recipe for Holiday String-Ups. Blend in **2 ounces (2 squares) unsweetened chocolate,** melted and cooled, after the eggs are added. Mix in **1 cup finely chopped pecans** after the last addition of dry ingredients.

German Molasses Cookies

1 cup butter
1¼ cups light molasses
¾ cup firmly packed light brown sugar
4 cups sifted all-purpose flour
1 teaspoon baking soda
1 teaspoon salt
2 teaspoons ground ginger
1 teaspoon ground cinnamon
½ to ¾ teaspoon ground cloves

1. Melt butter in a saucepan; add molasses and brown sugar and heat until sugar is dissolved, stirring occasionally. Pour into a bowl; cool.
2. Sift remaining ingredients together; add to cooled mixture in fourths, mixing until blended after each addition.
3. Turn dough onto a floured surface and knead until easy to handle, using additional flour if necessary.
4. Wrap in moisture-vaporproof material; refrigerate and allow dough to ripen one or two days.
5. Roll one fourth of dough at a time about ⅛ inch thick on a floured surface; cut with a 3-inch round cutter or fancy cutters. Transfer to ungreased cookie sheets.
6. Bake at 350°F about 7 minutes.

About 8 dozen cookies

Note: For gingerbread men, roll dough ¼ inch thick and cut with a gingerbread-man cutter. Bake about 13 minutes.

Kolacky Cookies

1 cup butter
8 oz. cream cheese, softened
¼ teaspoon vanilla extract
2¼ cups sifted all-purpose flour
½ teaspoon salt
Cherry preserves, apricot preserves, or prune filling

1. Cream butter and cream cheese with extract until fluffy.
2. Blend flour and salt; add in fourths to creamed mixture, mixing until blended after each addition. Chill dough thoroughly.
3. Roll dough ¼ inch thick on a floured surface; cut with 2-inch round cutter or fancy-shaped cutters. Transfer to ungreased cookie sheets, make a small indentation in center of each round, and fill with ½ teaspoon preserves.
4. Bake at 350°F 10 to 15 minutes, or until delicately browned.

About 3½ dozen cookies

Fruity Polish Mazurek

2	cups sifted all-purpose flour
1	cup sugar
½	teaspoon salt
½	cup butter or margarine
1	egg
¼	cup half-and-half
1⅔	cups seedless raisins, chopped
1½	cups pitted dates, chopped
1¼	cups dried figs, chopped
1	cup chopped walnuts
⅓	cup sugar
2	eggs
½	cup orange juice
3	tablespoons lemon juice

1. Sift flour, 1 cup sugar, and salt together into a bowl. Cut in butter.
2. Beat egg and cream together and add to flour mixture. Mix lightly with a fork until mixture forms a ball.
3. Spread dough in a greased 15x10x1-inch jelly roll pan.
4. Bake at 350°F about 30 minutes, or until dough is lightly browned around edges.
5. Meanwhile, prepare fruit topping by combining the chopped fruits and walnuts with a mixture of the ⅓ cup sugar, 2 eggs, and fruit juices; mix thoroughly. Spread over partially baked dough in pan.
6. Return to oven and bake 20 minutes.
7. Remove to wire rack; cool. If desired, garnish with **candied fruit** such as candied cherries, candied pineapple, and/or candied orange peel. Cut in 2x1-inch pieces.

About 6 dozen cookies

Scottish Shortbread

2	cups sifted all-purpose flour
6	tablespoons sugar
2	tablespoons cornstarch
¾	cup butter

1. Sift flour, sugar, and cornstarch into a bowl. Cut in butter until mixture becomes a soft dough (requires working beyond the stage when particles are the size of rice kernels).
2. Shape dough into a ball; knead lightly with fingertips until mixture holds together.
3. Roll half of the dough at a time ¼ to ½ inch thick on a floured surface.
4. Cut into 1½x½-inch strips, or use fancy cutters. Place on ungreased cookie sheets.
5. Bake at 350°F 25 to 30 minutes; do not brown.

2½ to 4 dozen cookies

Berlin Wreaths

1	cup butter
½	teaspoon vanilla extract
½	cup sugar
2	uncooked egg yolks
3	hard-cooked egg yolks, sieved
2	cups sifted all-purpose flour

1. Cream butter with extract; add sugar gradually, beating until fluffy.
2. Add uncooked egg yolks, one at a time, beating thoroughly after each addition; mix in hard-cooked egg yolks.
3. Add flour in fourths, mixing until blended after each addition. Chill dough thoroughly.
4. Shape small amounts of dough into strips 4 inches long and ¼ inch thick; the ends of strips should be slightly pointed. Form wreaths on ungreased cookie sheets, overlapping ends of strips about ¼ inch.
5. Brush wreaths with slightly beaten **egg white;** sprinkle lightly with crushed **loaf sugar.**
6. Bake at 350°F 10 to 12 minutes.

About 5 dozen cookies

Lemon Angels

	Red, yellow, and green food coloring
1¾	cups flaked coconut
1	cup butter
1	teaspoon vanilla extract
1½	cups sifted confectioners' sugar
1	egg
2¼	cups all-purpose flour
½	teaspoon baking soda
¼	teaspoon salt
1	tablespoon grated lemon peel

1. To tint coconut, use 3 jars, one for each color. Blend 2 or 3 drops food coloring with a few drops of water in each jar. Put one-third of coconut into each jar; cover and shake vigorously until coconut is evenly tinted. Turn into shallow dishes and set aside.
2. Cream butter with vanilla extract in a bowl. Add confectioners' sugar gradually, creaming well. Add egg and beat thoroughly.
3. Blend flour, baking soda, and salt; add gradually to creamed mixture, mixing well. Stir in lemon peel.
4. Divide dough into thirds and chill until easy to handle.
5. For each third, roll teaspoonfuls of dough in one color of coconut, form balls, and place on ungreased cookie sheets.
6. Bake at 325°F 10 to 12 minutes. Remove immediately to wire racks to cool.

About 8 dozen cookies

Moravian Scotch Cakes

4	cups sifted all-purpose flour
½	cup sugar
2	teaspoons caraway seed
1½	cups butter

1. Combine flour, sugar, and caraway seed in a bowl. Cut in butter until mixture becomes a soft dough (requires working beyond the stage when particles are the size of rice kernels); shape into a ball.
2. Roll a third of dough at a time ¼ inch thick on a floured surface. Cut into 2-inch squares. Transfer to lightly greased cookie sheets.
3. Bake at 325°F about 20 minutes.
4. Cool cookies; spread with **Snowy Icing,** *next page,* and sprinkle with **colored sugar.**

About 3½ dozen cookies

Snowy Icing

1 cup sugar
¼ cup water
Few grains salt
1 egg white
1 teaspoon vanilla extract

1. Mix the sugar, water, and salt in a small saucepan; stir over low heat until sugar is dissolved.
2. Cook without stirring until mixture spins a 2-inch thread (about 230°F) when a small amount is dropped from a spoon.
3. Beat egg white until stiff, not dry, peaks are formed. Continue beating egg white while pouring hot syrup over it in a steady thin stream. After all the syrup is added, continue beating until icing is very thick and forms rounded peaks (holds shape).
4. Blend in extract.

About 2½ cups icing

Sesame Seed Cookies

2 cups sifted all-purpose flour
½ teaspoon baking powder
½ cup sugar
⅔ cup lard
2 eggs
½ cup toasted or untoasted sesame seed*

1. Sift flour, baking powder, and sugar together into a bowl. Cut in lard with a pastry blender until particles are the size of rice kernels. Add 1 egg and mix until a dough is formed. Knead gently until smooth.
2. Form the dough into ½- to ¾-inch balls and flatten until about ¼ inch thick.
3. Separate remaining egg. Beat egg yolk and brush over top of each cookie; dip cookie, brushed side down, into the sesame seed and press the seed gently into the dough.
4. Brush lightly with remaining egg white, slightly beaten. Place on ungreased cookie sheets.
5. Bake at 325°F 12 to 15 minutes.

About 7½ dozen cookies

*To toast, put sesame seed into a pie pan and place in a 300°F oven for about 10 minutes, or until lightly browned; stir occasionally.

Butter Crisps

1 cup butter
3 oz. cream cheese
1 teaspoon vanilla extract
1 cup sugar
1 egg yolk
2¼ cups sifted all-purpose flour
½ teaspoon salt
¼ teaspoon baking powder

1. Cream butter and cream cheese with extract; add sugar gradually, beating until fluffy. Add egg yolk and beat thoroughly.
2. Sift flour, salt, and baking powder together; add in fourths to creamed mixture, mixing until blended after each addition.
3. Following manufacturer's directions, fill a cookie press with dough and form cookies of varied shapes directly onto ungreased cookie sheets.
4. Bake at 350°F 12 to 15 minutes.
5. Cool on wire racks.

About 8 dozen cookies

Note: Dough may be tinted different colors, and before baking, the shapes may be sprinkled with colored sugar or with cinnamon-sugar. Cooled cookies may be decorated with tinted frosting.

Spritz

1	cup butter
1	teaspoon vanilla extract
½	cup sugar
1	egg yolk
2	cups sifted all-purpose flour
½	teaspoon baking powder
¼	teaspoon salt

1. Cream butter with extract; add sugar gradually, beating until fluffy. Add egg yolk and beat thoroughly.
2. Sift flour, baking powder, and salt together; add to creamed mixture in fourths, mixing until blended after each addition.
3. Following manufacturer's directions, fill a cookie press with dough and form cookies of varied shapes directly onto ungreased cookie sheets.
4. Bake at 350°F 12 minutes.

About 5 dozen cookies

Chocolate Spritz: Follow recipe for Spritz. Thoroughly blend **¼ cup boiling water** and **6 tablespoons cocoa;** cool. Mix in after addition of egg yolk.

Nut Spritz: Follow recipe for Spritz. Stir in **½ cup finely chopped nuts** (black walnuts or toasted blanched almonds) after the last addition of dry ingredients.

Chocolate-Tipped Spritz: Follow recipe for Spritz. Dip ends of cooled cookies into Chocolate Glaze (below). If desired, dip into finely chopped **nuts,** crushed **peppermint stick candy,** or **chocolate shot.** Place on wire racks until glaze is set.

Marbled Spritz: Follow recipe for Spritz. Thoroughly blend **2 tablespoons boiling water** and **3 tablespoons cocoa;** cool. After the addition of egg yolk, remove a half of the creamed mixture to another bowl and mix in a half of the dry ingredients. Into remaining half of creamed mixture, stir cocoa mixture; blend in remaining dry ingredients. Shape each half of dough into a roll and cut lengthwise into halves. Press cut surfaces of vanilla and chocolate flavored doughs together before filling cookie press.

Spritz Sandwiches: Spread **chocolate frosting** or **jam** on bottom of some cookies. Cover with unfrosted cookies of same shape to form sandwiches.

Jelly-Filled Spritz: Make slight impression at center of cookie rounds and fill with **¼ teaspoon jelly** or **jam** before baking.

Chocolate Glaze: Partially melt **3 oz. (½ cup) semisweet chocolate pieces** in the top of a double boiler over hot (not simmering) water. Remove from heat and stir until chocolate is melted. Blend in **3 tablespoons butter.**

Holiday Spritz

1	cup butter
½	teaspoon almond extract
½	cup sugar
1	egg
2	cups all-purpose flour

1. Cream butter with almond extract. Add sugar gradually, creaming well. Add egg and beat thoroughly. Add flour gradually, mixing until blended.
2. Chill dough until easy to handle. Chill cookie press.
3. Following manufacturer's directions, fill cookie press with dough and form cookies of varied shapes directly onto cool ungreased cookie sheets. Decorate with **colored sugar** or **multicolored nonpareil decors.**
4. Bake at 350°F 8 to 10 minutes. Remove to wire racks to cool.

8 to 9 dozen cookies

Semisweet Chocolate Spritz: Melt **2 squares (2 ounces) semisweet chocolate** and set aside to cool. Follow recipe for Holiday Spritz; blend chocolate into creamed mixture. Proceed as directed.

Almond Spritz

1¼	cups butter
⅔	cup sugar
3	egg yolks (¼ cup)
¼	cup grated almonds
2½	cups sifted all-purpose flour

1. Cream butter; add sugar gradually, beating until fluffy. Add egg yolks, one at a time, beating thoroughly after each addition.
2. Stir in almonds. Add flour in fourths, mixing until blended after each addition.
3. Following manufacturer's directions, fill a cookie press with dough and form cookies of varied shapes directly onto ungreased cookie sheets.
4. Bake at 375°F 8 to 10 minutes.

About 6 dozen cookies

Bread Crumb Cookies

⅔	cup shortening
1	cup brown sugar
2	eggs, well beaten
½	cup molasses
2½	cups fine bread crumbs
1	cup cake flour
½	teaspoon soda
¼	teaspoon cloves
½	teaspoon cinnamon
1	teaspoon baking powder
	Flour, Milk

1. Cream shortening and sifted sugar thoroughly.
2. Add beaten eggs and molasses.
3. Sift together dry ingredients and add slowly to the liquid mixture. Mix thoroughly.
4. Add enough additional flour to make a stiff dough. Chill and roll thin.
5. Use a simple cookie cutter.
6. Glaze by brushing tops with milk.
7. Bake at 350°F 6 to 8 minutes.

156 cookies of 2-inch diameter

Queenies

1	cup shortening
¾	cup confectioners' sugar
2	cups cake flour
1	cup chopped nuts
½	cup flour
2	tablespoons confectioners' sugar

1. Cream shortening and sugar thoroughly. Add flour and nuts. Blend together.
2. Roll ¼ inch thick on a pastry cloth which has been dusted with a mixture of ½ cup flour and 2 tablespoons sugar.
3. Cut into small fancy shapes with cookie cutters.
4. Arrange on a greased cookie sheet and bake in a hot oven (400°F) 10 minutes.
5. Sprinkle top of cookies with confectioners' sugar as soon as they are removed from the oven.

100 cookies

Variation—Add ¼ teaspoon cinnamon to dough, blend well. Roll, cut and decorate with tiny red cinnamon candies.

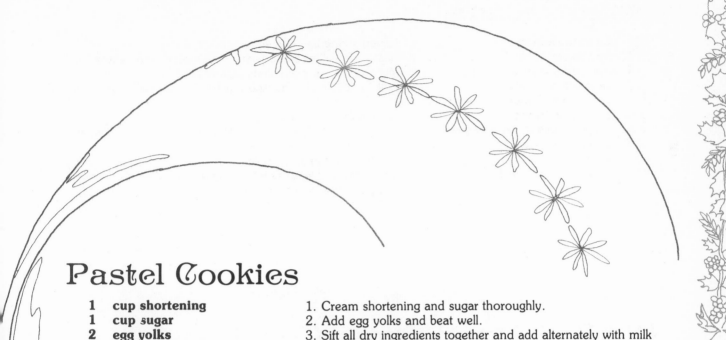

Pastel Cookies

1	cup shortening
1	cup sugar
2	egg yolks
3¼	cups cake flour
1	teaspoon baking powder
¼	teaspoon salt
6	tablespoons milk
	Food colorings

1. Cream shortening and sugar thoroughly.
2. Add egg yolks and beat well.
3. Sift all dry ingredients together and add alternately with milk to the creamed mixture.
4. This foundation makes the following:

Checkerboard: Use ½ of recipe and divide into 2 portions, one portion slightly larger than the other. To the smaller quantity add 1 square of melted chocolate. Divide the white dough into 5 balls of equal size and the chocolate dough into 4 balls of equal size. Shape each ball into a roll 8 inches long, then flatten sides to form rectangle ½ inch thick. Stack on waxed paper: a white roll, a dark roll and then a white roll. The stacked rolls will be 3 squares wide and 3 squares high and the colors will be alternated to make a checkerboard. When stacking the rolls moisten each side before placing the next roll in position. Wrap the resulting cube in waxed paper and chill for at least 3 hours. Slice ⅓ inch thick and arrange on a well greased cookie sheet. Bake at 375°F 9 minutes.

80 cookies

Pinwheels: Use ¼ of the recipe and divide this into 2 portions. Color as desired. Any 2 colors can be used; however it is preferable to have one dark and one light, such as the chocolate and white combination for checkerboards. Roll out the dark layer first making it almost ½ inch thick. Moisten the surface of the dark dough, place the light dough on top of the dark and press together lightly. Moisten the top of the light layer and with the aid of a sheet of waxed paper roll tightly into a long roll. Chill thoroughly for at least 3 hours and slice about ⅛ inch thick. Arrange on a well greased cookie sheet and bake at 375°F 9 minutes.

50 cookies

Ribbon Cookies: Use last ¼ of recipe and divide into 3 portions. Color each differently. Roll out the doughs about ⅓ inch thick, cut in 2-inch strips and stack 2 inches high alternating colors. Trim sides, press together slightly, wrap in waxed paper and chill. Slice ⅛ inch thick, arrange on a greased cookie sheet and bake at 375°F 9 minutes.

50 cookies

Lemon Snaps

⅓	cup shortening
1	cup sugar
5	egg yolks or 2 whole eggs
3	tablespoons milk
1½	teaspoons lemon extract
3⅔	cups cake flour
2½	teaspoons baking powder
¼	teaspoon soda
½	teaspoon salt
	Egg for glaze, Milk

1. Cream shortening and sugar.
2. Beat eggs well and add with the milk and lemon extract.
3. Mix and sift dry ingredients and add. Chill.
4. Roll ⅛ inch thick. Cut and brush tops with egg diluted with milk.
5. Bake in moderate oven (375°F) 10 minutes.

150 cookies 2½-inch diameter

Note: If desired top each cookie with ½ almond before brushing with diluted egg. Decorate with narrow strips of candied ginger, pine apple, citron or lemon peel.

Old-Fashioned Sugar Cookies

1	cup shortening
1	cup sugar
2	eggs, beaten
2	teaspoons vanilla
1	cup sour cream
5	cups cake flour
2	teaspoons baking powder
1¼	teaspoons salt
1	teaspoon soda

1. Cream shortening and sugar.
2. Add eggs and vanilla to sour cream.
3. Sift together the flour, baking powder, salt and soda and add alternately with the liquid to shortening and sugar mixture. Chill thoroughly.
4. Roll out on pastry cloth ¼ inch thick. Cut with large cutter, sprinkle with sugar and press in lightly.
5. Bake in moderate oven 375°F 15 minutes.

100 2½-inch cookies

Honey Orange Crisps

¾	cup shortening
½	cup sugar
1	egg, beaten
½	cup honey
1½	teaspoons ginger
2	tablespoons orange juice
½	teaspoon orange extract
3	cups cake flour

1. Cream shortening and sugar together. Add egg, honey and ginger, mixing until smooth.
2. Mix in orange juice and extract.
3. Sift flour and add slowly, beating well between each addition. Chill thoroughly.
4. Roll out very thin on a lightly-floured pastry cloth and cut with various shaped cookie cutters.
5. Bake on ungreased cookie sheet in moderate oven 350°F 8 to 10 minutes.

Approximately 10 dozen 2-inch cookies

Note: Sprinkle ground fresh coconut over the top of the unbaked cut-out to give attractive flavor, or frost with Cream Cheese Spread, top with candied peel.

Stone Jar Ginger Cookies

¾ cup shortening
1½ cups molasses
5 tablespoons boiling water
4 cups cake flour
2 teaspoons soda
¼ teaspoon salt
1½ teaspoons ginger
½ teaspoon cinnamon

1. Cream shortening, add molasses and water and blend.
2. Sift the dry ingredients and add to mixture.
3. The resulting dough is very soft and must be chilled overnight.
4. Roll out ⅛ inch thick on a well-floured pastry cloth. Use any shape cutter.
5. Bake at 375°F 12 minutes.

144 cookies 2-inch diameter

Spicy Ginger Crunchies

2¼ cups sifted all-purpose flour
2 teaspoons baking soda
1 teaspoon salt
1 teaspoon ground cinnamon
¾ teaspoon ground ginger
½ teaspoon ground cloves
¾ cup butter
1 teaspoon vanilla extract
1 cup sugar
1 egg
¼ cup molasses

1. Sift flour, baking soda, salt, and spices together; set aside.
2. Cream butter with extract; gradually add sugar, beating until light and fluffy. Add egg and molasses; beat thoroughly.
3. Gradually add dry ingredients to creamed mixture, mixing until blended. Chill several hours.
4. Shape dough into ¾-inch balls, roll in *sugar* and place 2 inches apart on greased cookie sheets.
5. Bake at 375°F 7 to 8 minutes.
6. Immediately remove to wire racks to cool.

6 to 7 Dozen Cookies

Gingersnaps

1	cup shortening
1	cup sugar
⅔	cup hot coffee
⅔	cup molasses
5	cups cake flour
1	teaspoon salt
1	teaspoon soda
2	teaspoons ginger
1	teaspoon cloves
1	teaspoon cinnamon

1. Cream shortening and sugar thoroughly.
2. Add hot coffee to molasses and add to creamed mixture.
3. Sift dry ingredients together.
4. Add gradually to liquid mixture. Chill thoroughly.
5. Roll out on a pastry cloth ⅛ inch thick, cut out and bake in a moderate oven 350°F 17 minutes.

14 dozen 2-inch cookies

Desserts

Holiday Bread Pudding

3 cups milk

4 cups bread cubes (5 to 6 slices)

3 tablespoons melted butter or margarine

½ cup (3 oz.) mixed candied fruits

½ cup (about 3 oz.) golden raisins

½ cup (about 2 oz.) coarsely chopped black walnuts

10 maraschino cherries, quartered and well drained

3 eggs, slightly beaten

½ cup sugar

½ teaspoon nutmeg

½ teaspoon cinnamon

½ teaspoon allspice

1. Butter a shallow 2-qt. casserole.
2. Scald milk.
3. Meanwhile, toast bread slices until very crisp.
4. Cut toast into ½-in. cubes; put into casserole. Turning cubes lightly with a fork, drizzle over butter.
5. Add candied fruits, raisins, black walnuts, and cherries gradually and mix thoroughly with fork. Set aside.
6. Blend eggs, sugar, nutmeg, cinnamon and allspice. Add milk gradually, stirring constantly and vigorously. Pour over bread cube mixture; turn with fork to blend well.
7. Bake at 325°F 35 to 40 min., or until a metal knife comes out clean when inserted in pudding halfway between center and edge.
8. Meanwhile, prepare Custard Sauce (below).
9. Serve pudding warm with warm custard sauce and sprinkle with nutmeg.
10. Serve immediately.

7 or 8 servings

Custard Sauce: Scald **2 cups milk.** Beat 2 eggs slightly and blend in **¼ cup sugar** and **⅛ teaspoon salt.** Gradually pour milk into egg mixture, stirring vigorously at first; strain through a fine sieve into top of double boiler. Cook over boiling water, stirring constantly and rapidly, until mixture coats a metal spoon. Remove from water at once; blend in **1 teaspoon vanilla extract** and ½ **teaspoon almond extract.**

New Orleans Holiday Pudding

1½ pts. heavy cream
5 cups water
1¼ cups (about ½ lb.) prunes
1 cup (about 6 oz.) dried apricots
1½ cups (about 7½ oz.) golden raisins
1 lb. (about 2¼ cups) candied cherries
⅓ cup (about 2 oz.) diced candied citron
⅓ cup (about 2 oz.) diced candied lemon peel
1 cup sugar
1 teaspoon cinnamon
1 teaspoon nutmeg
1 teaspoon allspice
1 cup orange juice
3 tablespoons brandy
1½ cups (about 6 oz.) walnuts
1½ cups cold reserved prune-apricot liquid
3 env. unflavored gelatin

1. Set out a 9- or 10-in. tubed pan and a 3-qt. saucepan with a cover.
2. Chill in refrigerator a bowl, rotary beater and heavy cream.
3. Meanwhile, pour 3 cups water into the saucepan.
4. Add prunes and apricots to the water. Bring to boiling; cover and simmer about 20 min., or until fruit is tender.
5. Bring 2 cups water to boiling in a small saucepan.
6. Add raisins and bring water again to boiling.
7. Drain raisins and put into a large bowl with cherries, citron, and lemon peel. Set fruit mixture aside.
8. Turn prune-apricot mixture into colander or large sieve to drain. Reserve liquid in a measuring cup (add water if needed to yield 1½ cups liquid); set aside to cool. Pit prunes.
9. Force prune-apricot mixture through sieve or food mill into the saucepan to make a puree. Stir in a mixture of sugar, cinnamon, nutmeg and allspice until sugar is dissolved.
10. Blend into candied fruit mixture with orange juice and brandy. Cover and set aside for about 1½ hrs., stirring occasionally.
11. Coarsely chop walnuts and set aside.
12. Pour reserved prune-apricot liquid into a heavy saucepan. Sprinkle gelatin evenly over liquid.
13. Set saucepan over low heat and stir constantly until gelatin is completely dissolved. Blend the dissolved gelatin into the fruit mixture. Mix in the chopped walnuts. Set mixture in refrigerator while whipping cream.
14. Pour one third of chilled heavy cream into the chilled bowl. Beat with the chilled rotary beater until cream is of medium consistency (piles softly). Turn whipped cream onto fruit-gelatin mixture.
15. Beat remaining heavy cream as above and turn onto previously whipped cream. Gently fold together, blending thoroughly. Carefully spoon into prepared pan. Chill in refrigerator until firm. Unmold onto a large serving plate.
16. This dessert will keep for several days in the refrigerator.

20 to 24 servings, depending upon size of tubed pan

For Festive Topping—Cover bottom of pan with chopped nuts. Reserve 12 cherries and arrange in clusters of three, moving nuts to let cherries touch bottom of pan. When spooning mixture over nuts and cherries, gently press mixture over nuts to cover entirely.

Nesselrode Pudding I

1½	doz. single ladyfingers (or use sponge cake cut in 4x¾x½-in. pieces)
2	egg yolks
½	cup sugar
¼	cup (2 oz.) sherry
1¾	cups chilled heavy cream (beat only one half at a time)
⅓	cup confectioners' sugar
1¼	teaspoons vanilla extract
2	egg whites
⅛	teaspoon salt
1	jar (10 oz.) Nesselrode mixture (about 1¼ cups)

1. Set out a 9x5x3-in. loaf pan. Put a medium-size bowl and a rotary beater into refrigerator to chill.
2. Set out ladyfingers. Line sides of the loaf pan with the ladyfingers and set aside.
3. Put egg yolks into a large bowl and beat until very thick and lemon-colored.
4. Add sugar gradually, beating well after each addition.
5. Add sherry gradually, beating constantly.
6. Set egg yolk mixture aside.
7. Using the chilled bowl and beater, beat heavy cream until cream is of medium consistency (piles softly).
8. Beat confectioners' sugar and vanilla extract into whipped cream with a few final strokes. Set in refrigerator while beating egg whites.
9. Using clean beater, beat egg whites and salt until stiff, not dry, peaks are formed.
10. Blend Nesselrode mixture into the egg yolk mixture.
11. Spread the whipped cream and egg whites over the egg yolk mixture and gently fold together. Turn mixture into the prepared pan and spread evenly.
12. Freeze until firm, about 12 hrs.

About 8 servings

Note: If desired, omit ladyfingers and freeze mixture in refrigerator trays.

Nesselrode Pudding II

8	cook chestnuts, broken into small pieces
	Maraschino syrup
3	cups milk
½	teaspoon salt
1½	cups sugar
5	egg yolks, beaten
2	cups heavy cream, whipped
¼	cup pineapple juice
1½	cups cooked chestnuts, pressed through a sieve
½	cup chopped candied fruit
¼	cup seedless raisins

1. Soak broken chestnut pieces overnight in maraschino syrup.
2. Scald milk in top of double boiler.
3. Beat salt, sugar and egg yolks together and add milk gradually, stirring constantly. Return to double boiler and cook until thickened, stirring constantly.
4. Strain, cool and add whipped cream, pineapple juice and chestnut puree. Turn half of mixture in mold or freezing tray of refrigerator.
5. To the remaining half, add candied fruit, raisins and broken chestnut pieces. Fill mold or tray with this mixture and freeze.
6. When firm, unmold and serve with whipped cream flavored with maraschino syrup and small pieces of cooked chestnuts.

Serves 8

Note: The maraschino syrup, pineapple juice and seedless raisins may be omitted.

Nesselrode Pudding III

2	egg yolks
½	cup sugar
⅓	cup confectionrs' sugar
1¼	teaspoons vanilla extract
1¾	cups heavy cream, whipped
2	egg whites
⅛	teaspoon salt
1	jar (10 oz.) Nesselrode mixture

1. Beat egg yolks with sugar until very thick.
2. Blend confectioners' sugar and extract into whipped cream.
3. Beat egg whites with salt until stiff, not dry, peaks are formed.
4. Blend Nesselrode mixture into egg yolk mixture. Spread whipped cream and egg whites over egg yolk mixture; gently fold together. Spoon into a 1½-quart mold or refrigerator trays. Freeze until firm.
5. If desired, garnish with nut and maraschino cherry halves.

8 servings

Frozen Christmas Pudding

1½	cups macaroon crumbs (about 14 small macaroons, crushed)
½	cup chopped pecans
½	cup chopped pitted dates
¼	cup chopped candied pineapple
¼	cup chopped candied orange peel
1¼	teaspoons grated lemon peel
¼	teaspoon ground cinnamon
¼	teaspoon ground nutmeg
8	marshmallows, quartered
¼	cup orange juice
¼	cup sugar
1	cup heavy cream, whipped

1. Combine crumbs, pecans, dates, pineapple, orange and lemon peels, cinnamon, and nutmeg in a bowl; set aside.
2. Heat marshmallows, orange juice, and sugar together in the top of a double boiler over boiling water until marshmallows are melted, stirring occasionally. Blend into fruit mixture. Fold in whipped cream.
3. Put 10 paper baking cups, 2¼x1¼ inches, into refrigerator trays or muffin-pan wells. Spoon mixture into cups; freeze until firm.
4. When ready to serve, garnish each with a holly spray formed with red cinnamon candies and pieces of green gumdrops.

10 servings

Note: If macaroons are moist, dry and toast them slightly in a 325°F oven before crushing.

Swedish Christmas Porridge

6	cups milk
1	cup rice
3	tablespoons sugar
½	teaspoon salt
1	whole blanched almond
	Cool milk
	Sugar
	Cinnamon

1. Put milk, rice, sugar and salt into the top of a double boiler. (The Rice Industry no longer considers it necessary to wash rice before cooking.)
2. Cover and cook over simmering water 2½ to 3 hrs., or until rice is entirely soft when a kernel is pressed between fingers and mixture is quite thick. Remove cover for last 10 min. if mixture is not thick enough.
3. Mix in almond just before serving.
4. Serve with cool milk, sugar and cinnamon or with fruit sauce.

6 servings

Steamed Pumpkin Pudding

1¼ cups fine dry crumbs
½ cup sifted all-purpose flour
1 cup lightly packed brown sugar
1 teaspoon baking powder
½ teaspoon baking soda
½ teaspoon salt
½ teaspoon ground cinnamon
½ teaspoon ground cloves
2 eggs, fork beaten
1½ cpus canned pumpkin
½ cup cooking or salad oil
½ cup undiluted evaporated milk
Lemon Zest Creme

1. Combine bread crumbs, flour, brown sugar, baking powder, baking soda, salt, cinnamon, and cloves in a large bowl. Set aside.
2. Beat eggs and remaining ingredients together. Add to dry ingredients; mix until blended.
3. Turn into a well greased 1½-quart mold. Cover tightly with a greased cover, or tie greased aluminum foil tightly over mold.
4. Steam about 3 hours (see below).
5. Remove pudding from steamer and unmold onto a serving plate. Decorate the plate with drained *cinnamon-apple rings, whipped cream,* and *sugar cubes* soaked with *lemon extract.* Immediately ignite the sugar cubes. Accompany with a bowl of Lemon Zest Creme.

One 2¼-Pound Pudding

Lemon Zest Creme: Cream ½ **cup butter or margarine** with ½ **teaspoon ground ginger** and ¼ **teaspoon salt** in a bowl. Add *two cups confectioners' sugar* gradually, beating constantly. Add ¼ **cup lemon juice** gradually, continuing to beat until blended. Mix in ½ **cup chopped nuts.**

About 2½ cups Creme

How To Steam Pudding

1. Use a mold or tin can large enough that the batter will fill mold one half to two thirds.
2. Grease the mold and the cover. If mold has no cover, use aluminum foil, parchment paper, or a double thickness of waxed paper tied on tightly.
3. Place filled mold on trivet in a steamer or deep kettle with a tight-fitting cover.
4. Pour boiling water into the steamer to no more than one half the height of the mold. Add more boiling water during the steaming period, if necessary.
5. Tightly cover steamer.
6. Keep water boiling gently at all times.
7. If pudding is to be stored several days before serving, unmold onto wire rack. Let stand until cold. Wrap in foil and store in a cool place.
8. To resteam, heat pudding in a double boiler over simmering water or set foil-wrapped pudding on a trivet in steamer over a small amount of boiling water. Steam thoroughly.

Molded Holiday Pudding

3	cups boiling water
1¼	cups prunes
1	cup dried apricots
1	cup sugar
1	teaspoon ground cinnamon
1	teaspoon ground nutmeg
1	teaspoon ground allspice
1¼	cups orange juice
3	env. unflavored gelatin
1½	cups golden raisins, plumped
2¼	cups candied cherries
⅓	cup diced candied citron
⅓	cup diced candied lemon peel
1½	cups walnuts, coarsely chopped
3	env. (2 oz. each) dessert topping mix, or 3 cups heavy cream, whipped

1. Pour boiling water over prunes and apricots in a saucepan. Return to boiling, cover, and simmer about 45 minutes, or until fruit is tender. Drain and reserve 1 cup liquid. Set liquid aside until cold. Remove and discard prune pits.
2. Force prunes and apricots through food mill or sieve into a large bowl. Stir in a mixture of the sugar, cinnamon, nutmeg, and allspice, mixing until sugar is dissolved. Blend in the orange juice and mix thoroughly.
3. Soften gelatin in the 1 cup reserved liquid in a small saucepan. Stir over low heat until gelatin is dissolved. Stir into fruit-spice mixture. Chill until mixture is slightly thickened, stirring occasionally.
4. Blend raisins, cherries, citron, lemon peel, and walnuts into gelatin mixture.
5. Prepare the dessert topping according to package directions, or whip the cream. Gently fold into fruit mixture, blending thoroughly. Turn into 9- or 10-inch tubed pan. Chill until firm.
6. Unmold onto chilled serving plate.

20 to 24 servings

Note: If a less sweet pudding is desired, decrease sugar to ½ cup. To develop flavor of dessert, prepare 2 to 4 days in advance of serving.

Macaroon Mousse

½	cup butter or margarine
1	teaspoon vanilla extract
¾	cup sugar
4	eggs, well beaten
1¾	cups fine almond macaroon crumbs
1	teaspoon unflavored gelatin
¼	cup cold water
1	cup icy cold water
1	cup instant nonfat dry milk
2	tablespoons lemon juice

1. Cream butter with extract until softened. Gradually beat in the sugar until thoroughly blended. Add the eggs in thirds, beating thoroughly until light and fluffy.
2. Add the macaroon crumbs and beat at high speed with electric mixer about 5 minutes.
3. Soften gelatin in ¼ cup cold water. Stir over low heat until dissolved. Set aside to cool.
4. Mix the 1 cup cold water and dry milk in a bowl. Beat until soft peaks are formed, 3 to 4 minutes. Very gradually add the dissolved gelatin, beating constantly. Add the lemon juice and beat until stiff peaks are formed, 3 to 4 minutes.
5. Fold macaroon mixture into whipped milk and turn into a 1½-quart mold which has been rinsed with cold water. Freeze overnight or until firm.
6. Unmold onto a chilled serving plate and garnish plate as desired. Serve immediately.

8 to 10 servings

Note: If macaroons are moist, dry and toast them slightly in a low oven befor crushing. Crumbs may be prepared in an electric blender, crushing a portion at a time.

Cheese and Fruit

Bel Paese—a soft, mild cheese of the North and often served with ripe cherries or plums.

Gorgonzola—the most popular of the dessert cheeses, a creamy, tangy cheese veined with green mold; often served with sliced fresh pears, ripe Italian bananas, or quartered apples.

Stracchino—a tangy goat's milk cheese of Milan which may be accompanied by any number of fruits including peaches and grapes.

Provolone—whether the pear-shape Provolone, round Provolette, or sausage-shape Provolone salami, this is a favorite when accompanied by quartered apples and small slices of watermelon.

Caciocavallo—typifying a tapering beet root, this smoked cheese is delicious when served as a dessert with small crackers.

Ricotta—a soft, bland pot cheese often used in baking, this can be served as a dessert when accompanied by berries and figs.

Holiday Pears

8	**medium canned pear halves (17-oz. can)**
1	**cup reserved pear syrup**
1	**teaspoon grated lemon peel**
2	**tablespoons lemon juice**
½	**cup currant or cranberry jelly**

1. Set out an 11x7x2-in. baking dish.
2. Drain pear halves, reserving syrup. Place in the baking dish, cut-side up.
3. Mix pear syrup, lemon peel and lemon juice in a bowl. Pour over pears. Place currant or cranberry jelly in core cavities.
4. Bake at 375°F 8 to 10 min., or until jelly melts.
5. Beat **1 pkg. (3 oz.) cream cheese** with **3 tablespoons milk** until light and fluffy. Spoon onto each serving.

4 servings

Baked Apples with Red Wine

8	apples, cored
	Cherry or strawberry
	preserves
½	cup sugar
½	teaspoon mace or nutmeg
1	cup red wine
½	teaspoon vanilla extract

1. Place apples in a buttered casserole or baking dish. Fill each with preserves.
2. Blend sugar and mace; stir in wine and vanilla extract. Pour over apples. Cover.
3. Bake at 350°F 1 hour.
4. Chill 2 to 4 hours before serving.

8 servings

Twelve-Fruit Compote

3	cups water
1	pound mixed dried fruits including pears, figs, apricots, and peaches
1	cup pitted prunes
½	cup raisins or currants
1	cup pitted sweet cherries
2	apples, peeled and sliced or 6 ounces dried apple slices
½	cup cranberries
1	cup sugar
1	lemon, sliced
6	whole cloves
2	cinnamon sticks (3 inches each)
1	orange
½	cup grapes, pomegranate seeds, or pitted plums
½	cup fruit-flavored brandy

1. Combine water, mixed dried fruits, prunes, and raisins in a 6-quart kettle. Bring to boiling. Cover; simmer about 20 minutes, or until fruits are plump and tender.
2. Add cherries, apples, and cranberries. Stir in sugar, lemon, and spices. Cover; simmer 5 minutes.
3. Grate peel of orange; reserve. Peel and section orange, removing all skin and white membrane. Add to fruits in kettle.
4. Stir in grapes and brandy. Bring just to boiling. Remove from heat. Stir in orange peel. Cover; let stand 15 minutes.

About 12 servings

Marzipan (Marcepan)

1 **pound blanched almonds**
1 **pound confectioners' sugar**
2 **tablespoons orange water or rose water**
Food coloring
Decorations (colored sugar, dragees, or chocolate shot)

1. Grind almonds very fine. Combine in a saucepan with sugar and flavoring. Cook until mixture leaves side of pan.
2. Roll almond mixture on flat surface to ½-inch thickness. Cut out small heart shapes. Or, shape into small fruits or vegetables.
3. Paint with appropriate food coloring or coat as desired, for example, with red sugar for "strawberries" and cocoa for "potatoes." Decorate with dragees or chocolate shot. Place on waxed paper to dry 2 hours.

2 pounds

Fruit-Nut Candy Squares

1 **cup (about ⅓ lb.) dried figs**
1 **cup (about 6 oz.) pitted dates**
1 **cup (about ⅓ lb.) dried apricots**
½ **cup (about 2 oz.) nuts**
½ **cup moist flaked coconut**
2 **teaspoons grated orange peel**
3 **tablespoons orange juice**
½ **teaspoon cinnamon**
Confectioners' sugar

1. Lightly grease an 8-in. square pan.
2. Rinse figs, dates and apricots and put through coarse blade of food chopper.
3. Coarsely chop nuts.
4. Combine fruits and nuts with coconut and a mixture of orange peel, orange juice and cinnamon.
5. Mix well. Turn into pan and press evenly over bottom. Chill well in refrigerator.
6. Sprinkle with confectioners' sugar.
7. Cut into 1-in. squares. Remove with flexible spatula.

64 squares

Sesame Seed Candy (Pasteli)

½   cup honey
2   cups sugar
½   cup water
3   cups sesame seed, toasted

1. Blend honey, sugar, and water in a heavy skillet. Cook over low heat, stirring frequently. Bring to a firm ball state, 250°F on a candy thermometer (syrup will be a light gold color). Stir in sesame seed.

2. Spread in a buttered 12x8x1½-inch pan. Break into pieces.

2 to 3 dozen pieces depending on size

Christmas Candy Balls

2   medium potatoes, scrubbed (do not pare)
1   cup sugar
1   teaspoon vanilla extract
2   cups chopped pecans
1   cup confectioners' sugar
1   teaspoon ground cinnamon
    Candied red or green cherries, cut in halves

1. Cook potatoes in their skins, peel, press through ricer or food mill. Mix in sugar, vanilla extract, and nuts. Chill.

2. Form little balls; coat them with confectioners' sugar mixed with cinnamon. Put into small fluted paper cups and garnish with cherry halves.

3. Store in refrigerator until ready to serve.

About 2 dozen balls

Snowballs Adrift

1   cup moist shredded coconut
1   qt. ice cream

1. Ice cream of any desired flavor may be used for snowballs. It must be firm before shaping balls.

2. Spread coconut in a chilled shallow pan.

3. With a scoop, rinsed each time in hot water, quickly form 6 to 8 balls of ice cream.

4. After forming each ball, roll immediately in the coconut. Place snowballs in chilled refrigerator tray and cover with waxed paper. Before serving, spoon chocolate syrup into individual dishes and in each one float a snowball.

6 to 8 servings

Christmas Squares

Almond Paste

1½	cups ground almonds
1⅔	cups confectioners' sugar
2	egg whites
2	oz. candied cherries
2	oz. candied orange peel
2	oz. candied lemon peel
4	oz. semi-sweet chocolate
2	oz. coconut flakes

1. Make almond paste. Mix ground almonds and confectioners' sugar, then add egg whites and blend until smooth. Mix in candied fruit.
2. Roll out almond paste to a stick. Flatten it on four sides so that each side is about 2″. Chill.
3. Cut the stick into slices. Melt the chocolate over a double boiler and brush on the slices. Sprinkle the coconut flakes on top. Chill again.

The Hedgehog

2	batches of almond paste (see Christmas squares)
1	cup hazelnuts, coarsley chopped
1	cup seedless raisins, coarsley chopped
4	oz. semi-sweet chocolate
4	oz. slivered almonds
1	red cherry
2	hazelnuts

1. Mix the almond paste and hazelnuts. Add raisins and mix well.
2. Shape the almond paste to look like a hedgehog. Chill.
3. Melt the chocolate in the top of a double boiler and brush all over the hedgehog.
4. Decorate with slivered almonds for quills. Use a red cherry for the nose and 2 whole hazelnuts dotted with chocolate for the eyes. Chill before serving.

Christmas Balls

3	cups almond paste (see Christmas Squares)
2	lbs. almonds
1	box paper candy cups
6	oz. semi-sweet chocolate

1. Work almond paste until smooth. Roll paste in small balls and work a whole almond into the center of each. Place in paper candy cups.
2. Melt chocolate in the top of a double boiler and pour 1 tbs. over each cut. Let them set.

A variation is to divide the almond paste into 3 parts. Mix yellow, red and green food coloring into the almond paste. Roll into small balls and place in paper cups. Decorate with hazelnuts or walnuts.

Kicki's Best Caramels

1 cup heavy cream
2 cups sugar
3 oz. brown sugar
3 oz. molasses
3 oz. unsweetened cocoa

1. In a heavy saucepan mix all ingredients. Bring mixture to a boil while stirring with a wooden spoon. Simmer for 20 minutes stirring occassionally. Test when a drop of the mixture sets in cold water the mixture is ready. The drop should be easy to form into a ball.
2. Pour the mixture into a greased baking pan and let it stand for a while. Cut the mixture into squares before it has set and wrap in greaseproof paper.

Cream Puff or Choux Paste

1 cup hot water
½ cup butter
1 tablespoon sugar
½ teaspoon salt
1 cup all-purpose flour
4 eggs

1. Put hot water, butter, sugar, and salt into a saucepan and bring to a rolling boil.
2. Add the flour all at one time. Beat vigorously with a wooden spoon until mixture leaves sides of pan and forms a smooth ball. Remove from heat.
3. Add eggs, one at a time, beating until smooth after each addition. Continue beating until mixture is thick and smooth.
4. Dough may be shaped and baked at once, or wrapped in waxed paper and stored in refrigerator overnight.
5. Complete as directed in the following variation.

1 Dozen Large or 4 Dozen Miniature Puffs or Eclairs

Cream Puff Christmas Tree: Prepare recipe for Cream Puff or Choux Paste. Force dough through a pastry bag and tube, or drop by spoonfuls 2 inches apart onto lightly greased baking sheets. Bake at 425°F 20 minutes, or until golden brown. Turn off oven. Prick puffs with a fork and return to oven for 20 minutes. Remove puffs to wire racks and cool completely. Cut off tops of puffs. Spoon about 3 tablespoons *Eggnog Pineapple Filling (below),* into each shell. Replace tops. On a serving plate. arrange puffs to form a tree.

18 to 24 Cream Puffs

Eggnog Pineapple Filling

1½ tablespoons cornstarch
2 tablespoons cold water
3 cups dairy eggnog
½ teaspoon vanilla extract
1 can (8½ oz.) crushed pineapple, well drained
1 cup quartered maraschino cherries
¼ cup flaked coconut

1. Mix a blend of the cornstarch and water and eggnog in a heavy saucepan. Stirring constantly, bring rapidly to boiling. Cook and stir 2 to 3 minutes. Remove from heat.
2. Immediately turn into a chilled bowl; do not scrape pan. Mix in remaining ingredients. Cool over ice and water, stirring occasionally. Use to fill cream puffs.

About 3½ cups filling

Pots de Creme Chocolat

2 cups whipping cream
1 tablespoon sugar
4 ounces sweet chocolate, melted
6 egg yolks, beaten
1½ teaspoons vanilla extract

1. Heat the cream and sugar together in the top of a double boiler over simmering water until cream is scalded. Add the melted chocolate and stir until blended. Pour mixture into beaten egg yolks, beating constantly until blended. Stir in vanilla extract.
2. Strain through a fine sieve into 8 small earthenware pots or custard cups. Set pots in a pan of hot water.
3. Bake at 325°F 20 minutes. (Mixture will become thicker upon cooling.)
4. Set cups on wire rack to cool; chill thoroughly.

8 servings

Creme Brulee

4 egg yolks, slightly beaten
¼ cup sugar
2 cups whipping cream, scalded
2 teaspoons vanilla extract
½ cup firmly packed brown sugar

1. Combine egg yolks with sugar; blend thoroughly. Gradually add hot cream, stirring until sugar is dissolved. Strain into a 1-quart baking dish.
2. Blend in vanilla extract. Place baking dish in a shallow pan with hot water and bake at 325°F 50 minutes, or until a knife inserted in custard comes out clean.
3. Remove from oven and set baking dish on wire rack to cool; chill thoroughly.
4. Before serving, sift brown sugar evenly over top. Place under broiler with top a least 5 inches from heat; broil until sugar is melted. Watch carefully so sugar will not burn.
5. Cool and refrigerate until ready to serve.

About 6 servings

Trifle

Pound cake
½ cup brandy or rum
¼ cup sugar
1 envelope unflavored gelatin
⅛ teaspoon salt
5 egg yolks
1¾ cups milk
1 teaspoon vanilla extract
3 egg whites
¼ cup sugar
¼ cup chilled whipping cream, whipped

1. Cut pound cake into 1-inch pieces. Arrange in a layer over bottom of a 2-quart shallow casserole. Pour brandy over cake pieces. Set aside.
2. Combine ¼ cup sugar, gelatin, and salt in the top of a double boiler; blend thoroughly. Beat egg yolks with milk in a bowl until thoroughly blended. Combine with the gelatin mixture in top of double boiler.
3. Set over boiling water and cook, stirring occasionally about 5 minutes, or until the gelatin is completely dissolved. Remove from heat and stir in vanilla extract. Chill until mixture mounds slightly when dropped from a spoon; stir occasionally.
4. Beat the egg whites until frothy. Add ¼ cup sugar gradually, beating thoroughly after each addition. Continue to beat until stiff peaks are formed.
5. Spread egg whites and whipped cream over gelatin mixture and gently fold together. Turn into casserole. Chill until firm.
6. When ready to serve, garnish with **candied cherries, slivered almonds,** and **pieces of angelica.** If desired, garnish with a border of sweetened whipped cream forced through a pastry bag and star decorating tube.

About 12 servings

Chafing Dish Oeufs a la Neige

Meringues:
3 egg whites (at room temperature)
⅛ teaspoon salt
6 tablespoons sugar
¼ teaspoon vanilla extract

Custard:
6 egg yolks
¼ cup sugar
⅛ teaspoon salt
2½ cup milk
1½ teaspoons vanilla extract
Grated orange peel
Strawberries, sliced

1. Pour hot water to a depth of 2 inches in water pan of chafing dish. Heat to simmering.
2. To make meringues, beat egg whites and salt in a small bowl until frothy. Gradually beat in sugar, 1 tablespoon at a time. Continue to beat until stiff peaks form, beating in vanilla extract with last few strokes.
3. Drop meringue by heaping tablespoonfuls onto simmering water, poaching 6 at a time. Cover, and poach meringues 3 to 5 minutes, or until puffed and slightly dry to the touch. Remove from water using a slotted spoon and place in blazer pan.
4. Remove some of the poaching water so blazer pan will not touch water when set in place. Keep water warm.
5. To make custard, beat egg yolks in a heavy 2-quart saucepan. Stir in sugar and salt. Gradually stir in milk. Place over low heat and cook until custard coats a metal spoon, stirring constantly. Stir in vanilla extract.
6. Pour custard around meringues in blazer pan, allowing meringues to float. Sprinkle orange peel over meringues and garnish with strawberries.
7. Place blazer pan over warm water. Serve dessert warm; do not overheat or custard will curdle.

6 servings

Chocolate-Mocha Cream Pudding

2 ounces (2 squares) unsweetened chocolate
1 cup double-strength coffee
2/3 cup sugar
1/4 cup flour
1/4 teaspoon salt
1 cup milk
3 egg yolks, slightly beaten
2 tablespoons butter or margarine
2 teaspoons vanilla extract

1. Heat chocolate and coffee together over low heat until chocolate is melted; stir to blend.
2. Meanwhile, combine the sugar, flour, and salt in top of a double boiler. Blend in milk.
3. Add the hot coffee-chocolate mixture gradually, stirring until blended. Continue to stir and bring rapidly to boiling; boil 2 minutes.
4. Stir a small amount of hot mixture into the egg yolks. Immediately blend into mixture in double boiler. Cook over simmering water 5 minutes; stir to keep it cooking evenly.
5. Remove from simmering water and blend in butter and vanilla extract. Chill thoroughly before serving.

4 to 6 servings

Rich Chocolate Pudding

2 ounces (2 squares) unsweetened chocolate
2 cups milk
1/2 cup sugar
2 tablespoons cornstarch
1/4 teaspoon salt
2 teaspoons vanilla extract
2 teaspoons butter or margarine

1. Put chocolate and milk into the top of a double boiler. Cook over simmering water until chocolate is melted, stirring occasionally.
2. Combine sugar, cornstarch, and salt; gradually add to chocolate mixture, stirring constantly.
3. Cook and stir over boiling water until thickened. Remove from heat; stir in vanilla extract and butter. Pour into serving dishes and chill.
4. Serve with **whipped cream** or **whipped dessert topping.**

About 4 servings

Semisweet Chocolate Pudding

1 package (6 ounces) semisweet chocolate pieces
1/4 cup water
1/2 cup firmly packed golden brown sugar
4 egg yolks
1 teaspoon vanilla extract
4 egg whites
1 cup chilled whipping cream
2 tablespoons golden brown sugar
Sliced almonds

1. Combine chocolate pieces, water and 1/2 cup brown sugar in the top of a double boiler. Heat over simmering water until chocolate is melted. Beat until smooth. Cool.
2. Beat egg yolks with vanilla extract. Stir in chocolate mixture. Beat egg whites until stiff. Fold chocolate mixture into egg whites. Spoon into individual serving dishes. Chill 3 hours.
3. Combine whipping cream and 2 tablespoons brown sugar. Whip until stiff. Top pudding with the whipped cream and sprinkle with almonds.

6 servings

Double-Boiler Chocolate Souffle

1 cup milk
2 ounces (2 squares) unsweetened chocolate
3 tablespoons butter or margarine
3 tablespoons flour
½ cup sugar
4 egg yolks
1 teaspoon vanilla extract
4 egg whites
¼ teaspoon cream of tartar

1. Combine milk and chocolate in a saucepan; cook over low heat, stirring occasionally, until chocolate is melted and mixture is blended.
2. Meanwhile, melt butter in saucepan; stir in the flour and cook until mixture is bubbly. Remove from heat and stir in the milk-chocolate mixture; blend in the sugar. Return to heat and bring the mixture to boiling, stirring constantly.
3. Beat egg yolks until very thick. Adding gradually, beat chocolate mixture into egg yolks until thoroughly blended. Mix in vanilla extract. Cool to lukewarm.
4. Beat egg whites until frothy; add cream of tartar and continue beating until stiff, not dry, peaks are formed. Gently fold in the chocolate mixture until thoroughly blended.
5. Butter inside of top section of a 2-quart metal double boiler; turn mixture into it. Cover and set over boiling water (water should rise to no more than one half of the height of double-boiler top).
6. Keeping water gently boiling, cook 60 to 70 minutes, or until a metal knife inserted halfway between center and edge of souffle comes out clean.
7. Run a spatula around edge of souffle and invert onto a serving plate, or spoon into individual serving dishes. Serve immediately; garnish with **sweetened whipped cream.**

About 6 servings

Viennese Chocolate Souffle

6 egg yolks
¾ cup sugar
10 tablespoons sifted cake flour
2 cups milk
3½ ounces (3½ squares) unsweetened chocolate, grated
1 tablespoons vanilla extract
9 egg whites

1. Beat egg yolks and sugar until very thick in the top of a double boiler. Add the flour gradually, beating until smooth. Gradually add the milk, continuing to beat until blended.
2. Place over rapidly boiling water. Cook and stir 5 minutes, or until thickened. Remove from water; add the chocolate and stir until blended. Mix in vanilla extract. Set on wire rack; allow to stand until mixture cools to lukewarm.
3. Meanwhile, butter a 2-quart souffle dish (straight-sided casserole). Sprinkle tightly with sugar to coat bottom and sides. Make an aluminum foil collar for souffle dish (see note).
4. Beat the egg whites until stiff, not dry, peaks are formed and immediately fold with the chocolate mixture. Gently turn into the collared souffle dish and immediately set in oven on rack (placed so top of product will be about at center of oven).
5. Bake at 375°F 45 to 50 minutes.
6. Remove from oven and carefully remove foil collar. Serve at once with a bowl of Ice-Cream Sauce.

8 to 12 servings

Ice-Cream Sauce: Using equal parts of **vanilla ice cream** and **whipped cream,** fold the cream into softened ice cream just before serving.

Note: To make a aluminum foil collar, cut a length of aluminum foil long enough to encircle dish plus 4 or 5 inches. Fold in half lengthwise and wrap around dish so that collar extends at least 2 inches above the rim. Bring the ends together and fold until collar is tight; tie securely with cord.

Indian Pudding

3 cups milk
½ cup yellow cornmeal
¼ cup sugar
1 teaspoon salt
1 teaspoon ground cin-
   namon
½ teaspoon ground ginger
1 egg, well beaten
½ cup molasses
2 tablespoons butter
1 cup cold milk

1. Scald the 3 cups milk in the top of a double boiler. Stirring constantly, slowly blend into milk a mixture of the cornmeal, sugar, salt, cinnamon, and ginger. Stir in a blend of the egg of molasses.
2. Cook and stir over boiling water 10 minutes, or until very thick. Beat in the butter.
3. Turn into a well-buttered 1½-quart casserole. Pour cold milk over top.
4. Bake at 300°F 2 hours, or until browned.

About 6 servings

Quick Indian Pudding

2 eggs, slightly beaten
¼ cup yellow cornmeal
¼ cup sugar
1 cup sugar
¾ teaspoon ground cin-
   namon
¼ teaspoon ground ginger
2 tablespoons cold milk
¼ cup light molasses
2 cups milk, scalded

1. Combine all ingredients except scalded milk in a bowl. Mix well and add the scalded milk gradually, stirring constantly. Turn mixture into a double-boiler top.
2. Cook and stir over direct heat until mixture thickens. Place, covered, over simmering water and cook 15 minutes longer.
3. Serve hot with **ice cream, whipped cream,** or **fruit.**

4 to 6 servings

Beverages

Egg Nog

1   egg, beaten
1   tablespoon sugar or honey
     Salt
¾   cup milk
¼   teaspoon vanilla
     Dash nutmeg

1. Combine egg with sugar and salt, add milk and vanilla.
2. Serve cold in tall glasses and sprinkle with nutmeg.
3. For a fluffy eggnog separate egg, beat white until stiff, then fold into egg yolk mixture.
4. May be served hot or cold, for 1.

Wassail

3   cups water
½   cup orange juice
¼   cup lemon juice
3   whole oranges, studded
     with cloves (see Note)
1½   teaspoons whole allspice
2   sticks cinnamon
¼   teaspoon nutmeg
¼   teaspoon ginger
2   cups water
¾   cup sugar
¼   cup instant tea
½   gallon apple cider

1. Combine 3 cups water, orange juice, lemon juice, 1 studded orange, and spices in an electric cooker.
2. Cover and cook on Low 2½ hours.
3. Bake the remaining studded oranges in a 350°F oven 45 minutes; reserve until serving time.
4. Meanwhile, stir 2 cups water into sugar in a saucepan; bring to boiling, stirring only until sugar dissolves, and boil 5 minutes.
5. Add sugar syrup, instant tea, and apple cider to spiced fruit juice mixture in electric cooker.
6. Cover and cook on Low 15 to 30 minutes, or until heated through.
7. Strain, transfer to punch bowl, pierce baked oranges several times with wooden pick, float them in wassail, and serve in punch cups. Make sure that bowl and punch cups are heatproof.

About 3½ quarts punch

Note: To stud oranges, pierce with wooden pick at 1-inch intervals and insert cloves.

Spicy Cranberry Punch

4   pieces (3 in. each) stick cinnamon, broken in pieces
8   whole allspice
18   whole cloves
3   qts. cranberry juice cocktail
1   orange, sliced
6   bottles (7 oz. each) lemon-lime carbonated beverage, chilled

1. Tie spices together in cheesecloth bag.
2. In a large saucepan, combine the cranberry juice cocktail, orange slices, and spice bag. Bring to boiling, reduce heat, and simmer about 20 minutes. Set aside to cool; discard spice bag and orange; chill cranberry juice.
3. Just before serving, pour into chilled punch bowl; add lemon-lime carbonated beverage and stir to blend. If desired, garnish with additional *orange slices*.

About 17 cups

Hot Buttered Cranberry Punch

1½   cups water
⅔   cup firmly packed brown sugar
½   teaspoon cinnamon
¼   teaspoon allspice
⅛   teaspoon cloves
⅛   teaspoon nutmeg
⅛   teaspoon salt
1   can (18 ounces) unsweetened pineapple juice
2   cups water
4   cups fresh cranberries, rinsed and sorted
      Butter or margarine

1. Combine 1½ cups water, brown sugar, spices, and salt in a saucepan. Bring to boiling. Reduce heat and simmer 5 minutes.
2. Transfer mixture to an electric cooker. Add pineapple juice.
3. Cover and cook on Low 2 hours.
4. Meanwhile, bring 2 cups water to boiling in a saucepan. Add cranberries and cook, uncovered, until the skins pop.
5. Force cranberries through a food mill or sieve to make a puree. Stir puree into mixture in electric cooker.
6. Cover and ook on Low 15 to 30 minutes to combine flavors.
7. Ladle punch into serving cups or mugs and add dots of butter to each cup. Serve with cinnamon stick stirrers, if desired.

About 1½ quarts punch

Cranberry Punch

4   cups firm cranberries, rinsed
4   cups water
1½   cups sugar
2   tablespoons lemon juice
4   cups pineapple juice, chilled
1   cup orange juice, chilled

1. Combine cranberries and water in a saucepan. Cook over medium heat until cranberry skins pop.
2. Sieve cooked cranberries. Stir in sugar and lemon juice. Return to saucepan; bring to boiling and cook 2 minutes, stirring constantly. Immediately remove from heat; cool and chill thoroughly in refrigerator.
3. To serve, pour over ice cubes in a large pitcher or punch bowl. Stir in pineapple and orange juices. Serve in punch cups.

About 1½ Quarts Punch

Note: For a refreshing start to a luncheon or dinner, fill small glasses with Cranberry Punch and top each glass with a small scoop of *lemon sherbet*.

Mulled Cider

2   quarts sweet apple cider
20   whole cloves
½   cup sugar
12   sticks cinnamon
14   whole allspice
¼   teaspoon salt

1. Combine ingredients in the order listed.
2. Heat to boiling and simmer 15 minutes.
3. Allow to stand 12 hours.
4. Strain and serve hot.

Serves 8 to 10

Hot Spiced Cider

2   quarts apple cider
⅓   cup lightly packed brown sugar
2   sticks cinnamon
1   teaspoon whole cloves
1   teaspoon whole allspice

1. Put ingredients into an electric cooker; stir to mix thoroughly.
2. Cover and cook on Low 2 hours, or until as hot as desired.
3. Serve in hot mugs.

About 2 quarts spiced cider

Sage Cider Punch

"Sage brew"*
"Tea brew"**
1   qt. apple cider
1   cup sugar
2   tablespoons lime juice (1 small lime)

1. Prepare the sage and tea brews; set aside.
2. Meanwhile, combine cider and sugar in a saucepan; set over low heat and stir until sugar is dissolved. Cover saucepan and heat the cider to simmering.
3. Add the strained sage and tea brews and the lime juice; blend thoroughly. Cover and keep hot over low heat until ready to serve. (Do not boil.)
4. Serve in small glasses or mugs. If desired, float several *sage leaves* on each serving.

About 5½ cups Punch

*To prepare "sage brew," pour *1 cup boiling water* over *2 tablespoons leaf sage* in a small saucepan. Bring to simmering; cover tightly and remove from heat. Let stand about 10 minutes to brew. Strain through cheesecloth or a fine sieve.

About ⅔ cup

**To prepare "tea brew," pour 1 cup boiling water over *1 tea bag* in a small saucepan; cover tightly and let stand about 10 minutes. Remove tea bag.

About 1 cup

Mexican Coffee

1   quart water
2/3   cup firmly packed brown sugar
2/3   cup ground coffee

1. Heat water and brown sugar in a saucepan. When sugar is dissolved, add coffee. Let boil 2 minutes.
2. Remove from heat and stir well. Cover and keep hot until all the coffee is at the bottom; strain and serve.

About 12 servings

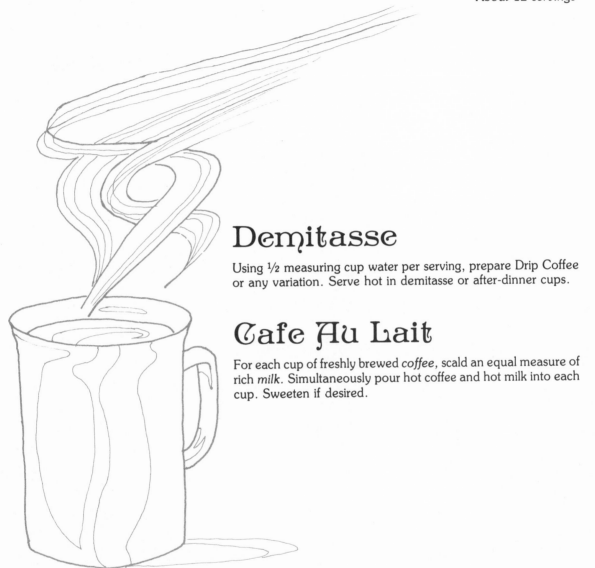

Demitasse

Using ½ measuring cup water per serving, prepare Drip Coffee or any variation. Serve hot in demitasse or after-dinner cups.

Cafe Au Lait

For each cup of freshly brewed *coffee,* scald an equal measure of rich *milk.* Simultaneously pour hot coffee and hot milk into each cup. Sweeten if desired.

Greek Coffee

1   heaping teaspoon Greek coffee*
½   teaspoon sugar
1   demitasse cup filled almost to the brim with water

1. Place coffee and sugar in a Greek coffeepot, a briki, or a narrow saucepot. Add the water and stir until well blended.
2. Place coffee pot on low heat and wait for coffee to boil. Remove from heat. Let coffee simmer down. Return to heat. Allow to reach boiling again. Remove from heat.
3. With a spoon skim a little of the foam, called "kamaki," off the top and gently place it in the bottom of the cup. Slowly pour the coffee into the cup, being careful not to disturb the kamaki.

*Greek and Turkish coffee are the same.

Index